ST. ODO OF CLUNY

THE MAKERS OF CHRISTENDOM

General Editor: CHRISTOPHER DAWSON

St. Odo of Cluny

*Being the Life of St. Odo of Cluny
by John of Salerno and the
Life of St. Gerald of Aurillac
by St. Odo*

TRANSLATED AND EDITED

by

DOM GERARD SITWELL

O.S.B.

SHEED AND WARD

LONDON AND NEW YORK

FIRST PUBLISHED 1958
BY SHEED AND WARD LTD
33 MAIDEN LANE
LONDON, W.C.2
AND
SHEED AND WARD INC.
840 BROADWAY
NEW YORK, 3

Made and printed in
Great Britain by
FLETCHER AND SON LTD NORWICH AND
THE LEIGHTON-STRAKER BOOKBINDING CO LTD LONDON

CONTENTS

INTRODUCTION

THE texts here translated are John of Salerno's *Life* of St. Odo of Cluny (*d.* 942) and the *Life* of St. Gerald of Aurillac (*d.* 909) by St. Odo himself. The monk John, who appears to have become abbot of a monastery in Salerno, and who at any rate dedicated his work to the monks of that place, came to know Odo well in his later years, when he had already acquired a wide fame and influence. Odo himself, it seems, never knew Gerald of Aurillac personally, though he was a younger contemporary. He knew, therefore, the world in which Gerald lived, and he tells us that he took the trouble to seek out those who had been in close contact with him. It is obvious, therefore, that both the lives have value as contemporary witnesses, but there is a difficulty about offering works such as these in a translation, for they come from the darkest part of the Dark Ages, and it cannot be denied that they show traces of their origin. They are, however, of great value for the history of Christendom, because they show Christian principles at work transforming society at a critical stage of its development. A whole civilization had perished, but a new civilization, of which we are the heirs, was about to be born. These men could not yet see the shape of things to come, but they laboured to fulfil the Christian ideal, and in doing so both of them—Odo obviously, Gerald less obviously but no less really—contributed to the formation of that new Europe which was to be Christian and Catholic. The fact that the documents which record their lives belong to the same world as they is, of course, what gives them value. They are not the sort of documents that we should write, if we set out with the same purpose as their authors, but the very differences in style and approach throw light on the age to which their subjects belonged, and therefore on the subjects themselves. There is much to be learnt from them, even though it may often be in noting what they take for granted or refer to casually rather than in what they set out to give. Odo is a great historical figure judged by any standards. Gerald of Aurillac has been largely for-gotten, yet he obviously impressed contemporaries greatly, and his life is a good example of the civilizing effect of Christianity on a rough age. He is only known to us in Odo's *Life*, and this must be left to speak for itself as far as the facts are concerned, but Odo's name is inseparably linked with that of Cluny and the movement for reform associated with it, and something must be said of the circumstances in which that movement began.

THE HISTORIC FACTS

The name of Cluny is famous in monastic history, and for most people it probably conjures up the idea of a great abbey with a vast number of monastic houses dependent on it—a huge but erratic growth in Benedictine history. Such indeed the later Cluny be-came, but its real title to greatness is to be found not in the size and wealth of the later organization, but in the tremendous in-fluence which the foundation had, in its early days, on contemp-orary monasticism, and through that on the whole Church; and the man who was responsible for this influence was its second abbot, St. Odo. Indeed it would be true to say that the influence for monastic reform associated with Cluny in its early days was in reality the personal influence of Odo. It was a remarkable suc-cession of great and long-lived abbots which at a later date gave it a unique place among the monasteries of Western Europe.

In order to understand the importance of Odo and the influence he had on the monasticism of his time, it is necessary to realize the state into which religious life had fallen in France and Italy, and indeed throughout Europe, in the second half of the ninth century. Lurid pictures of this are commonplaces of the history books, but it is probable that none of them is exaggerated, or even does justice to the conditions which existed. It is unnecessary to reproduce them here, for the present Lives provide not a little contemporary evidence which speaks for itself. It may, however, be useful to recall briefly the facts which led up to this state of affairs.

To confine ourselves to France in which Cluny was situated;

Gaul after its conquest by Caesar was a rich and prosperous Roman province, but beyond its eastern frontier there existed the great mass of the barbarian peoples. From an early period there was seepage into the Roman province, but in time pressure, exerted apparently by the Asiatic Huns for some reason yet unknown, set the whole Germanic world in motion, and finally the frontiers broke, letting in wave after wave of new nations. Except for the Huns, who remained always alien and ultimately retired whence they came, these peoples quickly came to identify themselves with the Roman civilization on which they imposed themselves, but they were not in a sufficiently developed state to produce an administrative class able to carry on government as it had been known under Rome. Consequently, even though early Merovingian government was centralized, there was from the start a tendency for society to break up into a number of units governed by local semi-independent lords—the germs of feudalism. The process was arrested by Charles the Great. The genius of this king did succeed in establishing, or re-establishing, some sort of central administration, but the time was still not ripe for it, and as soon as his personal influence was removed the machinery of government which he had established began to fall to pieces. Perhaps something might have been saved from the wreck, if Europe, and particularly the part of it which we now call France, had not been subjected to a new wave of barbarian invasions, that of the Norsemen. The effect of this, accentuated by dynastic squabbles among the descendants of Charles, was disastrous. Europe ultimately saved itself only by completing the process of disintegration. Defence came to depend on local magnates, who did indeed repel the invader, but at the cost of the loss of practically all central authority. Feudalism was finally established and the result was a society from which almost all traces of the ancient Roman civilization had been wiped out, and in which the population formed from the fusion of the Gallo-Roman and the Germanic peoples was scarcely less barbaric than the original invaders had been. Power was almost entirely in the hands of the landowners, who had become a military caste recognizing no authority except force. They oppressed the tillers of the soil on whom they were ultimately dependent for their wealth, waged constant war on each other, and were oblivious to the refinements of civilized life.

In such a society, without the machinery of government, and demoralized by internal feuds and external enemies, the Church was almost the only civilizing influence with which the people came in contact, but the Church itself was suffering from the effects produced by the degradation of society, as the present Lives bear witness. The point, however, to notice is that there was an awareness of the evils and a desire to put them right. Great abuses never fail to produce this response in the Church, and the power to cast out evil and to renew itself from within is indeed a necessary condition for its survival. Historians of a generation ago were inclined to speak of the Cluniac reform as though it were the origin of the whole movement for ecclesiastical reform which is associated with the name of Hildebrand in the second half of the eleventh century. It was so only in the sense that it was the first step in the process, but it is important to realize that it was by no accident that the movement began with a reform of the monasteries. It could perhaps have begun in no other way. Self-supporting and self-sufficing units in a fragmentary society, if the monasteries could be reformed, and above all freed from the control of local feudal lords, the full Christian life could be lived at least within their walls, if nowhere else. And although the monasteries fitted easily into the feudal scheme, the way was clear to make them independent of it. By being made directly subject to the apostle Peter—as the men of the time liked to think of him—in the person of the Pope, they could be freed from the encroachments of the local aristocracy, and prevented from becoming pawns in local politics. Men like Odo felt that they could do nothing until they had attained some such haven, and were free to develop their lives according to their own spiritual ideals. But it is of great significance, and it is the measure of his greatness, that Odo at any rate was no mere escapist. He sought a refuge in which he could foster his ideals, but he was clear that these constituted the only foundation on which society could endure. As Mr. Christopher Dawson has pointed out,[1] in his chief work, the

---

[1] *Religion and the Rise of Western Culture*, London 1950, p. 146.

Collations, he is concerned with evil within the Church, but he does not confine himself to ecclesiastical abuses. Strongly as he inveighs against these, he is equally strong in his condemnation of social injustice, the oppression of the poor by the rich, and it is further especially significant that in his view the only remedy for an evil that has its roots in the very nature of man is to be found in the fundamental principles of the Christian life. In his person we see how the re-establishment of the monastic life, which is basically the full Christian life, is related to the reform of society at large. It was because the aspirations of the age towards a better life found their fulfilment in monasticism that a number of new monasteries were founded at the end of the ninth and the beginning of the tenth century, but Cluny was the one of which Odo became abbot and something must be said of its origin.

One of the most powerful feudal lords, William of Aquitaine, decided to found a monastery on part of his personal property on the borders of Aquitaine and Burgundy. His history was perhaps no worse, but certainly no better, than that of most of his kind, but the desire to found a house in which the religious life should be worthily led was undoubtedly perfectly sincere. It was an example of that sort of innate decency in men whom circumstances had compelled to lead a violent life, which was the source of the whole movement. To advise and help him in his undertaking he sought the aid of one Berno, who was abbot of a number of monasteries in the neighbourhood. Berno, it would appear, was one of the few men at the time who were qualified to give the new foundation the sort of life it needed, for he represented the tenuous link which still existed with the earlier and short-lived monastic reform of St. Benedict Aniane. Apart from handing on this tradition of observance, he probably contributed a most important feature to the new foundation. One of the principle sources of trouble in the monastic life of the time arose from the fact that monasteries had come to be thought of like any other piece of feudal property. They belonged to their founders and could be inherited or disposed of as these thought fit. The result was that they were frequently provided with incompetent or unworthy abbots, or the lay owner himself settled in them with his wife and family. To avoid this highly undesirable state of affairs Berno subjected the monasteries of which he was abbot, and of one of which he was probably founder, directly to the Holy See. When William made his new foundation at Cluny a like provision was made in the foundation charter, and it is extremely likely, though I do not think there is proof, that it was the influence of Berno which was responsible for this. The monks were further to have the power of electing their own abbots. It was these conditions which gave Cluny the chance to preserve the monastic tradition which it had inherited. There is no indication that Berno and William of Aquitaine had any idea of doing more than founding a house at Cluny in which monastic life should be properly constituted and provided with safeguards. Berno ruled Cluny for sixteen years, from 910 to 926, and he was not concerned to do more than make it an observant house; and it was not in his day a rich one.

Such, then, is the inheritance to which Odo succeeded. What he made of it we learn rather from outside sources than from John of Salerno's *Life*. In 927 Rudolph of Burgundy, King of the Franks, gave the monastery a charter confirming its autonomy and giving it the right to coin money. In 929 his mother, Adelaide, gave it the monastery of Romainmoutier in the Jura. It is true that Cluny did not enter into possession of the gift for many years, but it was made. In 931 Pope John XI gave Cluny the right to receive into the community monks from other monasteries which had fallen into decay, and there were many gifts of land.[1] It is clear that the house was beginning to attract the attention of the great, but much more so was Odo himself.

Perhaps in the year 936, but certainly within a few years of that date,[2] he was summoned by the Pope to Rome to try to bring about peace between Alberic, the ruler of Rome, and Hugh, the King of North Italy. About this visit to Rome, John gives us a good deal of incidental information, but for the moment the interesting point is that Odo was summoned to Rome by the Pope on an important diplomatic mission. Cluny had been made directly subject

---

[1] Mabillon, *Acta Sanctorum Ordinis Sancti Benedicti*, ed. L. d'Achéry and J. Mabillon, Paris, 1668-1701, vol. vii, p. 139; *PL*, cxxxiii, 29-30.

[2] See p. 29, *n*. 2.

to the Holy See and it would not be by chance that the Pope was aware of its existence, but it can only have been a knowledge of Odo's personal attainments which caused the Pope to send for him to Rome and entrust him with such a mission. Most of the tenth-century Popes were heavily involved, to say the least of it, in the violent power politics of the Roman aristocracy, but they did show solicitude for the Church at large, and their recognition of Odo is not the least of their redeeming features. But in any case it is evident from the history of the last six years of Odo's life, from 936 to 942, that he was a man of outstanding ability and of an attractive character. During this period he was called upon to assist in the reform of some ten monasteries in France,[1] as well as the five or so in Italy that are mentioned in John's text. The fact is very significant, and it witnesses in the first place to Odo's personal reputation as a zealous, but surely also as an acceptable reformer—acceptable to the monks he was called upon to reform. And in the second place the fact that he was called in so often is a further witness to the widespread desire to improve the state of religious life which existed at the time. Old customs die hard, and several of the monasteries which were restored by Odo were in drastic need of reform again not long after his death, but that does not mean that the original impulse for reform may not have been perfectly genuine. But it must be understood that these reforms were personal to Odo. The monasteries retained their autonomy and there was no question of affiliation to Cluny. The growth of the Cluniac Congregation, of a large number of houses directly and formally subject to the Abbot of Cluny, only came later, and was not fully developed till the abbacy of St. Hugh in the second half of the eleventh century.

Such briefly is the part played by Odo in history. For our knowledge of him as a man we are mostly dependent on the *Life* here translated, and it will be well to say something about the literary quality and significance of this *Life* together with that of Gerald by Odo himself, for to a modern reader it may well be that they appear at first sight not easy reading.

[1] See Evans, *Monastic Life at Cluny*, 910–1157, Oxford, 1931, pp. 10–13.

The *LIVES* by John and Odo

SOME two hundred years after John of Salerno wrote his *Life* of St. Odo a monk of Cluny, Nalgodus by name, decided to write another one, or at least to rewrite John's *Life*, of which he was extremely critical. "So great was the verbal confusion and prolixity, so disorderly and preposterous the order of narration, that the series of events is hardly coherent in itself, or with reason, or with time. It displeased me much," he wrote of it. Perhaps Nalgodus was hardly the man to pass these strictures on John's work. His own *Life*, apart from its obviously derivative character, is of no outstanding literary merit, and while it avoids the worst faults into which John's falls, it also fails to reproduce his best qualities.

But John of Salerno certainly has faults as a writer. Perhaps his greatest, from a stylistic point of view, is that he feels compelled from time to time to be "literary". It takes the form, as always in those unaccustomed to writing (and we may judge that he was so), of indulging in laborious and extended metaphors. Only too often he cannot say simply what he means, and indeed it is difficult to know sometimes just what he does mean. In narrating anecdotes, for example, he frequently fails to make it clear to which of two parties he is referring. Thus in his description of the two monks captured by the Norsemen (ii. 12) it is impossible to be sure whether the *servi* are slaves of the Norsemen or servants of the monks. And if his command of language is sometimes inadequate to enable him to express his ideas clearly, it is also true that his narrative is somewhat disjointed and not without digressions, for which he periodically pulls himself up.

But before going further it is only fair to say that he has merits which do much to compensate for his defects. He only got to know Odo late in the latter's career, and he tells us himself that he spent less than two complete years actually in his company, but he had an unbounded admiration for him, and Odo on his side obviously thought much of John. When he is relating anecdotes in which he himself took part, he can tell them with considerable verve, as in

the story of the old man who carried a little sack full of garlic and
onions, whom Odo insisted on helping when they were crossing
the Alps on one occasion (ii, 6). John describes his discomfiture at
the smell of the sack, and how he was put to shame by Odo. Many
of his stories ring true—he will remark in passing that he knew one
of the characters—and we get some idea of what travelling in the
tenth century must have involved; snowstorms in the Alps or
Apennines; a party of horsemen crossing the Rhône, the horses
nervous and restive at being loaded on to a small boat, one of them
lashing out and kicking a hole in the side of the boat. Such things
must have happened. The results of the devastation of the monasteries by the Norsemen are vividly brought home to us, and his
account of the two wandering monks who insisted on being given
meat (iii, 3 and 4) is written concisely and with point. He is at his
best when he is describing a scene between persons, and his use of
direct speech is often effective, as in the all-too-human outburst of
the monk of some unnamed monastery that Odo was reforming,
who took offence at the Cluniac custom of washing shoes, and was
driven to desperation by the refusal of Odo's monk to break the
silence: "God did not make me a serpent that I should hiss as you
do, nor an ox that I should bellow, but He made me a man and
gave me a tongue to talk with." (ii. 23.) Unfortunately he did not
confine himself to anecdotes and on several occasions, notably in
this same chapter, he feels compelled to point the moral and illustrate it with texts. This laborious production of passages from
Scripture (the whole of Chapter 13 in Book II is given up to it)
is the more to be regretted because John obviously knew his Bible
well and can weave allusions and quotations into his narrative with
skill and effect,[1] though the aptness of some of the texts which he
quotes more explicitly is not always obvious.

But the whole difficulty about a work such as this of John's is
that he was writing within an inherited tradition which is not ours.
To us it is exasperating not to have some more insight into the
important work that Odo was doing, and to be put off with a story
about some berries he bought, when we should really like to know
how it was that he produced the impression he did on men of the

---

[1] The sort of passages I have in mind occur in i, 33, and iii, 12.

calibre of Alberic and Hugh. But to analyse and portray anything of this sort would have been far beyond John's powers, and moreover the idea would never have entered his head. He conceived it his duty, obviously, to give the facts of Odo's life up to the time he became an abbot, but after that he is concerned only with edifying anecdotes, and indeed the earlier narrative too is well seasoned with these.

Odo in his *Life* of Gerald has, of course, fundamentally the same approach as John, and if he does not lapse into quite the same kind of over-writing, he has in general a somewhat strained style, which is perhaps what we should expect as the result of his studies of the late Latin grammarians. Thus, his knowledge of Scripture is impressive, but unfortunately many of his frequent allusions to it are dragged in as obvious literary embellishments, a sanctified literary self-consciousness, as it were. He is even less able than John to say simply what he means. It might have been thought, for example, that when he sets out to give a description of Gerald's appearance (i, 12) he might achieve it fairly simply, but in the course of one of his longer chapters he tells us little more about Gerald than that he was of medium height and *euphormis*, that is, as he has to explain to his readers, well-made. One looks in vain for anything like Jocelin of Brakelond's description of Abbot Sampson.

But if there is plenty with which modern taste can find fault in these *Lives*, it would be a great mistake to think that there is nothing of significance in them. The general reader may very easily underestimate the brutality of the times and the civilizing effect which the behaviour of men like Odo and Gerald must have had. Much that to us now-a-days seems only common decency involved little short of heroic charity. There was a saying in thirteenth-century England that the villein, or the serf, was like the willow, the more it is cropped the more it grows.[1] If the thirteenth-century feudal lord thought of his serfs in those terms, his counterpart in the tenth century certainly did not think otherwise. The serfs at this time were really half-emancipated slaves. They were not chattels, but they were by no means free men, though the degree

---

[1] *Ancren Riwle* (Morton, p. 86).

of freedom which they enjoyed varied considerably. Gerald's behaviour to the men who were leaving their holdings (i. 24) or to the man who had left his service and prospered elsewhere (i. 30) may not strike us as extraordinarily benevolent, but it must have appeared so to the men of the time, and such acts must have demanded courage in flouting the opinion of his class. There were, we know, those who were ready to argue that such behaviour endangered the stability of society, and Gerald himself was aware of the problem (see iii. 4). When we read that even Gerald in his somewhat exaggerated fear of being praised threatened any free man with serfdom and any serf with maiming who supplied the much-desired water in which he had washed his hands (ii. 11), it brings home to us the temper of the age, as it does when we learn that the soldiers who on Gerald's orders captured a band of robbers put out their eyes forthwith, and his only regret was that one man was included in the party in error.

Living in the Welfare State it is difficult for us to bring home to ourselves the plight of those who for one reason or another fell outside the ranks of those who had a recognized means of livelihood, and the emphasis put by John on Odo's generosity to the poor may seem uncalled for, but it was the expression of a charity the need for which we cannot easily imagine, and which was seldom exercised, at any rate in the spirit in which he exercised it. Again, the stories of the feudal lords who made war on Gerald may seem to us to have the unreality of a fairy-story, but Odo names the people concerned and expected his readers to know them. Gerald's treatment of them strikes us as generous and magnanimous, but what we should expect. To Odo's first readers it must have seemed quite extraordinarily unusual and impressive.

But if all this seems to us only decent behaviour, though in the circumstances of the time it was far more, there is also to be noted in both Odo and Gerald a very real refinement of feeling which must have been quite as uncommon in the age in which they lived. It appears in so small a point as the fact noted twice by Odo (i, 15 and ii, 14) that Gerald would ask questions about the reading at table, but only of those who he thought would be able to reply. He had a delicacy of feeling which would not allow him to embarrass any of the company. He showed the same delicacy and tact with the bad-tempered cleric at Piacenza and skilfully smoothed out a difficult situation (i. 29). When the conversation at his table took a line of which he disapproved he would gently turn it back with a joke (i. 15).

All these are small points, but it is difficult for us to realize the civilizing influence which such men as Odo and Gerald must have had on a barbarous society, and the important thing to notice is that the effect they produced was the immediate result of their Christianity. Neither John nor Odo can give us any real idea of the spirituality of his respective subject. They can only describe the more directly religious aspects of their lives from the outside, but it is evident that prayer played a large part in the lives of both of them, and its fruits are manifest.

There is a further feature of these *Lives* which deserves special attention, and that is the place which the miraculous occupies in them, and this raises the whole question of the places of miracles in these early *Lives* of the saints. To one who believes in God as the Creator and Conserver of the universe there is no difficulty in admitting the possibility of His intervening in particular instances to modify what we call the laws of nature, but in this hagiographical tradition the number and also the apparently trivial nature of many of the miracles recorded is a difficulty, and it may be of interest to consider one aspect of the life of the time which may throw light on the problem. There can be little doubt that this great emphasis on the miraculous in the lives of the saints is an indication of a primitive mentality. In a stimulating book[1] Mr. R. W. Southern has recently pointed out the significance of the devotion paid to relics at this period. "When the machinery of government was simple or non-existent, these tangible elements of spiritual power [relics] had an importance in public life which they lost in a more complicated age. The deficiencies in human resources were supplied by the power of the saints."[1] That passage surely puts its finger on the reason why miracles figure so largely in this literature. We fail to realize how great were the deficiencies of human resources. It was not a lack of material resources so much

---

[1] *The Making of the Middle Ages*, London, 1953, p. 137.

as spiritual, or, more precisely perhaps, intellectual. In spite of
the knowledge of the Novels of Justinian which John alleges was
possessed by Odo's father, the fact is that the fine instrument of
Roman law was unusable by these people. They did not know
how to produce, or marshal, or preserve, evidence. Only too often
in the face of claims and counter-claims they were completely at
a loss, and hence they fell back on trial by ordeal, throwing the
responsibility back on to God, as it were, admitting their own
incompetence to decide the matter. By 1215 priests were forbidden
to take part in administering the ordeal, but at this period the
instruments for it, the cauldron for the boiling water and the rest,
were kept in church and blessed by the priest. It was a direct
appeal to divine intervention, indicating a lively faith no doubt, but
also an inability to deal with the complexities of life which belongs
naturally to the period of childhood. They were in fact simple and
childlike in a way which we find it difficult to realize. When the
process of human justice became once more developed, trial by
ordeal was dropped, and it was the canon lawyers who first dis-
carded it. The mentality of an age which sought to solve its practical problems of the administration of justice by appeal to the
ordeal is surely reflected in the stories of divine intervention in
human affairs which figure so largely in the *Lives* of the saints of
this period. If it was beyond the monastic discipline of the age to
stop monks eating meat, at least they should know that divine
retribution was liable to fall upon them if they insisted on doing so.

This attitude of mind, which we may call primitive or childlike
as we look on its darker or brighter manifestations—it is both, as
the child is in a sense primitive—is reflected also in the attitude
to the saints shown by John. There is vivid faith, but it is only
half spiritualized. St. Martin moves about the world; goes from
Rome to the coronation of Louis IV and stops off on the way to
visit Adhegrinus, and cannot stop too long lest he should be late
for the coronation (i. 27). St. Benedict is absent from the Office in
Fleury for a night, because he has to go to England in the interests
of the soul of an erring brother (iii. 11). When the behaviour of
the monks of Fleury becomes too trying he walks out, and the
monks ride round the countryside looking for him (iii. 8). We can

only call the attitude of mind betrayed by these anecdotes naïve, and so it is, but we should do well to remember that it was in fact the attitude which was natural to John and the people for whom he wrote. Mr. Christopher Dawson has pointed out its significance very clearly in his Gifford Lectures.[1] We may easily forget that, although the baptism of Clovis in 496 marked the official acceptance of Christianity by the Franks, the complete absorption of it by the nation as a whole was, as always with primitive peoples, a slow process. At the time these *Lives* were written more than four hundred years had elapsed since Clovis was received into the Church, but, as we have seen, for a variety of reasons the Franks were little more civilized at the end of this period than they had been at the beginning, while the Gallo-Roman substratum of society, possessed of a much higher civilization than the Franks at the time of the invasions, had been dragged down and submerged in the interval. In any case it is well to remember that the Roman civilization in Gaul was a predominantly urban one. The country-people, the inhabitants of the *pagi*, the districts—*pagani* as they came to be called—were neither Christian nor particularly civilized, when the Franks invaded the land. Their very name gave its origin to our word "pagan". Accordingly it was not to be expected that any of these people should be in a position to receive the profound theology of a St. Augustine or of the Eastern Fathers. They had to take Christianity on the level at which they could assimilate it, and it came to them not so much as a new doctrine, as the manifestation of a new power with a supernatural prestige, something which might easily, and frequently did, conflict with their own untamed instincts, but which nevertheless held out to them the hope of a divine salvation beyond the confines of the harsh world they knew. To a large extent it is probably true that, as Mr. Dawson says, "they could understand and accept the spirit of the new religion only when it was manifested to them visibly in the lives and acts of men who seemed endowed with supernatural qualities".[2] They saw the saints as supernatural beings who inhabited their sanctuaries and watched over their people in much the same way as they had been accustomed to thinking of their

[1] *Religion and Rise*, pp. 31 ff.   [2] Ibid., p. 33.

demi-gods as doing. In many cases the cult of a local saint was deliberately substituted for a local pagan cult. Their attitude was genuinely Christian so far as it went; they saw the saints as patterns of moral perfection whose prayers they invoked, but their conception of them was, as I said, only half spiritualized. Only very occasionally have we a hint of a different and more modern attitude. John was aware of the comic element in the story which he tells of the boar which came out of the forest and offered itself, in a moment of crisis, to supplement the commissariat of the monastery on the occasion of the consecration of the abbey church at Cluny, but he is heavy-handed and uncertain in his allusion to this element, (ii. 3), though not in his telling of the story.

John has a good many miracles to relate, but we may notice two things: (1) He never claims himself to have been a witness of a miracle by Odo, and (2) he states explicitly that he is not going to rely on miracles in extolling him. "Let those who like to do so praise exorcists, raisers of the dead, and all the other people famous for miracles. I ... will praise patience", etc. (i. 14.) This is a noteworthy passage in as much as it shows that John did realize that the moral virtues were more important than the power of working miracles.[1] Odo, it may be noted, adopts the same attitude to miracles as John, though rather more equivocally; nevertheless they both obviously believed in them and found them edifying. We may perhaps make two observations. (1) Granted the childlike mentality of the age—and it was childlike in spite of the violence (indeed this was only a manifestation of it, as children are violent in their way)—it is natural that they should have accepted and felt the need of frequent divine intervention in the world, and (2) they inherited a literary tradition which demanded the inclusion of many wonders in the lives of the saints. The second point is no doubt partly accounted for by the first. A literature is popular and successful because it gives people what they want, and the men of the Dark Ages wanted miracles. But other elements entered into this literary tradition, and behind it lay the devotion to the martyrs, which had flowered at the beginning of

[1] It may be compared with a passage from the *Discourse on the Life of St. Honoratus* printed in this series (*The Western Fathers*, London, 1954, p. 277), to which the editor draws attention.

the Church's history, and belief in the power of their relics. The first was humanly natural and theologically demanded by the doctrine of the communion of saints, the second has a profound dogmatic basis in the belief that man is composed of body and soul, which are complementary to each other; that the body is the instrument of the soul and destined to share in its glory. In view of this important truth honour paid to the relics of the saints is, of course, always valid. That the appeal to the miraculous should be made so frequently in this literature, then, need not surprise us. The question as to whether the miracles really took place is a thorny one and has to be left open, but it is not unreasonable to suppose that God may have worked many miracles for a generation which believed, and could hardly be taught in any other way.

Perhaps we may be allowed an attempt to sum up the characters of the two men as they appear in these *Lives*. John relates many anecdotes about Odo, and yet so remote from us is the feudal world of a thousand years ago, that they may easily have an air of unreality about them. Nevertheless a clear and very attractive picture of Odo's character does emerge. Perhaps the fundamental mark of sanctity which it bears is the ability to distinguish between the sin and the sinner. He was far from condoning the evils of his day, he was even preoccupied with them, and it has already been suggested (p. xiii) that his judgement on both the evils and their cure went deep, yet there is nothing harsh or unsympathetic about his treatment of individuals. He obviously had a gift of sympathy and understanding which enabled people to confide in him, whether it was John himself, who found his life as a canon in Rome unsatisfactory, or a notorious robber somewhere in the Alps or Apennines, a bishop whose consecration was delayed by ecclesiastical intrigue, or a young girl wanting to enter a convent. He was affable, indeed genial, with a sense of humour, he could be known to his monks by a good-natured nickname, and we can believe that people flocked round him, as John describes, not merely because he was generous with his alms but because he was genuinely kind and sympathetic. He had, too, that courage which comes from an utterly disinterested seeking after justice in its widest sense, and which he manifested in what must have been the most difficult reform he undertook, that of Fleury. We can be grateful that John has left this impression of his character enshrined in what seem so many trivial incidents, for it does not come out in his own writings. He must have talked, one would think, more easily than he wrote.

For this very reason perhaps, together with the fact that he never knew Gerald personally, we get a less clear idea of Gerald from Odo's biography of him, but we can, nevertheless, form some sort of picture of the man. As a feudal lord living an intense religious life he was an exceptional figure, and it is significant that he greatly desired to be a monk and was only restrained by devotion to the duties of his state. This perhaps accounts for a certain strain that we cannot help feeling accompanied his undoubted piety. It manifests itself in a rather exaggerated anxiety with regard to purity, perhaps in an undue sensitiveness in the matter of being praised, and in the expedients he found for being in effect tonsured but without letting the fact appear. Something has already been said of the significance of his upright, just, and charitable behaviour in his capacity as a feudal lord—characteristics which we might easily underestimate. Attention has also been drawn to the delicacy of feeling and consideration for others which he habitually showed. The picture of him, when his cavalcade had camped for the night on one of his journeys to Rome, standing outside his tent after his devotions were over, so that anyone who wished to speak to him should find him easily accessible, is one that it is pleasant to contemplate.

NOTE ON THE TEXTS

THE *Life* of St. Odo by his disciple John of Salerno was printed for the first time by Surius in his *De Vitis Sanctorum* (Cologne, 1575, vol. vi), and again by Dom Martin Marrier in the *Bibliotheca Cluniacensis* (Paris, 1614). The texts are substantially the same, but there is a good deal of verbal difference. That of Surius is rather shorter, and he confesses in one place that the copy he is using is deficient. The *Life* was printed again by Mabillon in the *Acta Sanctorum O.S.B.* (vol. vii. s.v.), in 1685. Mabillon used Marrier's text with a Compiègne manuscript, and this text was reprinted in Migne's *Patrologia Latina* (vol. cxxxiii). The present translation has been made from Migne's text, but reference has been made throughout to the Cluny edition. The differences are small but in some difficult passages Marrier's text seems in fact to be rather better. No reference has been made to manuscript sources.

There is another *Life* of St. Odo also printed by Marrier and Mabillon, which was written by Nalgodus, a monk of Cluny in the twelfth century. It does not claim to be more than a rewriting of the *Life* by John.

In 1889 Sackur discovered an anonymous *Life* of Odo in a Paris manuscript (Bib. Nat., 5566), and he also discovered an interesting recension of the *Life* by John of Salerno (Bib. Nat., 5386). The anonymous *Life* is addressed to St. Hugh, Abbot of Cluny in the second half of the eleventh century. Neither the anonymous *Life* nor the recension of John's *Life* has been printed, but Sackur gave some information about them in *Neues Archiv für deutsche Geschichte* (xv, pp. 103-16). Except for some information about Berno there is little new in the anonymous *Life*, but it is based on John's text in an altered and shortened form, some twenty-four chapters being omitted and the others rearranged. In another manuscript (Bib. Nat., 5386) Sackur found what is evidently the recension of John's *Life* on which the anonymous one is based. From internal evidence it seems that John himself was responsible for this recension and that it was made after the longer version. There are a few anecdotes peculiar to it which are not in John's *Life*.

The text of Odo's *Life* of Gerald here translated was published by the Cluniac monk Dom Marrier, with notes by the French antiquary André Duchesne, in 1614. The text was reprinted by Surius (1618), by the Bollandists (*AASS*, Oct., vi, p. 300, 1814), and, together with Duchesne's notes, in Migne (*PL*, cxxxiii, 639-704). There also exists a considerably shorter recension which has been printed by Bouange (1870) and, without the fourth book, by the Bollandists (*CCH*, 1890, pp. 392-401). There has been dispute as to which of these texts was really Odo's, but Poncelet would seem to have shown convincingly that the longer text is to be attributed to Odo, and that the shorter one is an abbreviation made possibly in Odo's own lifetime, perhaps by a monk of Aurillac. (*AB*, xiv, pp. 89-103).

ODO'S WRITINGS

IT may be useful to summarize the extant writings which can be attributed to Odo with any certainty.

1. The epitome of the *Morals* of St. Gregory the Great. See p. 22, *n.* 1.

2. The *Collations* in three books. See p. 40, *n.* 1.

3. Five sermons printed in Migne, *PL*, cxxxiii, cols. 709 ff.

(a)   *In cathedra S. Petri*, probably preached in the church at Cluny, which was dedicated to St. Peter. (Sackur, *Die Cluniacenser*, Halle, 1894, vol. ii, p. 334, *n.* 4.)

(b)   In honour of St. Mary Magdalen. Its authenticity has been questioned, but Sackur upholds it (vol. ii, p. 334, *n.* 5).

(c)   In honour of St. Benedict. This sermon became famous, and at the end of the 11th century was read every year at Cluny on the octave of the feast. (Sackur, vol. ii, p. 335.) It is interesting to note that part of it still appears in the Benedictine breviary as the Second Nocturn lessons for July 18th, the octave day of the feast of the Solemnity of St. Benedict.

(d)   On the burning of the basilica of St. Martin at Tours. Sackur (vol. i, p. 363) thinks that the occasion was in 938 rather than 903 as Mabillon suggests (note in Migne *ad loc.*).

(e)   A sermon for the feast of St. Martin.

4. Four hymns to St. Martin and one to the Eucharist. See p. 12, *n.* 2.

5. Twelve antiphons for St. Martin. See p. 12, *n.* 2.

6. *Life* of St. Gerald. See note on the texts.

7. The *Occupatio* (edited by Swoboda), a philosophical and moral poem in seven books. It deals with the theme of sin and grace from the creation and fall of the angels to the end of the world. The poem can only be described as gloomy and obscure to a degree. It has reminiscences of Virgil, Horace, and Juvenal, but more of Prudentius and Sedulius, and shows an extraordinary taste for unusual, frequently Greek, words. It is hardly fair to

illustrate a long poem by a single line, but the following example of its diction is by no means unique:

Hoc topon atque usian, telon dat rebus et archin.

On the whole the poem shows Odo at his worst. See Raby, *A History of Christian Latin Poetry*, Oxford, 1927, p. 312, and Evans, *Monastic Life at Cluny 910-1157*, Oxford, 1931, p. 104.

8. Rightly or wrongly Odo has his place in the history of music. We learn from John that he studied music under Remigius of Auxerre (i, 3), that he was apparently a skilled composer (i, 10), and that he must have taught music (i, 23). But there is much early manuscript testimony to him as an authority on music and as the author of a treatise, the *Dialogus de Musica* (printed *PL*, cxxxiii, 757. See also Gerbert, quoted *PL*, cxxxiii, 751). His authorship of the *Dialogus* has been questioned, but Grove's *Dictionary* says that "the generally received opinion is not lightly to be set aside". According to the same source, "of other treatises ascribed to Odo the best authenticated is a 'Tonarium' printed by Coussemaker (*Scriptores*, ii, 17.)" See also references to him in Reese's *Music in the Middle Ages*, London, 1941 (under "Odo" in index).

I should like to record my thanks to Abbot Justin McCann for much help and advice in dealing with the more recalcitrant bits of latinity produced by John and Odo, and to Mr. C. A. Robson for struggling with the identification of local Latin place-names, a problem eventually solved with the help of Mlle. Raïssac of Aurillac, to whom I am deeply grateful. Dom Julien Leroy of the Abbey of En-Calcat was kind enough to lend me the publications of M. Beaufrère, which would otherwise have been unobtainable, and Quarr Abbey lent me their copy of Bouange, not easily come by in this country. My thanks are due to Professor Wallace-Hadrill for advice on some passages dealing with technical points of feudalism, and finally to the General Editor, Mr. Christopher Dawson, for his patience and encouragement.

St. Benet's Hall,   GERARD SITWELL
   Oxford.

BIBLIOGRAPHY

The following is a list of the works referred to in the notes:

Acta Sanctorum Bollandiana, Brussels and elsewhere, 1643 onwards.

ALBERS, B., *Consuetudines Monasticae*, vol. i, Stuttgart and Vienna, 1900, vols. ii-v (Monte Cassino, 1905-12).

ARROYO, G., *S. Benedicti Regula Monasteriorum cum Concordantia*, Silos, 1947.

BÄUMER, S., *Histoire du Bréviaire* (Paris, 1905, 2 vols.).

BEAUFRÈRE, A., *Sépultures antiques du monastère bénédictin d'Aurillac*, Aurillac, 1944. *L'Eglise carolingienne du bon comte Géraud*, Aurillac, 1945.

BLUME, C., DREVES, G. M., and BANNISTER, H. M., *Analecta Hymnica Medii Aevi*, Leipzig, 1886-1922, 55 vols.)

BOISSONADE, P., *Life and Work in Medieval Europe*, trans. Eileen Power, London, 1927.

BOUANGE, G. M. F., *Histoire de l'Abbaye d'Aurillac, précédée de la vie de Saint Gérard*, Paris, 1899. First published 1869, vol. i.

BUTLER, C., *The Lausiac History of Palladius*, Cambridge, 1898, 1904, 2 vols.

Cambridge Medieval History, 1936, vol. ii.

Catalogus Codicum Hagiographicorum Latinorum qui Asservantur in Bibliotheca Nationali Parisiensi, ed. Bollandists, Brussels, 1890.

CONANT, K. J., *Early Medieval Church Architecture*, Baltimore, 1942.

CURTIUS, E. R., *European Literature and the Latin Middle Ages*, trans. W. R. Trask, London, 1953.

DALTON, O. M., *The History of the Franks*, trans. with intro., Oxford, 1926, 2 vols.

DAWSON, C., *Religion and the Rise of Western Culture*, Gifford Lectures 1948-9, London, 1950.

DICKINSON, J. C., *The Origin of the Austin Canons*, London, 1950.

DU CANGE, *Glossarium Mediae et Infimae Latinitatis*, ed. Henschel, Niort, 1883-7.

DUCHESNE, A., annotations to *Bibliotheca Cluniacensis* (Marrier).

EVANS, J., *Monastic Life at Cluny 910-1157*, Oxford, 1931.

Gallia Christiana, ed. Sainte-Marthe, D., Paris, 1720, vol. ii.

GANSHOF, F. L., *Feudalism*, trans. P. Grierson, London, 1952. *Mélanges offerts à N.Iorga*, Paris, 1933, pp. 295-307.

GIONO, J., *Notes sur l'affaire Dominici, suivies d'un essai sur le caractère des personnages*, Paris, 1955.

GREGOROVIUS, F., *History of the City of Rome in the Middle Ages*, trans. A. Hamilton, London, 1903, vol. iii.

GREGORY, ST., *Dialogues, The Old English Translation*, ed. E. G. Gardner, London, 1911.

GROVE, *Dictionary of Music and Musicians*, ed. Eric Blom, London, 1954.

HOARE, F. R., *The Western Fathers* (trans. and ed.), London, 1954.

KNOWLES, D., *The Religious Orders in England*, Cambridge, 1948-55, 2 vols.

LAVISSE, E. and others, *Histoire de France*, vol. ii (2) (A. Luchaire), Paris, 1901.

LECLERCQ, J., *Pierre le Vénérable*, S. Wandrille, 1946.

MABILLON, J., *Acta Sanctorum Ordinis Sancti Benedicti*, ed. L. d'Archery and J. Mabillon, Paris, 1668-1701. (John's *Life* was printed in this work and annotated by Mabillon, vol. vii, pp. 124 ff.) *Annales Ordinis Sancti Benedicti*, Paris, 1703-13, 5 vols. *Vetera Analecta*, Paris, 1675, 4 vols.

MCCANN, J., *St. Benedict*, London, 1937. *The Rule of St. Benedict* (ed.), London, 1952.

MARRIER, M., *Bibliotheca Cluniacensis*, annotated by A. Duchesne, Paris, 1614.

MIGNE, J. P., *Patrologiae Cursus Completus, series Latina*, Paris 1844-64.

PIGNOT, J. H., *Histoire de l'Ordre de Cluny*, Autun and Paris, 1868, 3 vols.

RABY, J. F. E., *A History of Christian Latin Poetry*, Oxford, 1927.

REESE, G., *Music in the Middle Ages*, London, 1941.

SACKUR, E., *Die Cluniacenser*, Halle, 1892-4, 2 vols.

SCHMITZ, P., *Histoire de l'Ordre de Saint Benoît*, Maredsous, 1942-9, 6 vols.

SMALLEY, B., *The Study of the Bible in the Middle Ages*, Oxford, 1952.

SOUTHERN, R., *The Making of the Middle Ages*, London, 1953.

SWOBODA, A., *Odonis Abbatis Cluniacensis Occupatio*, ed., Leipzig, 1900.

ABBREVIATIONS

AB   *Analecta Bollandiana*
AASS   *Acta Sanctorum Bollandiana*
CCH   *Catalogus Codicum Hagiographicorum Latinorum qui Asser-*
        vantur in Bibliotheca Nationali Parisiensi
PL   *Patrologia Latina*

THE LIFE OF ST. ODO OF CLUNY

by

JOHN OF SALERNO

THE LIFE OF ST. ODO OF CLUNY
BY JOHN OF SALERNO

I

To the fathers and brothers at Salerno John[1] the servant of Jesus Christ. As soon as I was urged by you to transcribe the book which the learned Palladius[2] wrote in the time of the Emperor Theodosius about the lives and virtues of the holy fathers who were hermits, I did not take it hard, but sat down at once, and, flexing my fingers, set about writing it; for I judged that there was nothing that I could do that would be more to your advantage. But while wishing eagerly to come to the end of the work, I began to be grievously afflicted with pains in the stomach. Just about this time it happened that the venerable Adelrad, our *confrère*, and John, the treasurer of the sacred palace at Salerno, had come to visit me, and in order to help me to bear my infirmities they recalled to my mind the holy and venerable and excellent memory of our most holy father Odo, knowing that it was before all things pleasing and sweet to me, either to narrate anything about him to others, or to gather something of use to myself. But remembering what was written: *The people shew forth the wisdom of the saints, and the church declares their praises*[3] [Ecclus. xliv. 15], I took up his story, and, as they were still with me, began to speak of his origin. When they had heard this, they urged me, if I loved him, as I professed, that without any more delay in words I should write down

---

[1] John tells us (i, 4) that he was a canon in Rome when he met Odo (for position of canons at this time see p. 13, *n.* 2), and that he became a monk at Pavia under one Hildebrand, who had been prior of Cluny. He himself became a prior, or perhaps an abbot (see p. 44, *n.* 3), and from this dedication and the indications in ii, 15 (see p. 59, *n.* 1) most probably at Salerno.

[2] This is the *Lausiac History* written by Palladius about the year 420. It is a series of biographical sketches of monks of the Egyptian desert whom he had known in person or by repute.

[3] Such is the translation of the verse as given by John, with verbs in the indicative. The Vulgate text has the verbs in the subjunctive—"Let the people ..."

this goodly inheritance for the benefit of posterity. I seriously considered the advice of these friends, and was much delighted with it, but at first I held back a little, as is the manner of monks, afraid lest with overbold speech I should rather bring dishonour to the life of so great a man by my tale, than describe it worthily; and I feared that my literary talent would not sufficiently grace the style; nor did I seem worthy to narrate the life of this great man, even if I had the ability.[1]

2

BUT having taken up the work, with heartfelt tears I invoked the Creator and Son of the Virgin, and the like Holy Spirit, the Giver of tongues and Distributor of words, who opens the mouths of the dumb and makes the tongues of infants to speak clearly, that He who once willed me to grow cold to the world and to be inflamed by the love of so great a Father, might inspire me, destitute of all literary talent as I was, to speak freely. And so, dear brothers, since at your exhortation I have dared to take up this great work, deign by your prayers to help me to bring it to an end. But I beg anyone who chances to read this, or hear it read, not to be offended, or to scoff, or to presume to say rashly that it is untrue, and that God has so far deserted the world that the Church, to whom Christ once promised, *Lo, I am with you all days, even to the consummation of the world* [Matt. xxviii. 20], is not now able to produce such a man.

I call Christ to witness that my master, Arnulf, used to relate on oath many things about Odo beyond what I narrate here, of which, according to his own testimony, he himself had been a witness; the same was true of Hutbertus, the Bishop of Tibur, and of one of our own brethren, by name Landricus. But of all this I have written nothing, for I did not wish to make use of their testimony,

---

[1] The protestation that the author lacks the ability and is unworthy to carry through the work he has undertaken was an inheritance from the tradition of classical oratory, in which affected modesty was used as a conscious device to put the hearers in a favourable state of mind. The sentiment was easily, if incorrectly, identified with Christian humilty, and it frequently appears throughout the Middle Ages. (E. R. Curtius, *European Literature and the Latin Middle Ages*, trans. W. R. Trask, London, 1953, pp. 83 ff.)

since these men were not constantly with Odo. If I had been willing to admit it, it would have sufficed, I think, for the praise of one of the old Fathers, or of an apostle. But it pleased me especially to put down those things which I remembered to have heard from his own lips as though he were narrating them of another, and after that those things which Dom Hildebrand, a reliable man, Prior of Cluny and my teacher in the discipline of the Rule, told to me and to many others. Meanwhile I beg you, beloved brethren, do not ask me the names of his forebears and of the Franks with whom he grew up, for I never saw them, nor had an opportunity of doing so. And since I was living under the Rule, it was not lawful for me to ask, and further, it was the land of Italy which gave me birth and nourished me in the cradle of the Church.

Book I

3

THE holy man Odo was a Frank by birth but was brought up in the house of William, the powerful Duke of Aquitaine.[1] At the age of eighteen he received the tonsure at St. Martin's[2] at Tours, and it was there that he got his literary education. After that he studied dialectic and music under a very learned man, Remigius,[3] at Paris, and in his thirtieth year went to Burgundy, where he led the monastic life for fifteen years under the abbot Berno[4] in the monastery of Baume. Afterwards he was made abbot himself and became a well-loved father of monasteries in France, Aquitaine, Spain, and the city of Rome.

[1] Aquitaine at this time was used as a comprehensive term to cover western France between the Loire and the Pyrenees and as far east as the Cevennes. It is the France of the *Midi*, a hard, sun-baked land with steep hills and rushing torrents, lacking natural unity, and profoundly distinct from the north, France proper, with its wide, fertile plains, and easy communications. The Franks had never established themselves very firmly in Aquitaine, and throughout the Middle Ages it remained largely a country apart, separated from the north in language and customs, though generally acknowledging at least the nominal suzerainty of the French kings. Its history is very involved during the internecine struggles of the descendants of Charles the Great, but it is at this time, the second half of the ninth century, that William's father, Bernard of Auvergne, emerges as Duke of Aquitaine and one of the most powerful feudal lords. William succeeded him in 888. Though known in later life, and to history, as the Pious, because of the large number of monasteries, including Cluny, which he founded in his old age, he was in fact a good example of the ruthless feudal lord. He would not recognize Odo, Count of Paris, whom the northern lords made king on the death of Charles the Fat in 888, and when in 893 he captured a vassal of Odo's who was fighting against him, and who begged for mercy, William ran him through with a spear with his own hand. If our Odo was born in 879 and joined William's household at the age of thirteen or fourteen, as is probable, he must have joined it just about the time this happened. (See J. H. Pignot, *Histoire de l'ordre de Cluny*, Autun and Paris, 1868, vol. i, pp. 1 ff.).
[2] See p. 13, *n.* 2.
[3] See p. 21, *n.* 3.
[4] See p. 25, *n.* 2.

4

IN the year of our Lord 939,[1] which was the sixtieth year of his age and the thirtieth of his monastic life, Odo came to Rome, and it was there that he met me. I was involved in wordly interests, and unhappy, and in his pity he caught me in his net and led me to the monastery of St. Peter at Pavia.[2] Being detained there for a little time by the king, Hugh,[3] he handed me over to be trained in monastic discipline by the above-mentioned master, Hildebrand.[4] But returning soon after to Rome he was kind enough to take me, unworthy as I was, as his companion; and the man whom on his departure he took from his relations as a canon, on his return he brought back as a monk. It was at that time, while we were on our way and conversing with each other, that putting aside my shyness, and contrary to the usual practice of monastic life, I boldly broke out and did not hesitate to inquire diligently from him his origin and way of life, at the same time begging him to expound them to me in detail. But he, as was always his manner, was silent for a little time; then going somewhat pale, and sighing from the depths of his heart, he began to tell me his history; but nevertheless his words were full of tears and groans.

5

"My father," he said, "was called Abbo,[5] but he was quite other in his standards of morality and in his behaviour than men of the present time seem to be. He knew by heart the ancient histories

[1] John is very precise about this date and it seems to provide an obvious sheet-anchor in the vexed sea of chronology, but it has been questioned (Sackur, *Die Cluniacenser*, Halle, 1892-4, vol. i, p. 359), and it seems probable that it should be 938 (see p. 49, *n*. 1), but in any case Odo must have been born in or around 879 and become a monk about 909.
[2] The texts have *Ticini*, Ticinum being the ancient name of Pavia, the capital of the Lombard kings of north Italy to whom Hugh had succeeded. It lies on the river Ticino, the part of the city lying to the south of the river being called Borgo Ticino to this day. The monastery of St. Peter there was called *S. Petri in Caelo-Aureo* owing to the gilded roof of the church.
[3] See p. 49, *n*. 3.
[4] See Prologue, 2.
[5] We know nothing of Odo's parents beyond what John tells. They both entered religion late in life (i, 35). See next note.

and the *Novella* of Justinian.[1] In his conversation there was always to be found something of the Gospel. And if strife of any kind had arisen between two parties, his judgement appeared so sound that from all sides men hastened to him to get a decision. And for this reason he was beloved by all, and especially by William, the great count who ruled Aquitaine and Gothia[2] at that time. He was accustomed to celebrate the vigils of the saints throughout the night, and that night in which peace was given back to angels and men, and Christ the Lord visiting the world came forth from the Virgin's womb as a spouse from his bridal chamber, he spent in silence with tears and prayers. While, therefore, he was diligently celebrating these watches, it came into his mind that he should ask God, in the name of the Virgin birth, to give him a son, and by the insistency of his prayers he merited that his wife should bear him one, though past the age when that might be expected. My father often related that in no other way had my nativity been brought about.

6

"When I was an infant it happened that he came into the room where I was sleeping and found me in my cradle unwatched. Looking around and seeing nobody he lifted me up in his arms, and raising his heart, 'Receive,' he said, 'O Martin,[3] jewel among

[1] One would like to know what John meant by the ancient histories in the ninth century. He may have been referring to the classical Roman historians, or to some of the later epitomizers, Orosius or Prosper of Aquitaine.

Justinian (483-565), of course, was the Emperor of the Eastern Roman Empire famous for his codification of Roman law. The *Novels* consisted of a collection of constitutions subsequent to the Codex.

It seems surprising on the face of it that anyone in the entourage of a ninth-century feudal magnate should have had the attainments attributed to Abbo, but we do not know what position he held—only that William of Aquitaine was willing to bring up his son as a "noble youth". Sackur (vol. i, p. 44, *n.* 4) refers to a Tours document of 898 which is signed by an *Abbo legislator* who he thinks was probably the man in question, and he may well have been. In all probability an interesting and exceptional man, but he barely comes to the surface of history.

[2] Gothia consisted at this time roughly of southern France from the Rhône to the Pyrenees. It corresponded to Septimania, and was the part of southern France which had been under Visigothic rule up to the Arab invasion early in the eighth century.

[3] St. Martin (*d.* 397) was the patriarch of monasticism in Gaul. The present work provides much evidence of the veneration in which he was still held five hundred years after his death. See *The Western Fathers* in this series.

priests, this child.' Then laying me down again on the bed from which he had taken me up, he went out. But he was unwilling to tell anybody what he had done.

7

"WHEN I was old enough, he handed me over to a certain priest, who dwelt in a remote place, to be educated and introduced to the study of letters. This priest afterwards confessed that at that time he had the following vision. The princes of the Church demanded the boy of him—and most insistently. When he asked for what purpose they wished to have him, and whether to take him back to his father's house, they said that they had come for no such purpose, but that they might take him into the regions of the East. The priest did not wish to let the boy go, and at the same time did not feel himself in a position to resist them, so he was at a loss to know what to do. Falling on the ground he turned to prayer, begging that they would exact retribution from him rather than take the boy. Now he said that he would suffer the vengeance of the father, now that he would be called by the parents the betrayer of their child. To this one of the apostles is said to have replied, 'Lest the father of the boy should take vengeance on the priest, let us allow him to remain for a time.' After this revelation the priest returned me to my parents. All these things which you inquire of me, my son, I heard from my father.

8

"BUT it happened that as I grew to be a youth, he whom you now see elderly and ill-favoured, was proclaimed a vigorous and good-looking young man, and as time went on my father began to withdraw me from the ecclesiastical life and to set me to military exercises, and with this purpose he sent me to serve as a page in the household of Count William. Gradually I gave up my literary studies and began to be occupied more and more in hunting and fowling. But Almighty God who shows salvation to the unwilling, and calls those who are not as well as those who are [Rom. iv, 17], began to terrify me in dreams, and to show how prone my life was to evil. He turned all my pleasure in hunting into fatigue, and the more I threw myself into sports of this kind, the more I returned dispirited, unsuccessful, and exhausted.

9

"ABOUT this time my father persuaded me to keep the vigils of the great festivals as he was himself accustomed to do. It was some years later that I was preparing to celebrate the vigil of Christmas, and when I had spent a part of the night in watching, it suddenly came into my mind to beseech the help of the mother of our Lord Jesus concerning my way of life. 'O holy Mother of Mercy,' I cried, 'on this night you brought forth the Saviour into the world; deign to intercede for me. I seek refuge, O most loving one, in the merits of your glorious and singular childbearing, and do you incline the ears of your piety to my prayers. I fear greatly lest my life should be displeasing to your Son, and because, O Lady, through you He manifested Himself to the world, through you may He hasten to have mercy on me.'

"So with prayers, and the divine Office, and the celebration of Mass, the night passed and the day dawned. According to custom the white-robed choir of canons was present, and while the intermingling voices were raised in praise of the great solemnity, impatient youth that I was, I sprang into the midst of them and joined them in singing the praises of the King who had been born. I know and I confess that I acted wrongly, and yet when I recall the saying of King David, *Praise the Lord, all ye nations: praise Him, all ye people* [Ps. cxvi, 1] it seems to me that perhaps I was justified in my presumption. Just at that moment I was seized by a violent pain in the head which overwhelmed me for a short time, but then departed. After the Gospel it returned again, and if I had not stretched out my arms to support myself against the screen I should have fallen down lifeless from my high place. The pain was so great that with each returning spasm I thought I should die. This happened to me in my sixteenth year, and during the three following years I was torn by this pain as the earth by a ploughshare. On account of this I was taken back to my parents' home, and for two years they tried every kind of remedy, but the more remedies I took the further I seemed to be from a cure. One day my father, weighed down with grief and sighing deeply, told me the story of my infancy, and he added, 'So, the gift which I offered freely, O blessed Martin, you require exactly. Certainly, as is fitting, you are ready to receive our vows, but you demand full payment.' Despairing at length of a remedy, I thought there could only be relief in one thing, namely to seek refuge with St. Martin, so that having received the tonsure I should serve him consciously to whom I had been offered without knowing it. And so it came about. There, my son, you have the story of my infancy and the beginnings of my way of life. Observe that I have never acted well of my own accord. Judge, then, my ill character as seems right, while you make known and praise the mercy which was always looking down on me."

10

FROM this time Odo's devotion to St. Martin was seen to be such that he loved him above all the saints, and daily commended himself to his protection. For he was always in his presence, keeping him in his heart and on his lips, serving him in his works. Not more than six years ago[1], while the ministers of the church were celebrating the vigils before the body of the saint, it happened that Odo was present. And because the antiphons of that office, as is clear to all, are short and the nights at that time long, wishing to extend the office till daylight, they were repeating the antiphon between each verse of the psalms. The labour became distasteful to them, and at length they came to Odo, and besought him unanimously, saying: "For a long time now, Father, we have awaited your coming, that you might free us from this heavy labour. Now that you are here we beg you to give us new antiphons

---

[1] Presuming that John was writing in 943 (see p. 64, *n*. 3) the dating is sufficiently accurate. It is evident that Odo was already a person of standing when these events occurred. The chapter, therefore, does not refer to Odo's early sojourn at Tours but to a later visit when he was an abbot, and is a digression, as John acknowledges at the end.

of the life of your master, St. Martin, whose length may relieve us
of the monotony of repeating these very short ones." He replied
that not only was he unable to do this, but that his years would
quite deny him the time to learn them, if they should have been
written by someone else. And he began meanwhile to praise the
brevity of the antiphons and to express disgust at the prolixity they
demanded. But they on the other hand averred that, if he acted
otherwise, he would offend Martin; adding that such an excuse
signified a hidden pride. Overcome by these mingled threats and
prayers Odo shortly set himself assiduously to this laborious task.
He composed in fact three hymns in honour of St. Martin,[1] only
one of which I have decided to include in this work.

> *Rex Christe Martini decus;*
> *Hic laus tua, tu illius:*
> *Tu nos in hunc te colere,*
> *Quin ipsum in te, tribue.*

"O Christ the King, Glory of Martin; He is Thy praise, Thou art
his: grant us to worship Thee in him, yea, rather, him in Thee."
He also composed twelve antiphons,[2] each of which contained

[1] Four hymns in honour of St. Martin are attributed to Odo—see Blume and
Dreves, *Analecta Hymnica Medii Aevi*, Leipzig, 1886-1922, vol. l, pp. 265-9.
One of these, *Martini renitet en speciosa dies*, is described by Mabillon (*Annales
ordini sancti Benedicti*, Paris, 1703-13, vol. iii, 461) as being written on his
deathbed at Tours, and internal evidence confirms this. He describes himself as
emigrans de saeculo and refers to Theotolon, the Archbishop of Tours at the time.
The other three hymns (of which that quoted here is one) are presumably the
three referred to by John in this chapter. Odo also seems to have written a hymn
to the Eucharist, but the hymn to St. Mary Magdalen printed in Migne
(*PL*, cxxxiii, 514) is thought by Dreves to be wrongly attributed to him.
[2] The twelve antiphons are to be found in Migne, *PL*, cxxxiii, col. 513. They
are presumably the antiphons for the twelve psalms at Matins for the feast of
St. Martin. In the *Customs of Cluny* written down by Ulrich about 1080 (bk. i,
ch. 43, *PL*, cxlix, col. 689) it is stated that the *new* antiphons are used at Nocturns
(i.e., Matins) on the feast of St. Martin, although the old ones are still used
during the octave. The new antiphons are explicitly stated to be those written by
Odo. It is to be noted that twelve antiphons would fit the twelve psalms at
Matins of the Benedictine Office. Since about 1200 the secular Office has had
nine psalms at Matins, but it seems certain that this number was not fixed by
the tenth century and at that date the difference between the Benedictine and
secular offices was negligible and sometimes non-existent. See Bäumer, *Histoire
du bréviaire*, Paris, 1905, vol. i, p. 297.
St. Martin's at Tours, incidentally, was originally a Benedictine house, but
after various vicissitudes it became definitely secularized, i.e., a house of
canons, in 816.

three variations, and in which the meaning and sound agreed so well, that it seemed that nothing could be added or taken away from the sense, nothing found more sweet in the modulations of the harmony.[1] They are retained to this day at Beneventum. Early or late the memory of the saint was never absent from his heart and mouth; O Martin, O holy one, how delightful to rejoice in you, and in such manner.

But since this is a suitable place for continuing the narrative, with the help of the Lord, I shall narrate what St. Martin was pleased to do through Odo when I have expounded his life more fully. For the present let us return to those things from which we have digressed.

II

ODO therefore, fleeing to St. Martin in his nineteenth year, took on the duties of a cleric.[2] About the many important persons who came to him, and with such great ceremony, I prefer to be silent

[1] From the way in which John speaks it is evident that Odo composed music for the antiphons as well, and this would be in keeping with his undoubted reputation as a musician. See introduction, p. xxvi.

[2] The position of the canons at Tours should be understood. It was neither that of the later twelfth-century canons regular nor that of a canon in the modern sense. In Gaul from the fifth century at any rate the clergy of cathedral or rural collegiate churches lived some form of common life, though one much less strict than that which Augustine had instituted for his clergy. All the inhabitants of these clergy houses were known as *canonici*, and would include junior clergy in minor orders. The decay of the Frankish Church during Merovingian times led to a considerable disintegration of this common life, though in the eighth century there was a strong movement to restore it; a movement which seems to have been a result of the reform of the Frankish Church by Boniface, though it was not directly initiated by him. His successor, Bishop Chrodegang of Metz (742-66), composed for his cathedral clergy the earliest *regula canonicorum*. Charles the Great and his son Louis the Pious did their best to support this movement and as a result of the Council of Aachen (816-17) under Louis the *Institutio Canonicorum* was drawn up by Amularius of Metz. This provided common residence with daily common worship, but the life of the canons differed fundamentally from that of monks and of the later canons regular in that it specifically allowed for private property.

For a time after 817 it seems likely that the Frankish houses of canons flourished, but there is no doubt that they shared in the general demoralization which occurred as the result of the combined effects of dynastic struggles and Viking raids in the second half of the ninth century. We have seen that the zeal shown by the canons of St. Martin's at Tours in the previous chapter (10) is to be referred to a later period at the end of Odo's life, say about 936, when the influence of Cluny itself may well have been instrumental in renewing their fervour (see n. 1, p. 11). Odo's sermon when the church of St. Martin at Tours was burnt down by the Norsemen in 903 indicates a falling-off in religious

than to speak, lest I should seem to do wrong to the poverty with which he was afterwards content. Among these people was the Count, Fulk, who had brought him up,[1] who gave him a cell next to the church of St. Martin, and provided for his livelihood from a canonry, which he gave him. But the holy man was a lover of poverty, and holding in contempt the glory of the world, he was concerned only to please God. For whole days he laboured at reading, and the nights he spent in prayer, having in mind that which is written: *If any man know not, he shall not be known.* [1 Cor. xiv. 38.]

12

AT this time, moreover, the skilful voyager, who has taught us by his leadership to cross the raging torrents of this world, himself passed over the great ocean of Priscian.[2] But when he wanted to read the songs of Virgil, there was shown him in a vision a certain vessel, most beautiful indeed outside, but full of serpents within, by which he saw himself suddenly surrounded, though without being bitten. He understood by the serpents the teaching of the poets, by the vessel in which they were contained the book of Virgil; but the way which he had entered so eagerly he understood to be Christ.

---

observance at that date (*Sermo IV*, *PL*, cxxxiii, col. 736), and this is corroborated by the interesting evidence in the third book of the present *Life*, where John quotes Odo's testimony to the abuses which had arisen in the house of St. Martin at Tours. For the position of canons in the eighth and ninth centuries see J. C. Dickinson, *The Origin of the Austin Canons*, London, 1950, Introduction.

[1] It seems to have been the father of this Fulk, one Ingeler, who came to the fore as Count of Anjou in the time of Louis the Stammerer (877-9) for the resistance he put up against the Norsemen. About 889 he brought back to Tours the relics of St. Martin, which had been removed for safety. In recognition of this he received for himself and his successors the dignity of Canon Treasurer of the Chapter of St. Martin's, together with various other honours (Pignot, vol. i, pp. 59-60). The position of the treasurership was doubtless honorary, but it would account for his son Fulk's being able to give so much patronage to Odo at Tours. John has not previously made any reference to Odo's having been in his household, but we must suppose that he sojourned there for a time.

[2] A Latin grammarian who lived about A.D. 500. He was purely a grammarian in a way that Martianus Capella was not. See p. 21, *n*. 1 and 2.

13

I SHALL now go on to describe briefly how much the virtue of patience began to shine forth in him. From this time onwards he left the songs of the poets, and taught by the Spirit from on high, he turned his attention wholly to those who expounded the Gospels and the prophets. Meanwhile almost all the canons began to inveigh against him, croaking like so many crows. "What are you doing?" they said, "Why do you wish to undertake this unaccustomed work? You are wasting your labour, and the flower of your youth along with it. Spare yourself, and leaving these inextricably involved writings, go to the psalms."[1] But the same spirit which had taught him to be silent from good things, now taught him to be silent from evil. With bowed head and stopped ears, his eyes fixed on the ground, he repeated in his heart that saying of David, *I will take heed to my ways, that I sin not with my tongue. I have set a guard to my mouth, when the sinner stood against me. I was dumb, and was humbled, and kept silence from good things.* [Ps. xxxviii. 2-3.] Nor was he unmindful of that precept and promise of the Lord, *In patience you shall possess your souls.* [Luke xxi, 19.] What remains to be said about his patience, with God's help, I will mention later.

[1] It is significant of the demoralization that had overtaken the religious houses of the time that the canons of St. Martin's at Tours at the end of the ninth century considered that any knowledge of the Scriptures beyond the psalms was uncalled for. It is clear that they themselves were only just sufficiently literate to read the psalms in Latin, and, though one would think that they must have had some knowledge of the Gospels, they apparently had no desire to deepen it. Conscious that their learning was inadequate, with an all-too-human weakness, they resented the fact that Odo surpassed them.

The ideal which the Carolingian Renaissance of the beginning of the century had set itself was the study of the Bible illuminated by the Fathers, the *De Doctrina Christiana* of Augustine providing the theoretical basis and the works of Bede the practical examples. At its best the system tended to produce a *florilegium* from the Fathers, and in the ninth century was too often dependent on previously existing ones. Rabanus Maurus and Walafrid Strabo were the outstanding exponents of the method in the first half of the ninth century, and Odo's own master, Remigius of Auxerre, in the second half. (See B. Smalley, *The Study of the Bible in the Middle Ages*, Oxford, 1952, ch. ii.)

14

Now I will pass on more quickly to his contempt of the world. Let those who like to do so praise exorcists, raisers of the dead, and all the other people famous for miracles. I, the least of all, will praise patience[1] as the first virtue of Odo, then his contempt of the world; and after that, zeal for souls, the reform of monasteries, and of the clothes and food of monks, the peace he brought to churches, the concord among kings and princes, his perseverance in watching and prayer, his care for the poor, correction of youth, honour for the aged, emendation of morals, the strength he brought to the continent, the mercy to the wretched, his perfect observance of rules; in a word, the example of all virtues. In the small space of his body the good Jesus constructed among the various groves of monks a paradise from whose fountain he might refresh the hearts of the faithful. For content with a little cell, and withdrawn from the eyes of men, his care was to please God alone. Having distributed to the poor all those things which he had brought with him for his temporal use, according to the Gospel precept he took no thought for the morrow. At night he deprived himself of the company of men, and betook himself alone to pray at the tomb of St. Martin, which was about two miles distant from his cell. Not relying on a colleague at his side and without the protection of a stick, he carried only in his hands two writing tablets joined by a frail band so that they could be opened but not taken apart, such as scholars are accustomed to carry at their right side. But the enemy of all good began to bring against him all manner of terrors. From the sides of the road foxes came out, at first following behind and watching him, and then throwing themselves in his way. But when they saw that they could not turn the eager youth from the straight path that he was pursuing, snarling and rushing at him with gaping mouths, they threatened to seize him by the throat. He neither fled nor resisted, but with legs together and shoulders hunched he defended himself only with his shoulders and arms.

[1] In choosing Odo's patience rather than his miracles as the object of his admiration John is surprisingly in line with modern taste, but he does nevertheless give a good deal of attention to the miracles. See introduction, p. xviii.

At length giving his whole body to their teeth he guarded only his throat from mortal wounds. Then suddenly a wolf came running swiftly and freed him from their attacks, and from thenceforth showed itself tame and acted as his companion. But if anyone finds this unlikely or difficult to believe let him read the life of St. Paul written by St. Jerome, and there he will find that the grave of the saint was prepared by lions.[1] And if this single example does not satisfy him, let him turn to the life of the blessed Ammon,[2] and he will find that his cell was guarded from robbers by two dragons. Then let him go again to the aforementioned Jerome and turn to Florentius[3] of Nursia whose life the blessed Pope Gregory described in his Dialogue, and he will find that Jerome merited to have a lion as the guardian of his asses, and Florentius a fierce bear to keep his flocks.

After this, however, Odo made his journey more safely. Always keeping Thy testimony, O good Jesus, in his heart, and exulting in Thee, he sang aloud: *Truly, Lord, thou art faithful in all thy words and holy in all thy works. Thou liftest up all that fall and setteth up all that are cast down.* [Ps. cxliv, 13-14.] For contrary to the usual order of things the wolf saved from being devoured what it is sometimes accustomed to devour, and frightened the foxes of which it is itself usually afraid. What and how great invisible temptations the devil raised against him may nobody ask me. However, to prove the matter, I think that the visible warfare which I have described may suffice to make all my readers believe what he may have had to bear through the invisible suggestions of the evil one. When at night he left the cell in which he dwelt in order

[1] The story of the two lions that dug a grave for St. Paul, the first hermit, occurs in St. Jerome's *Life of St. Paul*, ch. 16.

[2] The story of St. Ammon and his guardian dragons is given in the *Historia Monachorum in Aegypto*, which describes a series of visits paid to the hermits and monks of the Thebaid and Lower Egypt in the winter of 394-5. It is agreed, I think, that the Latin version is due to Rufinus of Aquileia (*c.* 345-410) and it is generally thought to be a translation from a Greek original. Its relation to the *Lausiac History* of Palladius, in which most of it reappears, is uncertain. See *The Lausiac History of Palladius*, ed. Dom Cuthbert Butler, Cambridge, 1898, vol. i, pt. i.

[3] The story of Florentius of Nursia and his bear is given in the third book of St. Gregory's *Dialogues*, ch. 15, and a long story about St. Jerome's lion which guarded the ass (there was only one) which belonged to his monastery at Bethlehem is given in the early *Life* by an unknown author which is printed in Migne, *PL*, xxii, col. 201 ff.

to pray, he did not close the door after him, because he did not fear to lose anything. For he was content to sleep with only a mat on the bare ground, and in the clothes he was accustomed to wear.

15

MEANWHILE it happened that in reading various books he came on the Rule of St. Benedict, and while he was going quickly through it he came on that place in which monks are ordered to sleep clothed [ch. 22]. But not understanding this passage aright, for three years he lay down in his clothes, and not yet a monk he bore the mild yoke of monks.[1] He took care to obey the precepts of the one saint, and desired to imitate the life of the other. For the Lord Jesus cast then the simple seed in the bare earth from which He foresaw yield a hundredfold.

16

IT was a remarkable thing that his body was not blackened by contact with the ground on which he lay, and the power of his spirit was not weakened by his long-continued fasting. For in these last two years when together we visited the holy places both inside and outside the city of Rome in order to pray, young as I was, I was unable not only to surpass but even to follow this venerable man who was sixty years of age.[2] When, tired out, I begged him to spare me, he said, "Indeed you see that I have lost all my strength. Advanced age has made my old bones dry. For thirty years I have been such as you see me now." Lamenting, he described his weakness in this way, but I with great astonishment was marvelling at his strength, and not without reason. And indeed it was not fitting that he who was not suffered to be overcome by his own weakness should be brought low by the weakness of another. He counted as little whatever strength he saw in himself;

---

[1] In Chapter 55 St. Benedict expressly says that the monks are to have two tunics to allow for a change at night.

[2] We know that Odo was in Rome shortly before his death (iii, 12), therefore in 942, but we do not know for how long before. If the events described really occurred within two years of the time of writing, then Odo must have been in his sixties, which no doubt is what John means.

he judged that as great which he could see in another. During this time of his youth he sustained himself on half a pound of bread and a handful of beans, and—what is contrary to the nature of the Franks—very little to drink. Having laid aside all this corruptible burden he stood forth stripped as a soldier of Christ bearing only his arms. The young beginner was seen by all to surpass the ranks of the old men, and trusting in Christ he succeeded in bringing back a glorious booty from the enemy. All these things happened at the church of St. Martin in Tours. It is a place full of virtues, remarkable for miracles, overflowing with riches, excelling in all the practice of religion. For that place deserves to be remarkable which deserved to have such a man dwelling in it. It is rich not only in a martyr or confessor, but in the light of the world and the most worthy of priests. Kings hasten there, princes of many nations come with gifts and votive offerings.

17

AND many of those who came to Tours visited Odo; those who already knew him that they might meet him again, those who did not know him that they might make his acquaintance. And he, as an overflowing fountain, offered to all the cup they so much desired, and as from an open book gave fitting instruction to all. To one he disclosed the virtue of chastity, on another he imposed sobriety; this one he taught to despise the world, that one he admonished not to covet the goods of another. To each he gave abundantly whatever was necessary. He deplored the wretched state of the world, and declared to its lovers that it would soon come to an end,[1] for it was indeed, he said, no better than Gomorrha. He admonished, therefore, all to live sparingly, and not to embrace the objects of an evil desire. Gluttony he urged men to curb entirely, saying that he who stuffs his belly nourishes

[1] As Professor Knowles has pointed out (*The Religious Orders in England*, Cambridge, 1948-55, vol. i, p. 122), the mental outlook which saw the forces of evil as all but visible and tangible, and which regarded catastrophe and judgement as always impending upon the world, was common to all minds in the Western Church between Augustine and Gregory VII. It was a mentality partly, if not wholly, brought about by the breakdown of the old civilization and the failure of the new nations during this period to attain to any sort of intellectual maturity. (cf. introduction, p. ix).

lasciviousness. To the libidinous he held up the abyss of the
dragon, saying: "Alas, how miserable these people are, for the
dragon draws after it the third part of the stars." [Apoc. xii, 4.]
He reminded drunkards and gluttons that Nabuzardan, the prince
of cooks,[1] destroyed the walls of Jerusalem. To the effeminate and
perverted he opposed the homicide of Herod and the exile of the
scribe.[2] By how much better, he said, the soul is than the body, by
so much is one who acts in this way worse than Herod. Herod slew
bodies, but sent souls to heaven; such a one separates men from
God, slays souls with eternal death. The scribe who exercised the
young soldiers was led captive into Egypt; the man who does these
things will after his death be led down to hell. He lamented the
headlong fall of the learned saying, "*Look, O Lord, how the city full
of riches is made desolate*", and again, "*Woe to you Behemoth; you
never cease to do evil. You strew gold under you like mire, and the
beams of the sun are beneath you*" [Job xli. 21]. When they heard such
words, those who were conscious of sin were terrified, but the
innocent rejoiced at his words of consolation; and as from one
storehouse diverse men took diverse provender. I call God to witness that from the mouth of a man I never heard such sweetness
of speech. That was fulfilled in him which the Lord says in the
Gospel: *The kingdom of heaven is like to a householder who bringeth
forth out of his treasure new things and old.* [Matt. xiii, 52]. So it
came about that, savoured with the divine salt and filled with
the heavenly banquet, all returned home giving thanks.

[1] The reference is to Jer. lii, 12-14, or to 4 Kings xxv, 8-10, where the same
events are described. In our Vulgate text Nabuzardan is always described as "the
commander of the army", *princeps exercitus*, or some equivalent phrase. Odo
presumably either got his *princeps coquorum* (which was necessary for his interpretation) from some curiously corrupt text, or, as his Bollandist editor suggested
(*AASS*, Oct., vi, p. 308) gave Nabuzardan this title in ironical reference to
4 Kings xxv, 14, where he is described as taking away pots and mazers, forks
and cups, the instruments of sacrifice, from the temple.

[2] This mysterious scribe comes from the same passage of Scripture. In
Jer. lii, 25, the Douai version following the Vulgate has, "a scribe, an officer of
the army, who exercised the young soldiers" (see below in John's text). The
corresponding text in 4 Kings xxv (v. 19) has, "Sopher, a captain of the army",
etc. The Hebrew word *sopher* means scribe, and it is possible that Odo had a
Vulgate text of Kings which translated *sopher*, as does our text of Jeremiah. It
looks in fact as though he must have had the text of 4 Kings in mind from what
he says lower down of the scribe's going into exile in Egypt, for there is nothing
of this in Jeremias. Even so his text of Kings must have varied from our Vulgate
text for in this Sopher, or the scribe, is slain (19 and 20), and it is others who
go into exile in Egypt (26).

18

HE was offered many gifts and presents, but he was unwilling to receive them, for he who had distributed all his goods knew not by what right he might receive those of others. But on one occasion the above-mentioned lord [Fulk] got the better of him, and whether he would or no he had to receive a hundred shillings which he sent. But the soldier of Christ did not suffer them to remain with him for a moment, but immediately gave them to the needy. The pupil began to take the lead in the ranks of his masters, and to become an example to those who followed after him.

19

ABOUT this time he went to Paris, where he studied dialectic in the work which St. Augustine wrote for his son, Adeodatus,[1] and he also read with attention Martian[2] on the liberal arts. As his teacher in all this he had Remigius.[3] When his studies were over, he returned to Tours, and

[1] The reference appears to be to a work known as *Categoriae Decem*, which was attributed to St. Augustine in the Middle Ages, and apparently already in the time of Charles the Great. Augustine nowhere refers to such a work, or to one written for his son Adeodatus, and it is generally agreed today that the Benedictine editors of his works were right in regarding it as spurious. For the evidence and their arguments see Migne, *PL*, xxxii, 1419-40, where the work is printed.

The dialectic of such treatises was dead, and Odo's age was not one which was intellectually forward-looking. Thirty years after his death the most distinguished scholar of the age, Gerbert (later Pope Sylvester II), who began his monastic life at St. Gerald's monastery of Aurillac, gave an impulse to the study of logic, which was later to be the great instrument of the scholastics, but even he, as Mr. Southern has pointed out (p. 176), was more interested in rhetoric as a means of conserving old truths than in logic as a means of discovering new ones. Unfortunately even the rhetorical tradition was a bad one, represented by Odo's study of the late grammarians.

[2] Martianus Capella wrote at Carthage between 410 and 429—approximately the time when Augustine was writing *The City of God*—the *Liber de Nuptiis Mercurii et Philologiae*. The first book celebrates the marriage of Mercury and Philology, the remaining seven celebrate the seven bridesmaids, Grammar, Dialectic, Rhetoric (the later *trivium*), Geometry, Arithmetic, Astronomy, and Music (the later *quadrivium*). The work was a summary of ancient learning, but not strictly scientific in form, and perversely mannered in style. It had, however, a great vogue which lasted until the school of Chartres began to go back to the classical texts in the twelfth century. Odo's master, Remigius of Auxerre, wrote a commentary on it.

[3] In an age which has some reason to be called dark Remigius of Auxerre had a considerable reputation for learning, which was displayed in commentaries

20

he was then asked by some of the brethren who were his friends
that he would summarize in one volume the *Morals*[1] of the blessed
Pope, St. Gregory. He protested that this was altogether beyond
his powers, adding that, even if he had ability, he ought not to do
it, lest he should seem to detract from the work of such a man, and
take away from its value. On the other side, they argued that they
had had to give in completely before they had been able to get
through this enormous work, and they judged it absolutely better
to leave it, and to go back to the other Scriptures, than to be overwhelmed by so great a mass of material. There was no little alterca-
tion about this daily. I know that many will be very indignant
about the matter, and to calm them I have thought it better to
relate what he told me. For he did not undertake this work out of
arrogance, but by the Lord's disposal, that the light which was
hidden under a measure should be set on a hill-top. This will
appear more clearly from the story I give below. For while they
were persisting in this request, it happened that on a certain night
Odo was persevering in his accustomed prayer in the church of
St. Martin, when suddenly he was overcome by sleep and saw in
a vision a choir of saints coming down from on high into the
church. When they had given praise to the Lord, they sat down in
order in the stalls, and in a short time one of them coming out into
the middle said, "Why do we remain in this place?" The others

---

on Scripture and the grammarians. He taught at Rheims and at Paris, and was
one of the more important masters of the cathedral schools from which the
universities were later to spring. Little serious work has been done on these
writers, but it is beginning. See Miss Smalley's *The Study of the Bible in the
Middle Ages*, Oxford, 1952, ch. ii. We learn from Chapter III above that music
was among Odo's studies at this time.

[1] When St. Gregory was acting as Nuncio in Constantinople before he became
Pope, he delivered a series of lectures on the book of Job to the small body of
monks which accompanied him. When he got back to Rome he edited these
lectures into the monumental work known as the *Magna Moralia*, or *Exposition
of the Book of Job*. Of exegesis in the modern sense the book contains nothing,
but it is a storehouse of theological and moral teaching and as such was greatly
valued throughout the Middle Ages.

Odo's epitome of the *Morals on Job* is printed in Migne, *PL*, cxxxiii, 105 ff.
It runs to 402 columns in Migne as against Gregory's 1417 in the same edition.

answered that they were awaiting Pope Gregory. When he heard this, Odo began to look about this way and that, searching eagerly if he might be able to witness the arrival of the saint. Then raising his eyes he saw St. Gregory as though coming from heaven, but much more splendid in appearance than those who preceded him. They all rose up when he came in, and bowing their heads asked a blessing. He, however, did not come down among them, but remained in the ambo of the church, and called Odo, who was prostrate on the ground, saying, "Rise up, brother Odo, and do not fear." When he had risen up, he noticed a pen sharpened as though by some expert's hand which was placed behind the saint's ear in the manner customary to scribes. Taking this Gregory gave it to Odo, saying: "Go forward with assurance and finish the work demanded of you. The book which you write will not be destroyed, but mine will last for ever." While he watched, Odo understood the vision, and so taking that great book he diligently worked through it, and arranged the more important parts in one volume. Thus he put an end to the grumbling.

21

At another time it happened that the aforementioned Count Fulk, in some way that I know not, took two vessels of gold from the treasury of St. Martin.[1] But caught in the toils of avarice, he was unwilling to give them up, and a heavy vengeance overtook him. Brought to death's door by sickness, he ordered himself to be carried to the tomb of St. Martin and there promised a great number of gifts, but even in this way he did not receive the gift of health. After some time, when he had become utterly exhausted, and failed so much that he looked forward only to death, Odo came to visit him and immediately said to him, "Give back, wretched man, the vessels of St. Martin which you have unhappily taken away, and you will be cured at once." He promised both to give them back and to present others, if Odo's words were proved true by the event. Then, lifted by the hands of our father and those

---

[1] If Fulk was indeed the Treasurer of the Chapter (see p. 14, *n.* 1) it might account for the temptation and the opportunity to appropriate the vessels.

who were with him, he was carried to the body of St. Martin, and prostrate on the ground he suffered no delay in the help promised to him; and he who was brought by the hands of others as though lying on a stretcher recovered and returned unaided. So it came about that, chastened by this experience, he did not commit such acts again, and faithfully fulfilled what he had promised. Meanwhile Odo began to admonish him that he should leave the world and act only so as to please God. But he replied: "You cannot persuade me to such a manner of life, but there is one of my followers, a man most dear to me, called Adhegrinus, vigorous in arms and wise in counsel, who if he hears you will at once obey your wishes." And this subsequently happened. In a few days, when he had recovered his strength, Fulk went home, and to the large number of people who came to congratulate him on his return to health he recited at length how much he had endured, and explained in addition how he had found renewed strength in the words of Odo.

22

ONE of those who were with him and who took note of what he said was this same Adhegrinus, who, struck with compunction of heart put aside all his possessions, and lost no time in giving himself to Odo. He received the tonsure and having laid aside his military dress became forthwith a soldier of Christ. Odo, therefore, took all that Adhegrinus had brought with him for his temporal use and gave it to the poor, as he had formerly done with his own possessions. The two former followers of the count dwelt together contented with a little hut. For seeing the evil condition of the world, and that its lovers were taking a way full of enticements which led to ruin, they sought daily to rise to the heights of the monastic life. For wherever they could hear of a monastery anywhere in France they either visited it themselves or sent investigators, but nowhere could they find a religious house in which they felt inclined to remain. At last Adhegrinus decided to go to Rome, and having started on his journey, he came into Burgundy, and to a certain village called Baume. In this place there was a monastery which had recently been restored[1] by the abbot Berno.[2] Adhegrinus turned aside there and was received by the abbot into the guest-house most hospitably, as St. Benedict laid down. And there for some time he chose to stay as a guest; not that he wanted anything from the monks, but that he might get to know their way of life and the customs of the place. For those who dwelt in this place were the followers of a certain Euticus,[3] the excellence of whose life there is no need for me to relate in this book, though later on I have thought it well to recall the death he merited to die.

[1] John's word is *constructum*. Mabillon considers this the equivalent of *instauratum* (*Acta Sanctorum Ordinis Sancti Benedicti*, Paris, 1668-1701, vol. vii, p. 70). Baume was not in fact a new foundation by Berno.

[2] There is a good deal of doubt about the details of Berno's life. What seems to be the stronger tradition (Mabillon, *Acta*, vol. vii, pp. 67 ff., followed by *Pignot*, vol. i, pp. 36 ff. and Evans, pp. 2 ff.) states that he founded Gigny, probably on his own property, and later obtained Baume and other houses. Whether he was a monk before he founded Gigny is not clear. The point is of some interest, for Schmitz (*Histoire de l'ordre de Saint Benoît*, Maredsous, 1942-9, vol. i, pp. 130 ff.) states that he was a monk of St. Martin's at Autun sent to restore Baume. St. Martin's itself had been restored about 870 from St. Savin near Poitiers, and St. Savin was a daughter-house of Aniane. This would account very nicely for the traditions of St. Benedict of Aniane which Odo found at Baume, but the question cannot be discussed here. Berno was the first Abbot of Cluny (see p. 41, *n*. 2), and his influence on the later development of that house seems to have been important in three respects. (1) He went to Rome about 895 and made his monasteries directly subject to the Holy See, a procedure which may well have influenced William of Aquitaine to make the same provision for Cluny in 910. (2) Wherever he got them, he handed on the traditions of St. Benedict of Aniane to Cluny. (3) In keeping a number of houses in his own hands—a procedure doubtless justified in the exceptional and unfortunate state of monasticism at the time—Berno may have been influential in forming the later Cluniac system of many houses subject to one abbot. Although the full Cluniac system did not develop in Odo's day, he certainly followed Berno in taking a number of monasteries under his charge, but perhaps the circumstances of the time would have made that inevitable in any case.

Baume lies about forty miles north-east of Mâcon, Cluny about twelve miles north-west of the same city; Gigny roughly half way between Mâcon and Baume.

[3] It is evident from the information which John goes on to give that this was St. Benedict Aniane. The son of a noble family in the south of France, he was born in 751. For a few years in his early manhood he seems to have lived a devout life as a layman at the courts of Pepin and Charles the Great, but he soon adopted the monastic life, ultimately building a monastery on his own estates at Aniane. In his early years as a monk he cultivated an extreme ascet-icism, but he soon modified this in favour of a more traditionally Benedictine manner of life. In a few years he began to be called in by bishops, abbots, and secular lords to reform a large number of monasteries, and Charles the Great's son, Louis the Pious, when he became Emperor, called him to Aix and built a monastery for him. Benedict did in fact, as John says, make a careful collection of monastic tradition, the *Codex Regularum*, and the *Concordia Regularum*, and in 816 Louis confided to him the inspection of all the monasteries of the Empire. Owing to the circumstances of the time the reform he instituted collapsed almost immediately and the present *Life* gives valuable and nearly contemporary

23

THIS Euticus lived at the time of the great Emperor Louis,[1] and
was well-loved by him, as he was by all, for he was of an attractive
character. As a layman he was learned in unusual studies,[2] but
giving up all those things in which human weakness is accustomed
to take pride, he devoted himself entirely to the rules and institu-
tions of the holy Fathers; and from these authorities he took
various customs and collected them into one volume. After a little
time he became a monk himself, and he was so esteemed by the
king that a monastery was built for him in the palace.[3] When his
life had run its course he gave up his spirit in the presence of all
the brethren. And it happened that while his disciples were getting
ready for the funeral of their beloved father, he who had been dead
came to life again.[4] While they were lost in astonishment and admiration Euticus said: "Thanks be to God, you know that in forty
years you cannot remember me on a single day to have taken my
food without tears. But today the Lord has taken away my sorrow
and consoled me, giving me a place of rest among the choirs of
angels." Saying these words he sank into eternal rest. This Euticus
was the founder of those customs which to this day are kept in our
monasteries. When the venerable Adhegrinus understood this, he
sent word immediately to Odo, who, taking a hundred volumes
from his library, went at once to the same monastery. And so it

---

evidence of the process (see bk. iii, ch. i). Less than a century after his death
his very name, it seems, had been forgotten, but nevertheless through this
monastery of Baume a tenuous thread of his tradition was maintained to be
picked up again by Cluny. (See previous note.) A *Life* by one of his disciples,
Smaragdus or Ardo, is printed in Migne, *PL*, ciii, cols. 355 ff.

[1] See p. 25, *n*. 3.
[2] John's expression is *peregrinis studiis*.
[3] Louis built a monastery for Benedict at Inde about eight miles from Aix,
which could hardly be described as *intra palatium*.
[4] John gives a rather colourful version of the story as told by Ardo. The latter
states that when he was dying, Benedict at his own request had been left alone
for some hours, and when the abbot visited him he said, "I have just been in
the presence of the Lord among the choirs of saints." It would be natural to
suppose that he had had some high form of mystical experience. Similarly, Ardo
quotes Benedict as saying that during his monastic life he had never broken
his fast until he had poured out tears to God, which may refer to no more than
a prayer of compunction. John's rather fantastic version of the story is apparently
his own.

came about that he who was first a follower became a leader. Adhegrinus, however, shut himself up in a small cell, and with the permission of the abbot, Berno, dwelt in it for three years. But on Odo, because he was an educated man, was imposed the heavy task of being master of the school.[1]

24

I CONFESS that I expected to pass easily and swiftly over the life of our most holy father, but my feeble genius rebels, and along with his life I would describe the men who, I understand, were his companions. For this reason I beg that, as I do not shrink from labouring under this burden, so it may not seem to you onerous to receive it. For it seems right and pleasing to God, and an added adornment of this narrative, that along with his life I should relate the example of those whom he conducted to their fatherland, leading them on their journey through this life by way of his happy resting-place.

25

THE venerable Adhegrinus, therefore, whose history we described above, after he had received permission, sought out a deserted place and was there enclosed in a little cave. It happened one day, when the trials that oppressed him seemed more than he could bear, and there was no one present who might bring him words of consolation or the example of the Fathers, that, according to the words of Wisdom, *Woe to him that is alone, for when he falleth, he hath none to lift him up*, [Eccles. iv. 10], he was brought almost to desperation, when suddenly there stood beside him a man splendid in appearance who asked him kindly what he desired and why he appeared so overwhelmed. He replied, "Ever since I gave myself completely to the service of the Lord, I have deserved to receive no consolation of any kind from Him. And for this reason

---

[1] It was usual, of course, to have a certain number of boys in the monastery, who would normally go on to become monks. The boys attended most of the Divine Office and formed in a most literal sense a choir-school. Odo would undoubtedly have taught them singing. See introduction, p. xxvi.

I suffer greatly, for I do not know if my service is pleasing to Him, or if I shall ever merit to receive a reward for such great labour." Immediately the other fell upon his neck and kissing him said, "Believe me, you shall never be unworthy of the good things of the Lord." And when he had consoled him with these words he departed.

26

AGAIN another time it happened that the tempter overtook him outside the cell in which he dwelt, and rushing upon him carried him to the top of an overhanging rock, and would have hurled him from it with great violence. What could the soldier of Christ do, carried to such an inaccessible place? He knew not how to resist; but when he was in the greatest danger of death, suddenly St. Martin stood beside him and taking his hand said to him, "What is this? How do you come to be here?" "I know not, my Lord", he replied. Then comforting him St. Martin restored him to his dwelling.

27

ABOUT five years[1] ago, when Odo was going to Rome to restore[2] at the desire of the Pope and the whole papal court the monastery belonging to the church of St. Paul, he decided to visit Adhegrinus again in order to consult him on the matter so that he might act according to the Scripture: *Do everything with counsel, and thou shalt not repent when thou hast done it.* [Ecclus. xxxii. 24.] While they were discussing the project and talking for a long time about spiritual things, Odo asked him if he would tell him about the divine revelations he had received. Then Adhegrinus remembering

[1] If we accept 943 as the date of writing (p. 64, *n.* 3) this journey would be about 938, a date at which Odo was probably in Rome (see p. 7, *n.* 1), but John deliberately makes the time that has elapsed approximate and it may be that it should be stretched somewhat, and that the reference is to a journey that Odo made in 936. See note 2, p. 29.

[2] In 846 the Saracens reached the walls of Rome and sacked both St. Peter's and St. Paul's, which lay outside them. It seems that St. Paul's was not restored till this time. (Gregorovius, iii, 87, *History of the City of Rome in the Middle Ages*, trans. A. Hamilton, London, 1903.)

their old friendship, and glowing with the fire of charity, replied, "On a certain day when I had finished the appointed psalms, St. Martin suddenly stood before me, and, when he had given me a blessing, his glorious appearance and assured familiarity presently gave me my chance, and after some little talk I inquired where he was going and whence he had come. 'I come from Rome', he replied, 'and I am going to France, and as my journey brought me near you, I turned aside to visit you.' I thanked him and besought him that as he had deigned to visit a sinner, he would deign to stay under his roof for at least a little time. But Martin replied, 'Today is the coronation of Louis,[1] King of the Franks, and I am hastening to be present at his anointing, so I am unable to delay.' To this I replied, 'If you do indeed wish to go, I beg that you will first give me your blessing.' 'You have no need of being blessed by me,' he replied, 'for He who blessed me has also blessed you.' When I continued to urge him, he insisted that on the contrary I should give him a blessing, stating moreover that he would not be at peace with me unless I did so. There arose no small contention of a friendly sort between us on the matter; he refusing because he was unwilling, I because I would not presume. Eventually when we had each given the other a blessing, he departed, leaving me very sad." Odo was a most faithful witness to the truth of this, for he ordered the day and the hour to be noted down, and afterwards diligently inquiring into everything he found the facts to be as Adhegrinus had said.[2]

[1] The Louis who became King of France late in Odo's life was Louis IV, *Outremer*, as he was called from the fact that he came to the throne direct from exile in England. A son of Charles the Simple (893-929), he was only a child when his father died, and in the turbulent state of France at the time it was impossible for him to succeed to the throne. Rudolph of Burgundy wore the French crown from 929 to 936, but on his death in the latter year Hugh the Great, the most powerful lord in France, preferred to bring back a Carolingian, who was still only fifteen years old and whom he could control from behind the scenes, rather than excite the envy of his peers by taking the crown for himself. *Ordinatio* is the word that John uses to describe the ceremony that St. Martin was going to attend. Although it seems that the barbarian Franks adopted the biblical custom of anointing their kings before they did that of crowning them, coronation was certainly the practice at this date. See *Cambridge Medieval History*, vol. ii, p. 659.

[2] Mabillon deduced from this chapter that the journey to Rome to which it refers took place in 936. He did this by supposing that Adhegrinus related this vision of St. Martin to Odo on the same day that it occurred. This was the day of Louis IV's coronation, which took place in 936. But John's Latin gives no

28

THESE things happened, if I am not mistaken, more than thirty years after he had retired into solitude. Only on Sundays and the principal feasts was he accustomed to come down to the monastery of St. Peter, which is called Cluny, because it lies about two miles from that place.[1] When he had collected a little flour from which he used to make his bread, and a few beans, he returned immediately to his solitude. He never took wine, and he did not season his food with fat or oil. In all seasons he suffered cold and heat; heat between his shoulders, cold in his hands and arms.

But while continuing the life of this man, let us return as quickly as possible to our tale, from which we have long digressed. For I remember that I promised first to expound Odo's patience (for that is the source of all the virtues), and then, as time went on, to show the others. So with the help of the Lord, as my powers allow, I will hasten to fulfil my promise.

---

grounds for identifying the day of the vision with that on which Adhegrinus related it to Odo. Adhegrinus tells Odo that "on a certain day", *illo die*, St. Martin appeared to him. Pignot, who follows Mabillon, gets out of the difficulty by boldly translating this passage in a quotation, "Today (*aujourd'hui*) ... St. Martin appeared", but there seems no justification for this. When John says *illo die* he means, I take it, a particular day specified by Adhegrinus though not by himself, and Odo was able afterwards to check that this was in fact the day of Louis' coronation.

Sackur (vol. i, p. 101, *n.* 3), however, is perhaps right in saying that the passage at the end of the chapter in which Odo is stated to have had a note taken of the day and the hour (but not the year) of the vision implies that this was done soon after it occurred, and historians seem to consider that Odo was in fact in Rome in 936, when a temporary peace was patched up between Hugh and Alberic (see p. 49 *n.* 3).

[1] In Chapter 23 John told us that Adhegrinus got permission from Berno to retire to a cell for three years soon after he went to Baume, and presumably the cell was near Baume. This would be about the year 909. When Odo went to Cluny as abbot about 926, Adhegrinus, we must suppose, went to a cell near that place. Baume was over forty miles away. John appears to have overestimated the time that had elapsed since Adhegrinus retired into solitude. In Peter the Venerable's time (twelfth century) it was still customary at Cluny to have some of the monks living as hermits. See Jean Leclercq, *Pierre le Vénérable*, S. Wandrille, 1946, pp. 98-102, and Evans, pp. 59-61. This is the first mention of Cluny, which was founded in 910. John tells us nothing about its foundation, but we learn later (ii, 1) that Odo only went there after Berno's death in 926. The events which are recorded in the rest of this book must therefore have happened at Baume between 909 and 926. From 910 Berno was Abbot of both Baume and Cluny.

29

THERE were certain of the brethren in this same community [Baume] whose life and morals will be apparent from the following story. Hearing that Odo had come in order to undertake the monastic life, they came to him feigning not to know his intentions and asked him why he had come there. When he told them, they said, "We are all trying to flee from this community in order that we may be able to save our souls, but are you on the contrary coming here to lose yours?" When he asked them why they said this, they replied, "Do you know how Abbot Berno is accustomed to behave?" "No," he said. "Alas, if you knew how severely he treats his monks. Blows follow his correction, and then those whom he has beaten he binds with shackles, tames them by prison, afflicts them with fasting. And when they have suffered all this, even so the wretched men cannot obtain pardon." When he heard this Odo began to have doubts about entering. Seeing this, Adhegrinus came forth into their midst and said: "Father Odo, do not fear. These are not the words of one who speaks himself, but of one who is a mouthpiece. Take notice and see that it is the devil who speaks through the mouths of these men." Immediately they retired in confusion, but Odo and his companion submitted their necks to the sweet yoke of Christ. It was for this reason that St. Benedict, who foresaw what would happen, ordered in his Rule [ch. 53] that no one should speak with a guest unless he had been given leave by the superior. How many deceived in this way have turned back from the beginning of their religious conversion, and from the ardour of inward desire have returned to the sluggishness of ill-will? And although Scripture says: *Try the spirits if they be of God* [I John iv. 1], nevertheless the trial of the faithful and of those who seek God should not be of this nature, for the Lord by His prophet says to those who are aflame with the fire of the Holy Spirit: *You that inhabit the land of the south meet with bread those who come from the north.* [Isa. xxi, 14.] But the soldier of Christ was neither caught by blandishments nor broken by terrors. Of such as he the blessed Job rightly says: *Let*

*them curse it [the night] who curse the day, who are ready to raise
up a leviathan.* [Job iii. 8.]

30

FOR the moment it will be well to put the story of Odo's life aside
for a while that I may explain the customs of the place a little and
thus make the succeeding narrative clearer. It was the custom there
that the master of the school should never go with only one boy
alone to any place whatsoever, not even for the purposes of nature,
also that no boy should presume to talk with the master alone, but
for the sake of good report he should always take another of the
boys or one of the brethren to accompany him or to talk with him.
But if it was night and one of the boys wished to withdraw, he
might not put a foot out of the dormitory without the light of a
lantern and another to accompany him. At meal times there was
always reading at both tables;[1] each one carefully collected his
breadcrumbs before the reading was finished, and consumed them
giving thanks, for when the reading was finished no one might
consume them or any other food. It was said that these crumbs
had more of a sacramental character than other food,[2] because they
had been the subject of a miracle about this time.

31

THERE was a certain very excellent brother in the monastery who
was beloved by all. When he came to die, he suddenly cried out to
the surrounding brethren who had come to commend his spirit to
the Lord with prayer, "Help me, I beseech you for God's sake. I
am now carried to the judgement and there the accuser of the
human race, the devil, has brought as evidence against me a sack

---

[1] In monastic refectories certain of the brethren are deputed each week to
wait on the others. These receive a snack before the main meal at which they
wait, and have their own meal afterwards. The two meals are known as first
and second table.

[2] It is an interesting fact—already noted by Mabillon—that in the so-called
Rule of the Master, which for the last fifteen years or so has been creating great
interest in scholarly circles among Benedictines, the crumbs left over at table
are also given a quasi-sacramental character, and they are there subjected to a
curious ritual (being made into a special pudding) in keeping with the rather
eccentric character of the document as a whole. See an article by Abbot Justin
McCann in *The Ampleforth Journal*, May, 1950.

full of breadcrumbs, which I refused to eat according to the custom, and which fell from the table." After a little time he cried out again in a terrible manner, "Behold the devil of whom I told you is here, and carrying the aforesaid sack." While the terrified brethren were lost in wonder, he cried again, "He is there, do you not see him?" Then he fortified himself with the sign of the cross and gave up his spirit with words of prayer. From that day the breadcrumbs were collected with all diligence.

32

THEY observed especially the custom of silence. At unsuitable times no one might speak or consort with another of the brethren in the cloister of the monastery, and on days when a twelve-lesson Office was celebrated no one might speak in the cloister before chapter on the following day. Within the octaves of Christmas and Easter there was strict silence day and night. This short silence, they said, signified the eternal silence. When there was necessity to ask for anything they made various signs to each other, which grammarians I suppose would call the language of the fingers and eyes. This usage had developed to such an extent among them that, if they were without the use of their tongues, the signs, I think, would suffice to indicate everything necessary. But on ferial days and in the other octaves of the saints there was this arrangement. On ferial days in the day and night Office together they sang one hundred and thirty-eight psalms, from which we subtract fourteen for the sake of the weaker brethren. But against this must be put the special prayers which our brethren say which are seen to exceed the psalter and also the two Masses and the litanies. At each of the canonical hours they knelt twice. During the other octaves which were mentioned, they sang seventy-five psalms only in the day and night Offices together, and they knelt once and rested twice. There are many other points which I think may be omitted lest they should weary the reader.[1]

[1] These details about the Divine Office are interesting. The Rule of St. Benedict legislates for forty psalms to be said on ferial and feast days. According to the Cluny Constitutions of about 980 (B. Albers, *Consuetudines Monasticae*, Stuttgart and Vienna, 1900, vol. i)* some 175 psalms were said daily, and more

* Given as those of Farfar, but see *Rev. Ben*, vol. xvii, pp. 165 ff, 1900.

33

WHEN Odo took over the mastership of the school, he soon had an opportunity of proving his patience. During the night one of the boys indicated by a sign that he wished to retire for the purposes of nature. The closet adjoined the dormitory and was so close to it that the lantern which burnt in the dormitory by rule lighted it fully. Odo therefore getting up and waking one of the other boys was content to accompany him without any other light. On the next day when the brethren came together in chapter according to custom, after the reading of the martyrology and the Rule, they began to speak sharply against him, asking why he had accompanied the boy without a candle on the night before. Because no one might set out his case before asking pardon, or defend his action afterwards, Odo falling to the ground begged pardon, stating that the dormitory light was sufficient. They gave him a hearing, yet condemned him as guilty of a grave fault. But the holy man, who had chosen the narrow way and had come in order to follow Him who "when he suffered threatened not". (I Pet. ii. 23), without indignation or murmuring, not complaining of the opposition, but taking the shortest course, prostrated himself on the ground and begged pardon. His abbot however wishing to prove his patience, pretended to be angry, and pronounced sentence of excommunication, saying that he should no more ask pardon on

---

at certain times of the year. The great increase in the number said at Cluny was of course the result of the special offices and groups of psalms (the penitential, gradual psalms etc.) which had been added to the canonical Office. It was St. Benedict Aniane (see above p. 25, *n.* 3) who introduced these new elements, and it is interesting to see the result recorded here in the practice at Baume, where his tradition was explicitly carried on (ch. 22 above). John's monastery evidently modified the psalmody customary at Baume (though not very much), but added substitutes; what we should describe as two conventual Masses, and the litanies of the saints. What John means by the special prayers which he says they added is not clear, as the most notable addition which might qualify for this description, the *Trina Oratio*, in fact consisted mostly of psalms. It was the custom then, as it still is, to say certain portions of the Office, not the psalms, kneeling.

The general reader will no doubt agree with John that further reference to this matter of office would have been wearying, but the historian of the liturgy must regret that he did not tell us more. A useful summary of the developments which the Divine Office, in a large sense, underwent between St. Benedict and the twelfth century is to be found in an article in *The Downside Review*, "The Monastic Horarium", by David Knowles, Oct., 1933.

that day. Odo revolving in his heart the saying of David: *I am be-come as a beast before thee; I am always with thee* [Ps. lxxii. 23], and again, *Thou hast laid afflictions on our back; thou hast set men over our heads* [Ps. lxv. 11 and 12], going out prostrated at the feet of the brethren and begged that they should go and ask pardon of the abbot in his place. At length the abbot, Berno, admiring such patience in a youth, called him to him, and according to the custom of the rule healed his trouble by a blessing, and after this Odo became still more dear to him.

34

In that same community some of the brethren, whom we have mentioned before, were childish both in mind and behaviour, and that which ought to have profited them worked rather for their loss. For they never missed an opportunity of doing Odo an injury or of bringing a false accusation against him. But the peace-loving Odo used to take them apart, and although innocent throw himself at their feet asking pardon as if guilty. And he did this not through human fear, but through fraternal charity, that his patience might correct those who he saw were incurring the divine vengeance. Sometimes they were overcome by his patience, but they soon returned, like flowing water, to their evil ways, and persecuted him whom they ought to have imitated.[1] The leader of this set was called Wido. Often when one of them instigated another to rail at Odo, the one who was sent would protest: "What is the use of doing this, since we cannot drive him away or provoke him to insulting words? You know that he is more learned than we are. Up till now he has willingly taught me what I wished to learn from him, but I am afraid that, crushed by these wrongs, he will begin to with-hold what he now freely imparts." The other would reply, "It is not so, for this Odo is such that he will put up not only with these or similar wrongs, but with even greater, and after all that he will still grant you what you wish." However, after a short time these men suffered the divine vengeance, and were struck down by the

---

[1] It will be remembered that Odo went to Baume because it was the only monastery that he could find where the religious life was lived in a worthy manner. What, it may be asked, were the bad houses like, if this was a good one?

just judgement of God, because they would not submit to fraternal correction. For when Berno, who was then the abbot of that monastery, was dead, having put off the religious habit they returned to the world, and later came to a terrible end.

35

OUR father Odo was accustomed to relate another miracle which occurred at this time. There was a certain brother in the community who, when he was at table, used to be completely absorbed in the reading. One day it happened that when he had collected his crumbs as usual, the abbot put a stop to the reading before he could consume them. He did not know what to do, for when the reading stopped he did not dare to eat them, nor yet to leave them lest they should be lost. He therefore closed his hand on them thinking it would be best to keep them to offer to the abbot when the community should have returned from their visit [to church], and so when they had come out of the oratory he immediately prostrated himself at the abbot's feet. On being asked why he was doing penance, he proffered the little heap that he had in his hand, and the crumbs were all found to have been turned into pearls. The community gave glory to God and were much amazed, but the pearls at the abbot's command were inserted into one of the church ornaments. Odo was accustomed to tell this story about himself as though it were of another.

At this time too he began to be much concerned about saving the souls of his parents, wondering how he might withdraw them from the bonds of this world. And so, having received permission, he went to visit his father and brought him to the monastery, where he became a monk. His mother also he induced to take the veil. But if I were to write her life this would appear as a history rather than a brief essay.

36

IT happened on another occasion that late one day he turned aside to rest at the house of a certain noble. His hosts were absent, but their grown-up daughter was there with the rest of the household. The whole evening this girl pondered most deeply on his way of life. Then full of compunction she went secretly to him by a back way, and prostrate at his feet told him she was condemned soon to be given in marriage, begging that for the sake of God, whose servant he professed to be, he might liberate her that same night. Hearing this the soldier of Christ was greatly perplexed, not knowing what to do or how he might satisfy this wish of the girl's. Considering, as he always did, his duty to God, but also his compassion for the tears of the girl, he put before himself on the one hand the judgement of God and the loss of her soul, and on the other the criticism that her parents and the people would bring against him, in that he a monk should have presumed to do such a thing. But overcome by the love of God and the sobs of the girl he at length consented to take her away. That night, when all the servants of the house were asleep, he and the brother who was with him, having mounted their horses, went on ahead, and on his orders the servants who accompanied him followed with the girl. The next day they approached the monastery. Now, not far from it there was an oratory[1] to which women were admitted to pray, and there he arranged for her to remain, while he himself went on to the monastery. On the following day, as is the custom, he told the abbot all that he had done. When the abbot heard of his action with regard to the girl, looking very upset, he began to rebuke him severely, asking why he had presumed to act thus without permission. Odo threw himself on the ground and prostrate at the abbot's feet begged pardon. The abbot told him to arise and repeated his question. At length Odo replied, "Father Abbot, from the time that you deigned to receive me a sinner, so far as I could tell your only care was for the saving of souls. Other abbots make it their business to amass property and to please men. But you, full of loving-kindness and mercy, are concerned only to please God and to save souls, and it was because I wished to be an imitator of you that I desired to win this girl to the praise of your name. For although her tears eventually overcame me, I was not unmindful

---

[1] Mabillon notes (*ad. loc.*) that he has seen many references to the fact that women were not allowed in monastic churches. I can only quote his authority.

of your rebuke, which I knew I could not avoid. But I preferred to be struck by the scourge of a loving father than to be held guilty of her soul. And would that I might gain all the women living in this province who are held by the chains of the flesh,[1] and that you in your love should scourge me for each one." With these and similar words he calmed the anxiety of the abbot, who, however, forthwith gave him this obedience: "Go, and as you have known how to withdraw her from the world, so take now her food to her daily and instruct her with holy admonitions, lest at any time she should repent and at the suggestion of the devil return to the world." So Odo took her food to her every day and instructed her by examples from the Fathers of old, till in a few days he was able to take her to a convent[2] and hand her over to the holy virgins. However, for the sake of good report all this was done in the presence of brethren. Not long afterwards she came to die, and when the sisters had gathered round to protect her spirit by prayer, and they thought that she was already dead, suddenly with such voice as she could muster she said, "Help me, I beseech you, to rise up." When they asked her why she made this request, she replied, "I see the most blessed Apostle Paul coming and I wish to go to meet him." She had hardly completed the words when stretching out her arms that she might rise more quickly, she repeated the same words again. The others thought that she was out of her mind, but meanwhile as far as she was able she raised herself on her knees and with head bowed sought a blessing from him who was coming, saying *Benedicite*, and immediately sank into eternal

---

[1] Odo's attitude towards marriage is calculated to cause surprise and even scandal to a modern reader. This is not the place to enter into a disquisition on the theology of marriage in the Dark Ages, but perhaps it will be useful to quote Abbo, a not very distant successor of Odo's at Fleury. He was born probably two or three years after Odo's death, and as abbot of the monastery which had given Odo so much trouble (see below, bk. iii, chs. 7 and 8) he attained considerable fame both for learning and sanctity. In his *Apologeticus* (*PL*, cxxxix, col. 463) he states that there are three degrees, *ordines* or *gradus*, in the Church. The first is good, the second better, and the third best. The first, which is good, is that of married people. We need not follow him into the other distinctions which he makes, but the point is that while he allows the married state to be good he very definitely makes his own St. Paul's saying about it being better not to marry. Odo would doubless have endorsed his opinions, though his words in the present chapter give a rather unduly strong expression to them.

[2] In the *Collations* (iii, 21) Odo tells a story of two nuns "from the monastery for women which lies near our monastery of Baume", and according to Mabillon there were two convents for women near (*Acta*, vol. vii, p. 68).

rest. So there was no doubt that she was taken by him who came to visit her.

37

ABBOT Berno, therefore, foreseeing what this most virtuous man was going to become, promoted him, and having summoned a bishop[1] had Odo, although unwilling, ordained priest.[2] Odo used to say of this bishop that no dog would dare to eat food that had been blessed by him, and if by chance one happened to do so it immediately died, as though it had taken poison.[3] But I beg that no one may hold it against me that I said he had been ordained against his consent, lest perchance he who attempted so to ordain him should seem to be among those who do not fear to buy or sell the gift of the Holy Spirit.

On the night after his ordination, when he awoke from sleep and found the stole given him by the bishop round his neck, as the custom is, not at first remembering that he had been ordained, he began to lament, as though some great misfortune had befallen him, and for a long time after through too great modesty he was ashamed to go outside the monastery. For this reason Abbot Berno, having found some pretext, sent him on a visit to this same bishop. After the bishop had spoken at length to his great consolation on the dignity of the priesthood, they were led on to discuss the state of the Church, and Odo began to expound Jeremias' lamentation over the priests. When he had finished, the bishop

---

[1] From the dedication of the book mentioned later in this chapter we learn that the bishop was Turpio, Bishop of Limoges.

[2] We are so accustomed today to thinking of a man pursuing a more or less comprehensive course of theology before ordination that it is interesting to recall what Odo's studies had been. There was the background of the late Latin grammarians and the dialectic of the pseudo-Augustine (see p. 21, n. 1), the considerable study of Gregory's *Morals* which he epitomized, and the further study of the commentaries on the "Gospels and prophets" (see p. 15, n. 1), disapproved of but apparently persevered in at Tours, and very likely continued at Baume. It was a good preparation at this period, for it must be remembered that before the scholastic movement of the twelfth and thirteenth centuries comprehensive treatments of speculative theology did not exist. That he had an extensive knowledge of the Bible is evident from his writings. The *Life* of Gerald in this volume will show a great number of quotations and allusions, and not a few reminiscences of phraseology.

[3] This "odd monkish tale" as Dr. Evans calls it (p. 2, n. 4) is introduced by John with characteristic irrelevance.

asked him to write down what he had said and to put it into the form of a book. But against this proposition Odo produced the Rule, which says that a monk may do nothing without the permission of his superior. The bishop accordingly went to the monastery, and being a firm friend of the abbot straightway obtained what he wanted from him. Then at the abbot's command Odo wrote three books on the prophecy of Jeremias, the text of which has already been sent to various churches.[1]

38

ABOUT this time Abbot Berno fell into a deadly sickness. At once summoning the neighbouring bishops he resigned his office, and with sorrow proclaimed himself a sinful man and unworthy of having held such a position. At the same time he asked the brethren that they would elect whom they wished as abbot. Then Odo was seized by the brethren and forcibly led to Berno, all crying out that he was the man to be made abbot. Even then he did not wish to give way and take on the office of pastor, but he was overcome at last by the threat of ex-communication from the bishops. Shortly after Odo had been made abbot Berno died.

[1] These are the three Books of the *Collations* (Migne, *PL*, cxxxiii, cols. 517 ff.). Their immediate connexion with the prophecy of Jeremias is not obvious. Odo makes no reference to their being in any way a commentary on the prophet, and the quotations from him are less numerous than from other books of the Bible. But in a general way they may well have been inspired by the temper of the Hebrew prophet, for the *Collations* might not unaptly be described as a Jeremiad. Odo could hardly fail to have been struck by the evils of his day, and we have already seen (ch. 17) how this was the subject of his preaching when he was at Tours. The theme of the *Collations* is twofold, the trials and afflictions which come to all men as the result of their fallen human nature, and the special trials which have been inflicted on his generation by divine Providence. And we can easily believe that it was the latter which led him to consider the former.

Book II

I

In the midst of many disasters and frequent weariness I have been able to narrate a few facts about our father Odo and what he did under his abbot, and from these you can easily perceive with what perfection he began his own career as abbot. Since, however, the beginning of a holy life is fraught with difficulties and labours, while the end of the contest brings glory and praise, I will hasten as by a direct route through his holy and peaceful life to his death.[1] As soon as he was elected and blessed as abbot his old persecutors,[1] whom I mentioned above, rose up against him. But he, preferring to give way and to be happily at peace than to live in contention, left the monastery and the things which Berno had collected and bequeathed to him in the manner of a father, and going to Cluny finished the monastery which had been begun there.[2] The senior monks of Baume, however, followed him.

2

At this time the money he had brought with him was all used up in putting up the monastic buildings. It was about the feast of

[1] Apparently these were the monks who made so much difficulty for Odo at the beginning of his life at Baume (ch. 34). It is certain, however, that he had difficulties too from another and more reputable source. Berno had come to be abbot of a whole group of houses, including the newly-founded Cluny. In the days of a less developed canon law he left by will (mostly translated in Evans, p. 8) the abbacies of Baume and Gigny, with some other dependencies, to his nephew Wido (not presumably the Wido mentioned in ch. 34), and to Odo the abbacies of Cluny, Massay, and Deols. He also transferred some property from Gigny to Cluny. Wido disputed the provisions of Berno's will and Odo appealed to the Pope, who upheld his claims. In any case Odo would presumably have left Baume now for one of the abbeys which had been given to him.

[2] The circumstances of the founding of Cluny were simply that William of Aquitaine wanted to found an abbey. Having heard of the good reputation of Berno he sent for him (910), and Berno chose the site of Cluny and became its first abbot, keeping the abbacies which he already held. William's charter for the foundation of Cluny is still extant (it is translated in Evans, pp. 4 ff.), and is important in making the abbey directly subject to the Holy See, and in giving the monks the right to elect their own abbot after the death of Berno. It is possible that this latter provision was also due to Berno.

We learn from the testament of Berno (Evans, p. 8) that the buildings at Cluny were not in fact completed in Berno's lifetime.

St. Martin, which feast we are accustomed to celebrate with an octave, and at the end of Lauds on the octave day, before it was light, and when all had retired to their beds to rest rather than to sleep, our father used to relate that this vision was granted to a certain poor old man. He saw a venerable figure with white hair, wearing a splendid stole and a cope, with a bishop's crozier in his hand. Coming nearer, the figure began to inspect closely the structure of the monastery. When asked who he was and why he was inspecting the building, he said: "I am the one whose octave day the brethren are celebrating, and I have come to visit them. Tell them not to give up, but to carry on with the work they have begun." To this the person who saw the vision replied that all the money he had brought with him was exhausted. "Let them not fear," the other replied: "I am now come from Rome and I am going to Touraine. I will make my way through Gothia and Aquitaine, and from these districts I will demand such payment as will abundantly suffice not only for the present time but also for the future." The brethren, therefore, delighted and feeling secure in the promise of such a one, began to give thanks to God with joyous hearts. Who the person was, who saw this vision, it is not for me to say, because it was our father's custom deliberately never to describe his own person. But if anything had appeared to him, great or small, he described what he had seen in this way—one of our brethren, or a certain poor old man, saw this or that. Whenever he told me this incident, he added that a few days after this revelation more than three thousand shillings were brought from Gothia. He was accustomed to relate to me great events of this nature which were done at the monastery of St. Benedict known as Fleury[1] in the same way as at Cluny. If I dared to write them down in full this little book would extend far beyond the meagre powers of its author. But while I am relating more simply the faithful fulfilment of St. Martin's promise, there suddenly occurs

[1] Fleury, now St.-Benoît-sur-Loire, is traditionally said to have been founded about 640. It acquired great fame from the fact that the bones of St. Benedict were said to have been brought there from Monte Cassino in 673. Monte Cassino was deserted during the whole of the seventh century after being destroyed by the Lombards in 581. Early testimony seems to be all in favour of the claims of Fleury. See J. McCann, *St. Benedict*, London, 1938, ch. 14; cf. below bk. iii, chs. 7 and 8.

to my mind the no small support of the wild beasts. It may be that the description of this will raise a smile in some readers, but since we are "made a spectacle to angels and men" [1 Cor. iv. 9], let those who disdain to imitate us, or are not able to do so, have at least a good laugh at us, seeing us go from good to better. And at last, leaving this sad life, may they follow us rejoicing to the joy of heaven.

3

WHEN the oratory of the monastery had been built, the brethren, according to custom, invited the bishop to consecrate it. He, however, not thinking of the poverty of the monks, came on the appointed day with a large body of ministers. When all these people arrived the brethren were much embarrassed, not having made fitting preparations to receive them. Early in the morning, however, before it was light, a huge boar from the forest approached the monastery. When the door-keeper of the church, who was outside the monastery admiring the beauty of the building,[1] saw it, he fled into the church and bolted the doors. But the beast, laying aside its ferocity, knocked for a long time at the porch as though asking to be let in, and anointed the stonework, in so far as it was able, with saliva from its mouth. But since no one dared to open to it, it stood there till the bishop came with his train, and

---

[1] This first church at Cluny, which must have been completed some time about 927, was replaced before the end of the century by one built under St. Majolus and dedicated in 981. This in its turn was replaced by the great church begun in 1089 under St. Hugh, which lasted substantially unaltered until the Revolution, when it was partly demolished and partly allowed to fall down, except for one transept, which remains. About this, which must have been the greatest Romanesque church in Christendom, much is known as a result of archaeological work carried out under Professor Conant for the Medieval Academy of America.

When the second church was built in 981, the early one was left alongside it and used as a sacristy, but it was pulled down before 1100. Professor Conant has made an interesting hypothetical reconstruction of the first and second churches (*Early Med. Church Architecture*, Baltimore, 1942, pl. xxxvi), but little is really known of Odo's church, which appears to have been a simple Carolingian building of the "shed" type. The second was much larger and more elaborate, in what is now known as the first Romanesque style, while the third must have been perhaps the greatest example of that style at its most developed. (See Conant, chs. 6, 7, and 8: *Speculum*, 1929, pp. 3, 168, 291, 443.)

it then offered itself willingly to be slaughtered,[1] thus fulfilling the word of the psalmist which says: *They that fear the Lord shall not be deprived of any good* [Ps. xxxiii, 11] and again: *They shall not be confounded in the evil time; and in the days of famine they shall be filled* [Ps. xxxvi, 19].

4

INDEED Odo sometimes confessed that his means always sufficed both to feed the brethren and to give alms to the poor. Never did a poor man turn away empty from the bosom of his mercy. Whenever I went out with him he was always careful to ask if we had something for the poor, and if we had all that was necessary, he went on his way happily and without hesitation. And because he gave to all who asked of him, by the power of God all things were supplied to him. He always had in mind that precept of Tobias: *See that you turn not your face away from that time, and give to all who ask of you.*[2] [Tobias iv. 7.] If anyone had brought him a gift and seemed from his dress to be a poor man, Odo immediately asked him what he wanted, or if he needed anything from him. If the man asked anything, he immediately estimated the value of his gift on an accurate balance and ordered him to be given double. I have many times seen him do this with all sorts of goods. I confess my fault in that I was often saddened by these transactions. Being abbot[3] I had, as it were, compassion on the poverty of the

[1] John ends this incident very tersely. Nalgodus, the monk of Cluny who re-wrote his story two hundred years later, drawing either on his imagination or possibly on tradition, is much more explicit. When the bishop's followers, approaching the church apparently from outside, saw the boar, they rushed away and armed themselves with clubs and spears, then, as a matter of course, they attacked and slew it.

[2] Tobias iv, 7 seems to be the reference but the translation of the Vulgate runs, "Turn not away thy face from any poor person", *ab ullo paupere*, which makes better sense than John's text. The second part of his verse is also different and seems only to be an explanation of the first part. He may have used a corrupt text, or his own may have been corrupted in copying.

[3] The Latin word used is *prior*. In his *Rule* St. Benedict calls the prior as we understand the term today *praepositus* and the word *prior* refers to the abbot or whoever is presiding (see G. Arroyo, *S. Benedicti Regula Monasteriorum cum Concordantia*, Silos, 1947). I think that the word here probably means abbot and that the monastery referred to is Salerno. If that is so, Odo's relation to John must have been that in which he stood to a number of abbots of monasteries reformed by him. It was a curious relationship, of which modern canon law takes no cognizance. The chroniclers of the time speak of the abbots of these

house, and, foreseeing the needs of the brethren and alleging our want, I told him that he was unjust thus to give everything away without discretion. I thought I was acting wisely, but involved in the darkness of foolishness I was pierced by the sword of obstinacy. But being a most skilful physician of souls he somehow touched the pulse of my error with the hand of discretion, and cured the wound of my mind by the following example. Concerning this matter he said to me "Be silent, you say these things to your hurt. There was a certain youth much given to literary studies, and on a winter night, while he was hastening to Lauds[1] in order to arrive before his fellows, he saw a poor man lying half-naked in the porch of the church. Moved with compassion at his poverty he took off the scapular which he had on over his habit and threw it down as he went past for the man's use. Thinking only of his good deed he put the fear of cold away from him, but when Lauds were finished he returned to his cell stiff all over. As he was about to lay his frozen limbs in bed to warm them, he found a pound of gold on his blanket, and from thenceforth he had abundance both for his own use and to give to others." I do not know of whom he told this tale, but with this and like examples he poulticed the wound of my perverseness.[2]

---

monasteries as being *co-abbates* with Odo (Mabillon, *Acta*, vol. vii, p. 133; *PL*, cxxxiii, 22). Later, when the Congregation of Cluny was constituted, the heads of the dependent houses were only priors, but it is to be noted that many of the houses which Odo took over in this way did not belong to Cluny when the Congregation was formed.

The last chapter was about Odo's early days at Cluny, but I suggest this one refers to when he was in Italy near the end of his life. The inconsequent switch from one period of Odo's life to another would be in keeping with John's disregard for chronology, of which Nalgodus complained.

[1] *Ad matutinos* is the expression which John uses, which at this time would naturally mean what we now call Lauds, *Vigiliae* being used for Matins. It would seem more likely that the incident took place before Matins as we use the term. These began probably about 2 a.m., and the choir would return to bed after they were finished. The point is not important.

[2] Pignot (vol. i, p. 70) puts this incident in Odo's Paris period, and it must belong there or to his time at Tours. In either case he would have been a cleric and not a monk, and hence could appropriately be provided with gold, which as a simple monk he could not. The tale obviously refers to Odo himself, as John is well aware in spite of his disclaimer at the end.

5

I WOULD pass to other things, but his many acts of mercy compel me to delay, and to say something more of his generosity. I know that I cannot do this without bringing shame on myself, but nevertheless I will set to and plunge the sword of rebuke into myself; henceforth I will reveal my faults to all, that if I may not now confess these things to him, because he has departed, at least I shall obtain you as intercessors with him. When he was on a journey he used to make any boys that he found on the road sing something and as though to pay their performance he would order them to be given a present. They deserved, he used to say, no small remuneration. He used to speak in this way that we might be encouraged by their cheerfulness, and that they might profit by his mercy. For his words were full of joy and his speech used to make us laugh with delight. But always holding the reins of moderation in his hand, he would quote that chapter of the Rule which says, not to love much or violent laughter [ch. 4], and again, that a monk should not be ready and prompt to laughter [ch. 7], because it is written: *The fool lifteth up his voice in laughter* [Ecclus. xxi. 23]. So he restrained us while his spiritual joy filled our hearts with inward rejoicing. But what can one such as I say that is worthy of him, or what can I relate of such great happiness? In truth when we could satisfy our minds in no other way we used secretly to kiss his garments. And what wonder that we should do this who were always with him, for when he went into the church of St. Peter,[1] the ministers and those who had gone there to pray coming out ran after him, and taking hold of the garment which covered him like a cape, kissed the fringe of it. He passed on with hurried steps as though in flight, and they followed him like persecutors. He was like a cornerstone with four faces, angelic and human, bountiful and pleasing, so that that seemed to be fulfilled in him daily which we read in the psalm: *Acceptable is the man that showeth mercy and lendeth* [Ps. cxi. 5], and again as the Apostle Paul says: *God loveth a cheerful giver.* [2 Cor. ix. 7 quoting Ecclus. xxxv. 11.]

[1] Presumably in Rome.

The blind and the lame, he said, would be the doorkeepers of heaven, therefore no one ought to drive them away from his house, lest in the future they should shut the doors of heaven against him. So if by chance one of our servants, not being able to put up with their shamelessness, replied sharply to them, or would not give them the usual alms, or denied them access to the door of our tent,[1] Odo at once rebuked him with threats: then in his presence he used to call the poor man and command him saying, "When this man comes to the gate of heaven, pay him back in like manner." He said this to terrify the servants, so that they should not act in this way again, and that he might teach them to love charity. If, as often happened, he found an old or feeble man by the roadside, he used immediately to get down from his horse and set the poor man upon it, ordering all to go on a little distance ahead; and he would command one of the servants to stay back and support him lest he fall. He himself continued on foot in the midst of us on horseback, and always singing the psalms himself, he made us sing them with him. If out of shame, or fear of him, any-one wished to get off his horse, Odo immediately ordered him to stay where he was, knowing that it was reverence for himself and not for the poor man that made him want to dismount. I have often seen him do this.

6

WHEN we crossed the Cottian[2] Alps with Gerald, the Bishop of Riez, and went to Rome[3] with him, I remember Odo did this with

---

[1] In the *Life* of St. Gerald there are many references to the party camping for the night on journeys. We should expect a feudal lord, even of so unworldly a mentality as Gerald, to travel with a considerable retinue, but Odo evidently did so too, and the conditions of the time must have made it necessary for safety. Odo's journeys, we know, were many and long, and they must have been slow.

[2] North of the Maritime Alps in the region of the Mont Cenis Pass.

[3] As the Cottian Alps lie between France and Italy the text here implies that John was accompanying Odo on a journey from France to Rome. We must therefore suppose that after their first journey to Pavia and back, mentioned in i, 4, John went with Odo to France, and presumably to Cluny; but they cannot have stayed there long. If the journey to Pavia in i, 4 took place in the spring of 938, the one to France might have been in the summer and autumn of that year. See p. 49, *n.* 1.

a certain woman who was possessed by the devil. She was immediately freed from the possession, and accompanied us to Sienna, but there she remained, as she had become ill with dysentery. Afterwards we saw her at St. Paul's in Rome, and by a sign he at once ordered her to be given money. For I asked him who the woman was who was sitting covered with confusion, with head bowed and eyes fixed on the ground. It is such a one, he replied, giving me signs by which I could more easily recognize her.

On that same journey a certain feeble old man crossed the Alps with us. He carried a sack filled with bread, and onions, and garlic, and leeks, the smell of which was more than I could stand. But the holy father, as soon as he saw him, put him on his horse, as his manner was, and took the evil-smelling sack himself. Unable to put up with the smell, I fell back from where I was walking at his side. When we had gone through the narrow pass at the top of the Alps and had begun to descend on the other side, I saw him standing a little way ahead and the poor man urging him to re-mount his horse. Even then he did not return the sack, but hung it on the pommel of his saddle. I passed those who were in front of me in order to come up to him more quickly, and I went full of shame. As I arrived he said to me, "Come on, for there are still some psalms that we must recite." When I replied that I could not stand the smell of the sack, he rebuked me saying, "Alas, this poor man can eat that which nauseates you. You cannot even stand the smell of it. The poor man can carry what you say you cannot even look at." It was of himself, the true poor man of Christ, that he said this. With such words he rebuked me, and so cured my sense of smell that after that I never noticed the presence of the sack.

7

AT this time[1] we were sent to Italy by Pope Leo[2] on a peace-making mission between Hugh,[3] the King of the Lombards, and Alberic,[3] the ruler of the city of Rome. Not without risk we came at length to Sienna and found that the city was suffering from famine. We had taken for this dangerous journey nearly thirty silver shillings, of which the greater part had already been spent. But I, remembering how it was his custom to keep nothing for his own and our use, and fearing that we and our horses would perish of hunger, if we had nothing with which to buy food, took what was left of the shillings, and slipping away without his knowing it passed through the city. When he himself came to enter it, he was accosted by beggars asking for the usual alms. Scrutinizing his whole party and seeing that I was not there, he guessed at once what I had done. Knowing that, although I was not present, I should not be far away, he signed with his hand for all to follow him, which they did. As they were crossing the square of the town, he noticed three men, who were dressed with a certain decency

[1] Italy in this sentence means the old Lombard kingdom with its capital at Pavia, where Hugh was king.

This journey was evidently not the one to Pavia mentioned in i, 4, as John holds a responsible position in the party and knows Odo well. If the occasion is to be connected with the expedition to Rome mentioned in the last chapter, then we must suppose that when Odo got to Rome the Pope asked him to go north again to Hugh, probably at Pavia, to try to make peace between him and Alberic. If this were so the journey might easily have occurred in the January and February following their return from France (see p. 47, *n.* 3 and next chapter); and if we follow Sackur in reading 938 (see p. 7, *n.* 1) as the year in which John met Odo, we have a possible chronological scheme:

938 Spring (say) Rome-Pavia-Rome, i, 4.
    Summer and Autumn, Rome-France-Rome, ii, 6.
939 January and February, Rome-Pavia-Rome, ii, 7 and 8.

[2] Leo VII, 936-39.

[3] This Hugh was King of Provence, or Lower Burgundy, one of the new small independent kingdoms which arose during the break-up of the Empire of Charles the Great. In the year 926 he became the nominal King of Italy, successor to the Lombard kings, and about 930 he tried to get control of Rome and the Papacy by marrying the infamous Marozia, who virtually controlled both. Conditions in Rome are illustrated by the fact that a son of Marozia, Alberic, headed a rebellion of the Roman populace and expelled Hugh and his mother in 932. From that date until 954 Alberic maintained his rule in Rome, giving himself the title of Consul. He was a strong, unscrupulous, but efficient tyrant of a type not unknown in later Italian history, and the period of his rule was almost the only period of law and order which the city knew in the tenth century. The Papacy was perforce entirely subservient to him, but was otherwise free from the grave scandals to which it not infrequently succumbed at this period, when it was largely controlled by the Roman nobility.

which raised them above the shamelessness of penury, but who were, nevertheless, in want. To these men he gave the occasion of becoming the recipients of his beneficence. Before the door of their house were set out little dishes full of laurel-berries. He straightway asked how much these were, and one of the men answered I know not what trivial price, to which Odo replied, "Hush; do not ask such a price, but say so many pennies"; which the man did, and forthwith received the sum. And so Odo enriched these men under the pretence of paying the price. Meanwhile I was watching for him to come out of the city, and I saw him coming a little way off surrounded and thronged like a soldier going to war by crowds of poor men and he was so filled with joy that he hardly noticed my greeting. Pretending not to know, I asked him who all these people were, and what they wanted. "These," he said, "are the servants of God and our labourers. Hurry up, therefore, and give them their wages." When I had distributed alms, I asked him what was the purpose of the berries and where he had got them. He answered us with such merry words that I have never heard the like, nor hope to. He made us laugh till we cried and were unable to speak to one another. With the tears still streaming down my face I leant forward and begged that we might no longer be burdened with the berries, but that he would send them back to those who sold them. "I will not do that," he said, "for I am afraid that they might send the price after us." With difficulty I at last got him to consent by pointing out the remoteness of the place we were in and the length of the journey we had come. It was on that day that he foretold that I would be abbot,[1] and many other things which afterwards happened to me. Then he began to tell me that among the other virtues it was patience especially that I ought to obtain and coming to his own history, he told me how much he had had to bear from his brethren at the time of his abbatial election.[2] But it is not fitting to write that now on account of the holiness of these men in later life.

[1] See p. 44, *n*. 3.
[2] John uses the word *ordinatio* which in modern usage would mean ordination to the priesthood, but he uses the word (in its verb form) when he is speaking of Odo's election (or possibly blessing) as abbot in ch. 38, bk. i, and at the beginning of bk. ii. In view of what he has told us of Odo's history it seems more likely to refer to election as abbot. (See p. 41, *n*. 1.)

8

ON this same journey, and before our money was quite exhausted, we met one of our brethren, the priest Peter, who was coming to stay in Rome.[1] His supplies were able to meet our needs, and we got from him enough money to complete the journey. All this happened in the months of January and February.[2] Our way lay by Monte Amiata,[3] and there were such snowstorms at the time that, although the road was known to us, we could not find it. We were so covered with snow and our limbs so frozen that we could not speak. When I noticed that Odo's aged limbs were shrivelled with the cold, I quickly made him a coat to protect and warm his vital parts. Our mission being completed, we were urged by the natives to return by the coastal road. At the place which is commonly known as Buriano,[4] the sun going down over the sea, we met a poor half-naked man, whose appearance I was unable to take in at the time or to recollect afterwards. But this I remember, that with bare feet and bare sides he was boldly crossing the waste of snow. When our father came up to him he stopped, and made all the others go on. Then he took off his coat and covered the poor man, and told me to give him enough money for him to finish his journey. I stopped a moment and asked the man where he was going, knowing that there was nowhere to stay in that great solitude. But he said that he would be able to reach a shepherd's encampment[5] while it was still day. From these words of his I found

---

[1] The expression John uses here is *conversationis gratia*. The word *conversatio* in a monastic context has either the meaning of "conversion", i.e. turning to the monastic life, or the medial meaning of "the monastic life" as a way of life. It is difficult to see how this Peter, who was already a monk, could be going to Rome to enter or to lead the monastic life, which he was already doing, presumably at Cluny. I have supposed that the word is to be taken here without any specifically monastic sense, and that it means in effect that he was coming to Rome on holiday. On the meaning of *conversatio* see *The Rule of St. Benedict*, ed. P. J. McCann, London, 1952, p. 202.

[2] See p. 49, *n*. 1.

[3] *Per Ammiates Alpes*; Alps, of course, are any high mountains, and the reference is obviously to Monte Amiata, which lies just beside the direct road from Rome to Sienna.

[4] *Burrianum*. There is a small place called Buriano near the coast road on about the same latitude as Monte Amiata.

[5] *Pastorale castrum*. Sackur (vol. i, p. 360) thinks that this is to be identified with Castello di Pietra, which lies about a day's journey north of Buriano.

out that there was something uncanny about the man,[1] for the
journey which he promised to make in an hour we hardly made in
a whole day. These events were shown to me in the same order in
a terrible vision on the preceding night. Odo was so filled with
mercy that he used not only to treat the faithful in this way, but
he held out his hand with palm extended even to his persecutors.
And I will give you an example of this which Firmus, a brother
of Abbot Baldwin,[2] witnessed.

9

WHEN the king Hugh was besieging[3] the city of Romulus on
account of his feud with Alberic, Odo went backwards and for-
wards trying to bring peace and concord to both parties; trying to
allay the fury of the king and to save the city from the siege.
During this time, while he was one day going past the monastery
of St. Andrew which is called *ad clivum Scauri*,[4] a yokel tried to
kill him for the sake of a small jar of water. According to the saying
of Scripture: *He that walketh sincerely walketh confidently* [Prov.
x. 9], Odo was going along as usual without doing any harm to
anybody, suspecting nothing, and with his head bowed. For to
such an extent had the custom of the Rule [ch. 7] grown habitual
to him, that wherever he was, standing, or walking, or sitting, he
always had his head bowed and his eyes fixed on the ground. For
which reason he was jokingly called by some of the brethren at
that time, the Digger. When this yokel aimed a blow at Odo's head
the bystanders with a loud cry seized him by the hands. Then our
most gentle father borrowed—lest I should make a mistake, I don't

---

[1] *Non fuisset homo purus.* The implication, I think, is that he was some sort
of sorcerer. Compare the *Life of St. Gerald*, ii, 31, where another man who
performed extraordinary physical feats was convicted of using incantations.

[2] He was the Abbot of St. Paul's in Rome and also of Monte Cassino, a Frank
by birth (Mabillon, note *ad loc.*).

[3] Hugh seems to have made attempts to dislodge Alberic from Rome in 933,
936, and 941. John does not speak of either of the two incidents which follow
as though he had witnessed them himself, so, if Odo did come to Rome in 936,
they might have occurred on that visit.

[4] The monastery of St. Andrew was that founded by St. Gregory the Great
in his monastery on the Caelian Hill. The *Clivus Scauri*, still known as *Clivo di
Scauro*, is a steep road running down the hill past the site of the monastery,
which is now occupied by the church of St. Gregory.

know how many—pennies, and rendering good for evil sent him away an ally. Afterwards this came to the ears of the afore-mentioned ruler, who wanted to cut off the man's hands,[1] but Odo hearing of it begged strenuously that this should not be done, and dismissed the yokel safe and unhurt.

10

ODO's treatment of a robber on one of his visits to Rome is known to many and certainly to you, but I would like to relate it, more to save it from being lost than to instruct such well-informed persons as you are. While Odo was praying in the city, it was seen by all that one of our brethren, Godfred, went out into the country to the men who were herding our horses. That night when all the herders were sound asleep, but he was awake and at his prayers, it happened that a thief came, and having caught one of the horses got on to it and made off. The brother, however, pre-ferred to lose the horse rather than to break the silence; for had he done so the thief would at once have let the horse go. What he did, however, was to go and awaken one of the herders by touching him and to show him by signs what had happened. When it was light the thief was seen at a little distance sitting on the horse, which was standing still.[2] He was captured and sent bound to Odo, who immediately ordered him to be given five silver shillings, saying that it was unjust to send him away without his due reward, because he had had great labour all through the night. Afterwards when by the grace of God I had come to the monastic life and in time had been elected abbot[3] by the brethren, they often recalled that thief to me, and, because he was the son of our miller, when-ever his father did anything against their wishes, they made me ask for that money back again.

[1] A good example of Alberic's ruthless methods of government.
[2] Nalgodus two hundreds years later is explicit that the thief was miraculously restrained by the merits of Odo.
[3] The word used here is again *prior*, but see p. 44, *n.* 3.

11

SINCE we have got on to the subject of silence, without which the
life of a monk is led to no purpose, it remains that we should go
back and treat of it a little further. For the life of a monk is of
value as long as he takes pains to keep silence. But when that is
lost, whatever he thinks to do well will be nothing, according to
the teaching of the Fathers.

12

WHEN the savage Norsemen were cruelly laying waste the country
round Poitiers and Tours, it happened that two respected members
of the community, for what reason I know not, were sent to Tours.
One of them, called Archembalbus, was well-known to me; the
other I did not know, but he was called Adalasius. They were men
of standing and have now become the fathers of many monks.[1]
While they were on their journey and had turned aside to rest for
the night, they were taken prisoner by the Norsemen, who had
captured a nearby town that same night, and one band of whom
had come with their captured booty to the very place where these
brethren were staying. The Norsemen were able to take them and
bind their hands and threaten them, but they could not break their
silence. The next day the band went to an agreed place in which
they had arranged to foregather. The monks separated themselves
a little from the rest and, bound as they were, threw themselves
on their faces on the ground, that having finished the appointed
psalms they might bring the time of silence to an end. But before
they had finished their prayer another band arrived with much
captured booty. Their leader, finding the two monks lying on the
ground, asked who they were. The others told him the whole
history of events, adding that in no way could they make these men
speak. But he, swelling with barbaric savagery, in his overweening
pride rushed upon them mounted on his horse, which was be-

---

[1] Archembalbus seems to have become Prior (*praepositus*) of Cluny and then
Abbot of Fleury with Odo (Mabillon, *Acta*, vol. vii, p. 149, *PL*, cxxxiii, 42),
Adalasius Abbot of Sarlat with Odo (Mabillon, *ibid.*, 43).

decked with medallions, and with his lance raised to strike threatened the monks with death, in order to test their courage. The rest
of them crowded round to witness this spectacle, shouting in their
barbaric way and clapping their hands. But the monks, constant
in spirit, remained unmoved in body, and this they did, not from
any deceit, but in observance of the holy Rule, under which they
desired to live and die, and from which they never wished to turn
aside. But the hand of the Almighty forthwith turned this exciting
spectacle into grief for the onlookers. For as soon as the barbarian
approached them, the horse on which he was sitting bounded back
sideways and flung its rider to the ground. Immediately, as a result
of the fall, a deadly fever set in. All were silent and, lost in wonder,
began to inquire among themselves what they should do. Having
taken counsel they decided, like the barbarians they were, that one
of the monks should be slain for the life of their leader, and they
cast lots for which it should be. But the lot of the devil cannot fall
on men of virtue who are numbered with the lot of Christ. Be-
wildered, the barbarians in admiration said that these were more
than men, on whom their lot was unable to fall; for in this way
they had put to death one of the monks' servants.[1] The surviving
servant knew the language of the enemy well and secretly told the
monks in Latin all that was said. And I believe that the Consoᵣ
of men preserved this man for their salvation, for the barbarians
now came to them and, loosing their hands, began to ask them
eagerly through the interpreter for the life of their leader; and
after that they no more dared to bind them. It was noteworthy,
too, that when they found a gold ring which one of the monks was
wearing round his neck they did not presume to take it; and the
monks enjoyed what food and drink they wished while they were
among them. So was fulfilled in them that most perfect joy which
works patience, of which the Apostle says: *And not only so: but we
glory also in tribulations, knowing that tribulation worketh patience,
and patience hope; and hope confoundeth not: because the charity of*

[1] This seems to be the sense, though from the Latin it is not clear whose was
the servant, or slave (*famulus*). There has been no previous mention of servants
accompanying the monks, though Odo always seems to have travelled with a
number of retainers, even before he was an abbot (cf. bk. i, ch. 36), and doubtless the conditions of the time made it advisable to travel in as large a body as
possible. On the whole this interpretation seems most likely.

God is poured forth in our hearts [Rom. v. 3-5]. And now therefore I beg those who wear the monastic habit to observe with me the example of these men, and to give themselves finally to the practice of silence. For of this good silence Isaias says: *In silence shall be your hope,*[1] and Jeremias: *It is good to wait with silence for the Lord* [Lam. iii. 26], and again: *It is good for a man when he has borne the yoke from his youth. He shall sit solitary and hold his peace: because he hath taken it upon himself.* [Lam. iii. 27-8.] So David proclaims: *I said; I will take heed to my ways, that I sin not with my tongue. I have set a guard to my mouth* [Ps. xxxviii. 2], etc.; and the Apostle Paul: *Now we charge them that are such, and beseech them by the Lord Jesus that working with silence they would eat their own bread.* [2 Thess. iii. 12.] I have quoted these sayings of the prophets of old that no one should think that this cult of silence is an invention of modern times, as some say in error. For these men were imitated by the Fathers of the New Testament;[2] by Paul, Anthony, Hilarion, John, and lastly by our holy father Benedict, apart from many others whom I will not name for fear of being tedious. Abundant reference to their practice of silence can be found in the history of their lives, if anybody wishes to look for it. Therefore lest there be some who object to the peacefulness of solitude in which these men passed their lives, I shall go on straightway to the teaching of the Evangelists and begin with the actions of our Lord Jesus.

13

The first witness is in Matthew: *And forthwith Jesus obliged his disciples to go up into the boat and to go before him over the water, till he dismissed the people. And having dismissed the multitude he went into a mountain alone to pray.* [Matt. xiv. 22-3.] The second is in Mark: *And immediately he obliged his disciples to go up into the ship, that they might go before him over the water to Bethsaida, whilst he dismissed the people. And when he had dismissed them he went up to*

---

[1] "In silence and in hope shall your strength be." (Isa. xxx, 15.).
[2] That is, the Fathers who lived under the dispensation of the New Testament. Paul, Anthony, Hilarion, and John (the Almsgiver) all figure in the *Vitae Patrum.*

the mountain to pray. [Mark vi. 45-6.] The third in Luke runs thus: *And it came to pass in those days, that he went out into a mountain to pray; and he passed the whole night in the prayer of God.* [Luke vi. 12.] And again in the same: *Watch ye, therefore, praying at all times, that you may be accounted worthy to escape all these things that are to come and to stand before the Son of Man. And in the day time he was teaching in the temple; but at night, going out, he abode in the mount that is called Olivet.* [Luke xxi. 36-7.] The fourth witness in John ends in this way: *And Jesus went unto mount Olivet. And early in the morning he came again into the temple* [John viii. 1-2]. If therefore the Word of God and the Creator of flesh, while He lived among men and preached the Gospel of life, was sometimes silent, you can easily understand what ought to be our practice, *since death and life are in the power of the tongue* [Prov. xviii. 21], and since Scripture says: *In the multitude of words thou shalt not escape sin* [Prov. x. 19], and: *A man full of tongue shall not be established in the earth* [Ps. cxxxix. 12]. If, therefore, these brethren of ours, when they were bound and beaten and threatened, did not allow the silence to be broken, they were imitating Him of whom it is written: *He was led as a sheep to the slaughter and was dumb as a lamb before his shearer, and he opened not his mouth.* [Isa. liii. 7.] Those who suffer no violence, and are not compelled by anybody, but of their own free will transgress the commands of the Rule, what shall they say in the presence of these men at the judgement, when the cause of both shall be examined in the sight of God and His angels? Of this judgement holy Church in the mouth of blessed Job pronounces terrible words, saying: *Thou renewest thy witnesses against me* [Job x. 17]. The vengeance is always terrible which overtakes those who are convicted by witnesses. And they receive the condemnation of the law, who knowing the law do not fear to turn away rashly from its ordinances. Of these the psalmist says: *They are cursed who decline from thy commandments* [Ps. cxviii. 21].

14[1]

THERE were two brothers in our community, whose names I do not care to mention, who used very often to ask Odo to order them medicinal remedies for their grave sickness—presuming that they were to have health. Unable to put up with their audacity he consented to their wish and gave permission for the requested medicine,[2] but first calling them to him he gave them this example in the form of a similitude. "Once I saw a brother suffering from a malady like yours, and he died before he could be restored to his former health." However, without any misgivings they went to a doctor, but after much suffering they still failed to regain their health. I know another brother who at the time of his conversion had no thought but to wipe away the stains of his former sins, and striving incessantly day and night with prayers and compunction and lamentation, gave up all other activities. When our wise father asked why he did not come with the others either to teach or to learn, he told him the truth and openly revealed the secrets of his heart, and begged Odo to give him permission to complete the work he had begun, being assured according to the teaching of the Rule [ch. 49] that whatever a monk does without the permission of his spiritual father is to be put down to presumption and vainglory and not reckoned meritorious. The father said to him, "It is better for you that this spirit [of compunction] depart from you

---

[1] The section included here in chapters 14-22, following Mabillon's edition, is to be found in Marrier's in Book III between Mabillon's chapters 6 and 7 (there are no chapter divisions in Marrier). But within this section Chapter 21 comes between chapters 15 and 16.

The strictures of Nalgodus on the lack of order in John's work are so far justified that there seems to be no significance in the change.

[2] Odo's attitude to medical remedies as here described is puzzling, and not, on the face of it, edifying to modern readers. St. Benedict devotes a chapter of his *Rule* (36) to the care which is to be had for the sick. Christ is to be seen in them as in guests and the poor, and it is a serious obligation on the abbot to see that this care is given. It is true that he says nothing about doctors or medicines, but he makes concessions to the sick in the matter of baths and eating meat. One cannot believe that Odo would be indifferent to the spirit of St. Benedict's teaching on this point, and it is reasonable to suppose that he was ready to give these men every consideration short of treatment by a doctor. But with regard to this one cannot avoid the suspicion that Odo's theology was at fault. He seems to have disapproved on principle to their having medical aid, and for this view he would have had, I think, no support from the theologians of any age.

for a time, for through it your heart is wounded by the pricks of vain glory." From this time the brother lost his spirit of compunction, and it was almost half a year before he merited, by imploring our father, to receive it again. Odo's words had always great weight, because filled with the divine fire the holy man could not speak in vain.

15

RECENTLY John, the Bishop of Nola, told our community and others who were with us, that three years before he had twice gone to Rome but had been unable to receive his episcopal consecration on account of the opposition of his enemies. Odo was going on pilgrimage to Gargano[1] at the time and noticing the sadness of the bishop he asked him what was the matter. When the bishop had told him all that had happened, and that despairing of receiving episcopal consecration he was in doubt whether to go to Rome a third time, Odo blessed him and said, "Go again with confidence, and know that God has fulfilled your wish." Then he dismissed him. But the bishop, after he had received a blessing, departed, and in fifteen days he was consecrated as our father had foretold. This leads us to state without doubt that Odo had the spirit of prophecy, since his words were confirmed with such authority.

16

I WOULD recall to your memory, brethren, that last year the pilgrim to Jerusalem, who told us that he belonged to our father's family, spoke to you two or three times about him. He said that in those years when the Norsemen were devastating the district of Tours, they captured Odo's nephew, who was still unbaptized, along with his nurse. Odo was in Tours at the time, and when this was told

[1] Monte Gargano—a peninsula on the Adriatic coast of Italy near which there is a famous shrine of St. Michael. Nola is not far from Naples and Odo might have gone through it, or near it, if he went from Salerno to Gargano. It certainly looks as if, when John speaks here of "our community", he means one in Salerno. There were in fact two Benedictine houses in Salerno at this time, and it is not known which of them was handed over to Odo. (*Annales Ordinis Sancti Benedicti*, Paris, 1703-13, vol. iii, p. 463).

him he at once set himself to prayer, and beseeched the Lord until he knew that the child had been set free. He was not more grieved about him than about the other captives, but he was very anxious about the state of his soul, fearing lest by chance the boy, not yet baptized, should be delivered to hell. But amongst the rest the testimony of the boy's nurse must not be passed over. The place, she said, to which the captives were led was on the other side of a certain river, which was so deep that it could not be crossed except in a boat or by swimming, and it was eight days' journey away from Tours. All hope of seeing the boy again disappeared. While the woman was in this predicament she was suddenly inspired by God to seize the child and depart, which she did. She went so safely through the bands of the enemy, that she was not only not detained, but not even questioned. She crossed the deep river dry-shod and made the long journey to Tours in three days, suffering from neither hunger nor thirst nor weariness. It was at once clear by whose merit this had happened, because as soon as the boy was brought to our father he had him baptized, and raising his eyes to heaven prayed that he should die, and three days later the child gave up his spirit to heaven. His father became a monk.

Our holy father himself related what follows, not as though it had been done by him or on his behalf, but as recounting the dangers from which the Lord had delivered the boy.

17

ON one occasion when he was crossing the Rhône in a boat, accompanied by the leading men of the district, it happened that one of the horses kicked at another and struck the side of the boat in a place where there was a knot in the planking. As soon as the side of the boat was pierced, so great a torrent of water came in through the hole that the boat was quickly filled, and in this state by the manifest help of God it reached the other bank. Odo remained in it until all had disembarked, and when last of all he had come out, the boat sank. The merit of this man is manifest, who was able by his prayers to obtain what Peter and Paul, and then our father Benedict, had previously merited.

18

AT this same time he visited Rome on pilgrimage,[1] and not long after, when he was on his way home, there was such a depth of snow in the Burdonian Alps[2] that the road became completely blocked, though at no time is the mountain without it. The region is inhabited by a race of men who are called Marrones,[3] taking their name I suppose from the Province of Marronea. Guides hired according to custom from among these people were leading him, for without a guide no one could cross these mountains in winter. Now, the sun had not yet set, but what was left of the day was turned to darkness by a heavy fall of snow. As they were going through this horrible and dangerous place, suddenly the horse on which our father was sitting slipped sideways and they both fell together down the steep slope. Leaving go of the reins Odo raised both his hands to heaven as he fell, and immediately his arms found the branch of a tree from which he hung suspended until those in front turned back at his cries and rescued him. But the branch of the tree was no more seen, because there is no tree to be found in that place, nor does any grow there. The horse was never seen again.

[1] Odo's journeys to Rome seem to be accounted for on other grounds than those of pilgrimage, but Mabillon thought that this might have been a special journey distinct from the others mentioned. (*Acta*, vol. vii, p. 140; *PL*, cxxxiii, 32.)

[2] I have been unable to identify these mountains. They may have been a part of the Alps proper, but Nalgodus places the incident in the Apennines.

[3] The name Marrones was applied to the Saracens (see Ducange) who had established themselves about 888 at Fraxinetum on the Golfe du St. Tropez, on the coast of Provence. From their fortified settlement at Fraxinetum they raided as far as Swabia, and in particular established themselves in the alpine passes, whence they laid waste much of the surrounding country and preyed on the bands of pilgrims going to Rome. It is interesting to note that they were not finally extirpated till they captured Odo's successor, Majolus of Cluny, in 972 as he was crossing the Great St. Bernard Pass. Cluny at once raised the enormous ransom demanded, but the event aroused such indignation that the feudal barons for once united and succeeded in finally getting rid of the menace. Odo, representing a still nascent and comparatively poor Cluny, was able to get by more easily than his successor. The sojourn of these people on the coast of Provence is commemorated in the name of the Chaîne des Maures.

19

WHEN his ardent zeal for peace between kings and princes, and for the reform of monasteries, caused him to travel much about the country, robbers often lay in ambush for him.[1] One day forty of them set upon him, and when their leader, by name Aymo, saw Odo and the brethren who accompanied him continually singing psalms as they went along the road, he was struck with compunction, and said to his companions, "I never remember to have seen such men, nor do I think their like has been seen elsewhere; let us leave them. There is an armed and vigorous man with them, and we cannot do them any harm without danger to ourselves." To this they answered: "Let us lift up this armed man on the points of our spears, and the others we will let go when we have robbed them." "Turn your weapons against me first," he replied, "otherwise you will have nothing to do with them while I am alive." So, divided amongst themselves, they retired. But the leader went after our father and did penance for his crimes, and afterwards gave up his evil life of robbery. But I do not think this happened immediately. Such graciousness of spirit filled those with whom he consorted that his good spirits not only enlivened the cheerful, but restored those who were sad to true joy, and gave them lasting happiness. His tongue, as the Scripture sings, was a tree of life, a peaceable tongue [Prov. xv. 4], and his lips the sweetness of honey, a dropping honeycomb [Cant. iv. 11], and the law of prudence was in his words.

20

ONE day his journey took him into the territory of some robbers, and one of them, who was still quite young, seeing the affability of his appearance, was struck with compunction of heart, and

---

[1] The Marrones of the last chapter, although they were apparently willing to act as hired guides on occasion, certainly indulged in much brigandage, but the lack of central authority in feudal times led to widespread brigandage amongst the native peoples as well. Aymo is a Frankish name, and it is likely that this man was a Frank or Burgundian. The conversion of a Saracen would have called for further comment.

falling on his face before him, begged him in humble tones to have mercy on him. Odo asked him what he wanted, he begged to be helped to the monastic life. Then our father asked him if anyone from that parish knew him. "All do so," he replied. "Go, then, for the present, and tomorrow when you come to visit me bring one of the elders of the place." So he went away and did as he had been ordered. The next day when they both came before him Father Odo began to ask the elder about the robber. "Father," the man replied, "this youth is a most notorious robber." Hearing this the father, who was full of discretion, said to the robber, "Go first and amend your behaviour, and then ask to be admitted to the monastic life." But he replied, "If I am rejected by you today I shall be lost, and God will require my soul of you." Then the holy father, moved by mercy, ordered him to go to the monastery, which he did. When he had been tested for some time according to the Rule, he was at length made a monk and was put under obedience to the cellarer, and because he was illiterate the study of letters was imposed on him in addition to the yoke of obedience,[1] and he devotedly carried the double burden. So that, while he stretched out one hand to the work of obedience, with the other he held his psalter, imitating that people of Israel who, while they rebuilt Jerusalem, held in one hand the sword to strike their enemies and gave the other to the labour of their craft [2 Esdras iv. 17]. So this brother led his life, and after a short time of exile it drew to an end. Having laboured to the last, he called his loving father and begged to speak with him alone. When he had begged pardon, Odo asked him if he had failed in anything after he had become a monk. "Since you ask me, I was at fault in giving my tunic to a naked man, and I took a hair rope from the store." When asked what he had done with this he replied, "To restrain the gluttony which I had formerly evilly contracted I wrapped it round my stomach." The loving father was amazed at this, but

---

[1] "The yoke of obedience" presumably means the ordinary round of monastic duties. As this would normally include a good deal of reading it is difficult to see how his elementary lessons in this could have imposed much extra burden. It is interesting to speculate on how he said the divine Office, if he could not read. Laybrothers, who were not expected to recite the choir-office, do not seem to have been introduced before the eleventh century (see *Catholic Encyclopaedia*, art. "Lay-Brothers").

when he wished to loosen it, the skin which adhered to it came away with it. He went on, "Last night, father, I was raised in a vision to heaven. A lady of most glorious appearance and great power met me, and approaching me said, 'Do you know who I am?' 'No, lady,' I replied. 'I am the Mother of Mercy,' she said. 'What do you command me to do, lady?' 'After three days come to this place at such an hour.' " And so indeed it happened, for on the third day at the hour which she mentioned he died. From this it was perfectly clear that what he saw was a true vision, because at the hour which she foretold he left the world. From that time our father was accustomed to call our Lady the Mother of Mercy.

21

ONCE[1] I was sent to Naples on the business of our monastery, and fate brought it about that it was convenient for me to return to Rome by ship. When I reached the city of Porto,[2] I was met by certain nobles who had come from Rome the day before. When I asked them about our father, as though rejoicing in a new friend, they told me this among other things that he had done while I was away. Last August[3] on the feast of the Assumption of our Lady our father was in the monastery on the Aventine.[4] He had been asked by Abbot Baldwin[5] if he would say Mass there that day in honour of our Lady and with his own hands give communion with the

[1] John begins this chapter *per idem tempus*, but I do not think much importance can be attached to connecting links of this nature, *sub eodem tempore, per illud namque tempus* and so on. An attempt was made to sort out the journeys to Rome in chapters 6, 7, and 8 of this book, and there are one or two more precise indications of time which will be noted (one in this chapter), but I take it that these vague expressions were used in much the same way as, and may even have been inspired by, the phrase *in illo tempore* with which passages from the Gospel in the liturgy are introduced.

[2] A harbour and town on the right-hand branch of the mouth of the River Tiber, originally constructed by Trajan to replace Ostia, whose harbour had silted up. The town was rebuilt and fortified by Leo IV (847-55).

[3] Presuming that John was writing after the death of Odo, which occurred in November, 942, this must refer to the August of that year, and it follows that John was writing before August, 943, so that his work is dated to about the first half of that year.

[4] Alberic's palace on the Aventine made over to Odo for a monastery. (Sackur, vol. i, p. 101.)

[5] The abbot of St. Paul's (p. 52, *n.* 2). What his relation to the monastery on the Aventine was we do not know, but he may well have been administering its beginnings.

Body and Blood of the Lord. He replied that he was unable to do this, but as the abbot persisted in his request he at length unwillingly agreed. He entered the church and when he had prayed a little he began to go out. They wished to keep him, but "I beseech you," he said, "allow me to go, because two of our brethren are at the point of death, and I must go quickly to them lest they should die while I am absent." Then he added, "See, one who has come for me is at the gate of the monastery." He had not completed the words when the messenger arrived as he had foretold. When he had come to St. Paul's he went at once and celebrated Mass for Brother Benedict, and gave him the Body and Blood of the Lord as Viaticum; and so the brother gave up his spirit to the Lord. The other, who was called Gislebert, was a cousin of mine, and he followed him on the eighth day. Now having come as it were in a circle, let us return to former times, and let us look a little at some more important examples.

22

THREE years ago[1] while we were at St. Paul's in Rome, Abbot Baldwin asked him to correct and elucidate with a commentary the book which Gallus and Postumianus wrote in dialogue form about the life of St. Martin the bishop.[2] He at once consented to his wish, and having called Brother Othegarius gave him the work of correction. Just then the bell went for Vespers, and according to the precept of the Rule they at once left what they were doing and went into church, leaving the book open where they had been sitting; and occupied with their prayers at Vespers they forgot about it. It was winter, and there was such heavy rain that night that all the precincts of the monastery were flooded. Now the place in which the book had been left is so situated that the water which falls on its roof and on three adjacent roofs higher up collects

---

[1] Say January or February of 940. Odo was in Rome in February, 939 (p. 49, *n.* 1), but where he had been in the meantime we have no means of knowing.

[2] The *Dialogues* of Gallus and Postumianus on St. Martin were in fact written by Sulpicius Severus, and it is possible, or probable, that Gallus and Postumianus were fictitious characters. See the volume in this series, *The Western Fathers*, pp. 63 ff.

and pours down like a torrent in that one place, and there the open
book remained till morning while floods of water fell around it.
The margin of the book was indeed wet but the writing remained
untouched. In the morning the book was displayed in front of the
brethren. We were all amazed and full of admiration, but the wise
father remarked, "Why are you surprised, brothers? The water,
you know well, was afraid to touch the Life of St. Martin." And
he said this with a certain pleasure. But one of the brethren who
was free of speech took up the book and said, "Look, this book is
old and damaged by moths, and it has been wet before, and is still
so damp that it is covered with mildew. Look at the marks, and
our father says that now the water feared to touch this book which
has been so wet. The case is otherwise." The modest father replied, "Be silent. There is no one who is so praised among all
peoples as Martin." So Odo turned to the praise of Martin what
the Lord had done for his own sake.

23

At that time our father's name, like a bright star, began to shine
far and wide. He became known to kings, was familiar to bishops,
beloved of the secular lords. For any monasteries that were built
in their territories they handed over to his rule that he might reform and regulate them according to our customs.[1] And so on one
occasion he came to a certain monastery with a small band of
monks, of whom one called Adolfus was known to me; he died
two years ago. At the end of the week, on Saturday evening, when
the brethren had begun to prepare for the *Mandatum*[2] according

---

[1] We have already seen something of the straits to which monasticism had
been reduced in France in the difficulty Odo had in finding a monastery to
which he might go, and we shall have further evidence from him later (bk. iii,
chs. 1-5). The situation was as bad in Italy. Odo's reputation was such that he
was soon called on to reform many houses in France and Italy, and this was the
beginning of the so-called Cluniac reform. The relation of the various houses
to Cluny varied, and they did not all remain subject to it. See Schmitz, vol. i,
pp. 136-9. Evans, ch. ii.

[2] This was the washing of the feet of the community performed by the
weekly servers according to the prescription in Chapter 35 of the *Rule* of St.
Benedict. The antiphon *Mandatum novum do vobis* was sung at this ceremony, as

to the Rule, it happened that one of the monks of the monastery passed through the place where this was being done. When he saw our brother washing his shoes according to our custom, he was filled with anger, and he broke the silence saying, "Tell me where St. Benedict orders monks to wash their shoes?" The brother, as our custom is, made him a sign to be quiet, because it was a time of silence, for he did not remember that which Wisdom says through the mouth of Solomon: *He that teacheth a scorner doth an injury to himself* [Prov. ix. 7], and again: *Rebuke not [a scorner] lest he hate thee.* [Prov. ix. 8.] Seeing that he got no reply the monk became very angry and began to pour out these reproaches: "O, you who formerly went through all the provinces of the world on business, now you have come to preach the Rule to us and to correct the life of your betters. By oaths and counter-oaths you pounce like a hawk on the property of others, and now you impudently seek to win approval from us as from men who do not know your behaviour. God did not make me a serpent that I should hiss as you do, nor an ox that I should bellow, but He made me a man and gave me a tongue to talk with." While he continued to bark out such remarks the aforesaid brother hurriedly retired. When all this was related at chapter on the following day, the wretched man not only did not ask pardon, but even maintained that he had done well, adding moreover that it was not fitting for such a person to accuse his better. Then our father, indignant at his pride, said with some emotion, "Today is Sunday, and no one should be made sad. Therefore let this discussion be held over till tomorrow." So it was done, and in a little while all rose from chapter. But he (the contumacious monk) was suddenly struck dumb, and in three days he died without having regained his speech. Such is the poison of arrogance, and we still find the lives of many monks wounded by this weapon, for they think they know that of which in fact they know nothing; according to the saying

---

still on Maundy Thursday. It was the custom in the early days at Cluny for the brethren to wash their shoes first, a custom which Peter the Venerable in the twelfth century did away with. As the monks of his day hardly ever went outside the cloister the shoe-washing had become a ceremonial sprinkling with a few drops of water. See Peter the Venerable, *Statutes*, chap. 28, *PL*, clxxxix, col. 1034.

of the Apostle they are made foolish in their assertions.[1] As Scripture says: He who does not wish to be a disciple of truth will be a master of error. And of these the Lord speaks through Amos: *They returned that they might be without yoke; they became like a deceitful bow.*[2] They are like this without doubt who strive to be called masters before they have become disciples, and who seek to attain the summit of power before they know how to submit. Not yet recruits they snatch the victor's crown, and with untrained hand are not ashamed to take up the arms of the strongest soldier, ignoring what the Scripture says: He who does not submit to rule ought not to take the lead among rulers. And because they do not wish to live according to the law they are not ashamed to turn away from its precepts. Of these the Lord speaks through the prophet: *They have turned their back on me and not their face* [Jer. ii. 27]. So Nicodemus the lawyer came to Jesus by night, because he wished first to be instructed that afterwards he might be able to instruct others. There is twofold evil in this disease: one sufferer, with secret presumption and under the pretext of sanctity, is incited to climb the heights of power; the other, already led astray, seeks to instruct others in the path of his errors, and (what we cannot say without grief) himself cast down, strives to draw those standing behind him to destruction, of which the Lord says in the Gospel: *They are blind [and] leaders of the blind. If the blind lead the blind, both fall into the pit.* [Matt. xv. 14.] A community of such people is rather to be called a tavern than a monastery, because there each one does what he pleases and leaves undone what does not appeal to him. Of such Solomon says: *The congregation of sinners is like tow heaped together.* [Ecclus. xxi. 10.] St. Benedict calls these the most detestable kind of monks [*Rule*, ch. 1]. Their way of life, he says, is most wretched, and so wretched that he considers it better to be silent about them rather than to speak.

---

[1] The reference perhaps is to Rom. i, 22, "Professing themselves to be wise they became fools". The Latin text has no stop before Scripture, but "as Scripture says" is an awkward tag at the end of the sentence, which already has the reference to the Apostle. The following sentence seems to be quoted as from Scripture, though it is not from the Bible No doubt Mabillon was correct in saying that here and later in this passage ("He who does not submit to rule", etc.) the author comprehends under the term Scripture the teaching of any authoritative writers, *solemni veterum more*.

[2] The quotation is in fact from Osee, vii, 16.

So leaving these let us return to the complaint of this monk, and let us see what St. Benedict ordained concerning the property of the monastery. Let them look, he says, on all the utensils of the monastery and its whole property as upon the sacred vessels of the altar [ch. 31]. And again: If any treat the property of the monastery in a slovenly or careless manner, let him be corrected [ch. 32]. What else are the shoes or clothes of the brethren than the property of the monastery? If elsewhere he orders the weekly servers to give back the vessels of their service clean and intact to the cellarer, and these are only cheap earthenware destined for service in the kitchen, what is to be thought of the shoes, which are costly and destined for the floor of the church? If it seems to be a grave fault for monks to be solicitous about other people's property, much more is it for them to neglect their own. If the rich man is reprehended because he dined splendidly every day, without doubt the servant of God is greatly reprehended who daily desires to feast, since in the sixth degree of humility St. Benedict lays it down that a monk should be content with the meanest and worst of everything. So he is negligent who is unwilling to wash his shoes, and throws them into some corner so that they decay with mud and mould, and at last are of no use to himself or the poor; for St. Benedict laid it down that all old things were to be given to the poor. I say this not that, like hypocrites, they should appear either slovenly or resplendent, but that they should keep all their clothes clean and washed; as some wise man said: "If you desire to be good and seek an honest life, love cleanliness of body and soul."

Finally there are these precepts of the Fathers. The Lord speaks through Moses: *Cursed be he that removeth his neighbour's landmarks.* [Deut. xxvii. 17.] Since this monk did not fear to move the landmark of the precept, he rightly falls under the malediction for that in which he sinned. And so that rich man who is said to have been buried in hell stated that he burned more in his tongue than in his other members. Hence the saying of some wise man: "A man shall be tortured by that through which he sins." And the Apostle James says: *The tongue is a fire, a world of iniquity. The tongue is placed among our members, which defileth the whole body and inflameth the wheel of our nativity ... the tongue ... is an unquiet evil, full of deadly poison.* [Jas. iii. 6 and 8.] The psalmist says of it: *May the Lord destroy all deceitful lips, and the tongue that speaketh proud things.* [Ps. xi. 4.] And so in Ezechiel: *I will make thy tongue stick fast to the roof of thy mouth, and thou shalt be dumb* [Ezech. iii. 26]. And would that he were dumb in tongue and not separated from the company of the faithful. What, I ask, is excommunication but separation from the good?[1] Among his other precepts St. Benedict put those concerning silence under pain of excommunication, and he did not leave it to the judgement of the superior. For which reason whoever comes to the heights of monastic life, let him take care how he acts and keep himself clear of that excommunication. Let him always remember what happened to those two virgins who followed the precept of St. Benedict carelessly, whom St. Gregory mentions in his *Dialogues.*[2] But we have delayed long enough over this, let us now turn to other matters.

[1] The reference to excommunication here is obscure and apparently uncalled for. It seems likely that John had in mind the passage in St. Gregory's *Dialogues* concerning the two virgins to which he refers just below. St. Benedict is quoted as saying to them, "Amend your tongues, or I shall excommunicate you." Hence, I suggest, the connexion in John's mind between the unbridled use of the tongue and excommunication; but of course he is not clear.

[2] The reference is to a story told by St. Gregory in the *Dialogues*, bk. ii, ch. 23. The two nuns were apparently anchoresses living near St. Benedict's monastery.

Book III

I

WHEN our father was instructing us in the discipline of the Rule he used to describe carefully to us, I will not say the death, but the miserable end, of many monks, in order to repress youthful impulses in us, and that in fear of his rod he might lead us like a shepherd to the joys of heaven. One day while he was expounding such things to us, with deference to his authority, I asked him to tell us whether it was only in Italy that the monastic life had fallen so low, or if it had fallen in a similar way throughout Europe, and how, and to what extent, and when this had happened. So he began to speak and told us the following facts. "Some years ago the monastic community at the church of St. Martin in Tours[1] began to depart from their way of life and their customs, and to transform their life and profession according to their own ideas. They gave up their proper and accustomed dress and began to wear coloured and flowing cowls and tunics, and to adorn themselves with a cloak. The shoes also which they used were coloured and glossy, so that they seemed to shine like glass. They got up in daylight lest they should dirty their shoes going to the night Office. In these and many similar ways they acted against their Rule. When God had decreed to put an end to these things, one of them who was awake in the night when all the others were sleeping, saw two men come into the dormitory, one of whom held a sword in his hand. Pointing out the sleepers one by one the other ordered this man to strike saying, "Strike this one, and this." When the striker approached him who was the witness of all this, he adjured him in a loud voice saying, "I adjure you by the living God not to kill me." At once the striker drew back his sword, and he alone escaped.

---

[1] The community at St. Martin's had originally been Benedictine. At the end of the eighth century they were apparently living as canons, but Alcuin, who was abbot from 796 till his death in 812, restored a modified Benedictine rule. It became definitely a house of canons in 816. The state of affairs to which Odo refers here must have existed in his own early days at Tours (see p. 13, *n.* 2) and no doubt accounts for the fact that he sought the monastic life.

2

ON another occasion I asked him what fault was to be imputed to
a monk who with a right intention made use of secular dress. At
once he gave me this example. "At the time when the sword of
the Norsemen was abroad in our country, many of our Order
found occasion in the presence of the enemy to leave their monasteries and to seek again those things which it is pleasant for men
to use, and which they had previously renounced. To replace the
fellowship of the brethren they had a multitude of relations and
friends, and to replace the goods of the monastery they sought to
be enriched by private possessions. When the clothes in which
they had left the monastery at length wore out, they did not put
on new ones like them, but ones of a blue colour. In those days,
then, a certain brother retreating in front of this scourge came to
our monastery and begged us to receive him. We met his wishes,
and he forthwith renounced everything that he had acquired and
gave it to the monastery. When the brethren told him to go and
collect his possessions he replied: 'I and all that I now possess are
subject to your authority; it is for you to require these things and
send for them; and for this reason I shall not go out of the monastery
alone, but order any of the brethren you please to fetch them, and
I in obedience to your wishes will go with him and will obey his
commands as well as I know how. But whether I remain here or
whether I go, henceforth I shall be stripped of all things.' In fact,
as the brethren persisted in their demand, he accompanied the
brother to whom they had given the obedience. When they had
come to the place where he had previously dwelt, he was suddenly
overtaken by sickness and died. As he was dying the brother who
was with him poured out ever more urgent prayers to God for his
soul as he perceived him to be nearer death. And so it came about
that both of them saw this vision. St. Benedict was seen seated on
a high throne, and before him was an innumerable army of monks.
The steps to the throne appeared to be covered with cloaks and on
the lowest step, as if begging pardon, lay the sick brother. To the
left and right there sat the aforesaid army of monks, and in the

middle was an open path leading up to the steps. When the brother had been prostrate for a long time, one of those standing near came to St. Benedict making supplication for him, saying that he deserved to be told to arise and make his request. St. Benedict appeared to reply that he saw a man but did not recognize his habit, and therefore it was not for him to discuss the cause or judge the life of a man of another Order. Hearing this our brother took off his habit and put it on to the sick brother, and compelled him to ask pardon—all this in the same vision. As soon as he had done this a voice came from above ordering him to arise and come up the steps. Then, waking from sleep, the brother at once carried out in action what he believed he had done in sleep, and as though now secure of the soul of his companion, he protected him in his dying as well as he could by prayer, and fortified him with Holy Communion. Attend therefore, son, to the word of the Apostle saying: *Faith if it have not works is dead* [Jas. ii. 17], and as it is written elsewhere: *He who saith that he knoweth Christ ought himself also to walk even as he walked.* (1 John ii, 4, 6.] So he who professes to be a monk ought in work and word to imitate the Father Benedict, because it is written: *Not the hearers of the law are just before God, but the doers* [Rom. ii. 13]. Purity of mind is not sufficient for a monk if indications or signs of other works are lacking, of which the Lord says: *So let your light shine before men that they may see your good works and glorify your Father who is in heaven.* [Matt. v. 16.] St. Gregory speaks more plainly of this in the first part of Ezechiel,[1] of which I will give one example. As men fall away from God in two ways, so they become apostates from God in two ways. For everyone falls away from his Creator either in faith or works. As, therefore, he who loses his faith is an apostate, so he who returns to what he has abandoned is, without any doubt, to be considered an apostate from Almighty God, even though he seems to retain his faith. One cannot be of use without the other; faith does not help without works, nor works without faith. Therefore let no one take offence because I said the above-mentioned brother could not receive pardon, nor merit to ascend on high, until he

---

[1] The reference is to the *Homilies on Ezechiel*, bk. i, hom. ix, 6: *PL*, lxxvi, col. 872.

had changed his dress. There is no doubt of the precept in the Law concerning the vestments of the sons of Levi, without which they might not go up to the sanctuary. [Exod. xxviii.] For who would dare to say that a rational could be used for a humeral, or a linen ephod be put on for a tunic? For each one has its colour, its purpose, and its particular characteristic. For the devil strove against Jesus, the great High Priest, until He was clothed in new vestments by an angel,[1] and David, when he wished to go up against the Amalecites,[2] twice consulted God and did not receive the reply to go up; the third time he wore the ephod and at once heard the voice ordering him to go up."

3

THUS he spoke, and then once more continued: "Do you wish me to show you from other stories how a very small thing may bring great disgrace and harm?" I replied that I desired this very much, and as he saw that I was eager for his information, he briefly gave me the following examples.

"Two brethren were overtaken by sudden death, not however in the same place or on the same day. One of them came to the house of a sister of his, and said that he had a great desire to eat, and asked her to give him some food. His sister replied that she had plenty of fish for him to eat whenever he liked. But he was indignant at this, and replied that he was tired of fish, adding that for many years he had eaten nothing else, and now he could not bear the sight of it. His sister replied, 'Well, we have meat ready, so eat what you like.' Then he ordered a joint of some animal to be roasted for him, but not being able to bear the delay of the roasting he seized a portion and threw it on to the coals. Then he ordered wine to be brought and greedily took the piece of meat. But what he took would not go down his throat nor could he eject it, but he lost his life together with the food.

[1] This curious expression is presumably a reference to the resurrection of our Lord.
[2] The reference is to 1 Kings xxx. 7 and 8, but there is nothing in the Vulgate about David first consulting the Lord without the ephod.

4

"THE other coming early one morning to the house of one of his relations immediately asked if they had anything they could give him to eat. When they replied that it was not yet the time for a meal, he burst out, 'I have been riding hard all night on a task that was given me by obedience, and have had no rest, and now do you make me fast? If you have anything, bring it to me.' When they told him that they had some fish, he was still more indignant, and full of disdain and arrogance looked around this way and that. Now there was at his feet a flock of fowls,[1] and in a fury he snatched up a small stick and struck the first one which came near, declaring in an angry voice, 'This shall be my fish today.' Those who were standing around asked in some confusion, 'Is it lawful for you to eat meat, Father?' 'Fowl,' he said, 'is not flesh, fowl and fish have one origin and are created equal, as our hymn[2] says.' At these words everyone was silent. Meanwhile the fowl which he had killed was roasted and put before him. He took a piece of it and put it in his mouth, but he could neither spit it out nor swallow it, and it deprived him of life. He received blows and buffets in scorn as a reward of his wickedness before he died."

If your spirit is moved at the death of these two brothers, as at that of the one mentioned before, I will show you now, by an example, that they deserved the deaths which came upon them.[3] For a few lentils Esau lost his birthright. [Gen. xxv, 33.] The people of Israel, when they were fed by manna, returned in their hearts to Egypt, desiring the fleshpots of which they had partaken under the yoke of an evil servitude. Of these the apostle Paul makes mention: *That we should not covet evil things, as they also coveted.* [I Cor. x. 6.] The men of our day said they were tired of fish, those murmured saying: *Our eyes behold nothing else out manna.* [Num. xi. 6.] It is

[1] *Grex cornicum quas nos gallinas vocamus.* Ducange quotes this text for the meaning of *cornix.*

[2] The reference is undoubtedly to the hymn *Magnae Deus potentiae,* which is the vesper hymn in the ferial Office for Thursday both in the Roman and Benedictine breviary. The hymn celebrates the work of the fifth day of Creation as described in Genesis i. 20-23.

[3] Similar cautionary tales to those in this chapter and Chapter 2 above are to be found in the *Collations,* iii, 20 and 22.

not that I condemn food as evil in itself, but those who make bad use of it. So Paul says: *Make not provision for the flesh in its concupiscences.* [Rom. xiii. 14.] What he denies to concupiscence he grants to necessity. The three children who were thrown into the fiery furnace at Babylon [Dan. i and iii], refusing the royal food, came out unhurt from the flames, but the same fire consumed and killed those that it found of the Chaldeans.[1] So Nabuzardan, the prince of cooks, destroyed the walls of Jerusalem.[2] Let no one be disturbed that Elias in time of famine was fed with meat morning and evening [3 Kings xvii. 6], but let him who questions the food consider the minister. (Demons often take the appearance of these foods).[3] Food of this nature was suitable to the ministry of ravens, and a sufficiency of it night and morning merited hunger. But when he ate bread, he had an angel to bring it [3 Kings xix. 5 ff.], and was so strengthened by it that for forty days he did not need other refreshment. I have said all this that I might show more clearly that evil is not in the food but in the appetite. The death of all these people resulted in the emendation of morals, for in so far as the monastic order among us has collapsed, it has been restored, and still is repeatedly restored, by many miracles, that by the power of God it may remain.

But while I have narrated the life and doctrine of our father more fully, as it were without noticing and not meaning to, I have fallen into excess, and so have digressed from my purpose, to which let us quickly return.

5

THE brethren who went before us used to relate that there was a certain brother of our father's community who, when occasion demanded, made use of blood-letting. He was disturbed at this, because although necessity compelled him, still he ought not to have presumed to do it without permission. But soon the vein

---

[1] He has confused two incidents here. The faces of the three children became fairer and fatter when they refused the royal food. (Dan. i.) They were thrown into the furnace for refusing to worship the statue of Nabuchodonosor. (Dan. iii.)

[2] See p. 20, *n.* I.

[3] The parentheses are mine, but seem called for.

through which the blood had flowed burst, and it could in no way be restrained until he died. The brethren added, moreover, that if Odo had foretold either good fortune or bad for anyone, he could by no means escape from them. Would that some of us had not experienced that in ourselves. But happy are those who deserved to see his presence while he lived. Unhappy I who merited to be associated with him for less than two complete years.[1]

<h2 style="text-align:center">6</h2>

As the time was approaching when in the dispensation of God we should no longer be able to see each other, and when his absence—which had to be—should greatly increase the flame of my love, on a certain day seeing me unduly sad, he began gently to console me, as his manner was. But when he saw that he could not still my mental anguish, beginning like the patriarch Jacob with the past,[2] he began to predict with a prophetic spirit the things that would happen to me. "Listen, most dear son, to what I say to you. I give God thanks that I have received punishment in this life for all the sins I have committed from my youth, except those which I have committed against my abbot, and I have always awaited the day and the time, beseeching the Lord that He would not reserve it for a future life. And now I believe that I have been heard, because those things which I have done against him I have received again from you. But be sure that you on your part will not get a mere equivalent, but tenfold. Be strong and patient, then, that you may be able to bear them quietly." He said this weeping, then kissing my head commended me to the Lord. But Thou, Almighty God, have mercy on the priest Caesarius who is paying me back in my turn a hundredfold and more, and if any remain of my sad evils graciously avert them.

---

[1] John means presumably that the total time he spent in Odo's company after meeting him amounted to less than two years.

[2] It would seem that the reference must be to Jacob's prophetical blessing of his sons in Genesis xlix, but what he means by "beginning with the past", *exordium sumens de praeteritis*, as applied to Jacob is not clear.

7

THE ruler Alberic, whom I have already mentioned, gave us the
monastery of St. Elias which is called Suppentonia, of which
St. Gregory makes mention in the book of the *Dialogues*.[1] But as
the same St. Gregory says, it is hard to take in new things with
an old mind, and we were not able to restrain the monks we found
there from eating meat.[2] Our father appointed a prior[3] in this
monastery from among our brethren, by name Theodard. Seeing
that neither force nor holiness could restrain them from this vice,
he began to buy fish from neighbouring regions, that perhaps in
this way he might satisfy their desire. (The horses which our father
sent him for this purpose were almost worn out going to and fro).
The aforesaid prior often tried to make known to our father the
depravity of the monks and his own labour. While all this was
going on Odo was beseeching the Lord, and it happened that the
valley on which the monastery looked and in part lay became
closed by the joining of two small hills which lay close together,
and the channel of a small stream which flowed through it was
blocked. A great quantity of water collected and formed a lake, and
the labour of the brother was saved, for there was no longer any
necessity to buy fish. But by whose merit this came about some
who are not instructed are unaware, because they have not appre-
ciated the public benefit for which it was done, and because they
did not hear the prayer of our father. It is hypocrites, not the
faithful, who say these things; that is to say those who speak thus
do not know that saying of the psalmist: *The Lord hath heard the
desire of the poor: thy ear hath heard the preparation* [*desire*] *of
their heart* [Ps. ix. 17], and again: *He will do the will of them that
fear Him; and he will hear their prayer* [Ps. cxliv. 19]. For Odo
had brought about the same thing when he was in France at St.

---

[1] Suppentonia is the modern Castel Sant'Elia between Nepi and Civita
Castellana about thirty miles north of Rome. It is mentioned in the *Dialogues*
of St. Gregory, bk. i, ch. 7. (See p. 262 in Gardner's edition.)

[2] The *Rule* of St. Benedict forbids meat to all except the sick, though it is
mitigated in this particular by the constitutions of most modern Congregations.
It seems that the abstinence from meat must have been made a sort of test case
in these monastic reforms. Cf. Chapter 9 below.

[3] The word used here is *praepositus*.

Benedict's [Fleury]; and we relate this with the more assurance as we have the faithful witness of the father himself. But first it must be told how he received this monastery [Fleury[1]], so that my pen may come as by a straight line to those things which are to follow.

8

WHEN the persecution of Nortmund, the savage King of the Norsemen, in France was ended, that it might be fulfilled which the Lord had foretold of His Church by Isaias: *For a small moment have I forsaken thee; but with great mercies will I gather thee. In a moment of indignation have I hid my face a little while from thee; but with everlasting kindness have I had mercy on thee* [Isa. liv. 7 and 8], the brethren of St. Benedict's [Fleury], who had been scattered far and wide through fear of the enemy, were gathered together and received back their monastery. But—and I cannot say it without sorrow—it was united in body but with divided minds that they occupied again that holy place. I pass over this quickly that my pen may not dwell on the lives of such men. And in truth I have enough to do to narrate clearly how our most blessed father Odo was called, elected, and indeed pre-ordained [to this abbey] by St. Benedict. One day when the brethren in this monastery were quarrelling, one of them, who was giving up his obedience, met St. Benedict outside the door, and the saint immediately gave him this command: "Go and tell the brethren that they give me no rest. I am leaving this house, and let them know that I shall not return till I bring from Aquitaine a man who shall be after my own heart." When the brother hesitatingly inquired his name, the saint replied, "You know that I am Brother Benedict." As soon as he had finished speaking he departed. The brother, therefore, made known what he had been commanded. But the wretched men, when deprived of such a father, did not have recourse to tears and prayers, which often allay the vengeance of the Lord, but getting on to their horses rode off hither and thither to find him [St. Benedict], and bring him back by force or entreaties. When

---

[1] See p. 42, *n.* 1. The following story gives a good indication of the demoralizing effects of the Norse invasions on monastic life.

they did not find him they began ceaselessly to mock at the brother. At that time Elisiardus, who was then an illustrious count but who has now taken the monastic habit, hearing of the infamy of these monks begged the abbacy from Rudolph, the King of the Franks,[1] and when he had received it he gave it to our father. Then taking with him two counts and the same number of bishops, together with our father Odo, he set out. When the brethren heard of their approach, some arming themselves with swords went up on to the roof of the building, as though to hurl stones and missiles on their enemies from the sky. Others took shields and swords to guard the door of the monastery, saying they would die before they allowed these men to come in, or would receive an abbot of another community. Meanwhile, come to their senses, they were saying: "Now we see what St. Benedict recently threatened us with. Alas, why did we not believe our brother? Everything which he told us has come about. Is not this Odo that Aquitainian of whom we often suspected that St. Benedict was speaking. Alas, why did we not ourselves send to him and invite him of our own will?" Meanwhile turning this way and that they sought by what means they could repel those who were approaching. There was among them a brother called Wulfaldus.[2] He was young, but of good disposition, and when he acted as ambassador between the two parties, the monks sent certain royal charters in which it was asserted that no one from another community should ever be head of their monastery. Our father replied: "I come peacefully—to hurt no one, injure no one, but that I may correct those who are not living according to the Rule." With these and similar words, even though carried by a third party, he strove to soothe their minds. But when they saw that their efforts were of no avail, they turned to other arguments, now invoking the king, now threatening to kill him. This went on for three days. Then the father Odo, unknown to any, mounted a donkey and set out quickly for the monastery. The bishops and the counts with their followers hurried after him crying: "Where are you going, Father? Do you

---

[1] He was Duke of Burgundy and seized the French crown from Charles the Simple, its rightful possessor, in 923 and held it till his death in 936.

[2] According to Mabillon (note *ad. loc.*) he succeeded Archembalbus (see p. 54, *n.* 1) as Abbot of Fleury and was afterwards Bishop of Chartres.

seek your death? Do you not see that they are prepared to kill you? The hour in which you go to them will be your last. Do you wish to give cause for rejoicing at your death to them, and to us deadly grief?" With such remarks they called after him. But as the Scripture says: *The just, bold as a lion, shall be without dread* [Prov. xxviii. 1]; once he had started on his journey nothing they could do would make him turn back. I am about to relate a wonderful thing. When he approached and was recognized by those who had known him previously, those who were then resisting were forthwith changed, so that I can say without doubt: *This is the change of the right hand of the most High.* [Ps. lxxvi. 11]. And indeed straightway throwing away their arms they went out to meet him and embraced his feet. There was no little joy for all on that day. The community received Odo as a father, and his escort returned home.

9

HE began now, moreover, to persuade them to give up eating meat, to live sparingly, and to possess nothing of their own, and that what they possessed in secret they should renounce before all in the manner of the apostles. But because they did not hold the property of the monastery in common, but divided it amongst themselves as they were able or as seemed good to them, when they saw that what they had been doing was no longer lawful, they wrongly preferred to present their unjust possessions to their friends, and even to profligates, than to renounce them according to the Rule. For, temporizing, they were striving to consume the very thing which they had given up [fish], together with what our father had brought with him, so that all having been used up he should at least unwillingly grant them leave to eat meat.[1] For this reason they persistently demanded fish. On the other hand the loving father gave them everything that was suitable, that he might prohibit them from the one thing. So it came about that with his giving and their eating almost everything was consumed. Nevertheless, our father remained constant in faith, secure in hope,

---

[1] The Latin of this passage is extremely confused.

fortified by charity, knowing that he would not be abandoned, according to the promise of the Gospels: *Be not solicitous* [*for your life*] *what you shall eat, or what you shall drink, or with what you shall be clothed.* [Matt. vi. 25.] While this was going on St. Benedict appeared to one of the brothers in a vision, and commanded him among other things to tell our father to be in no way anxious about the shortage of money, nor to be solicitous about acquiring goods, and then he added, "Tomorrow I will send him a hundred shillings and next week I will provide him with a variety of things that will suffice for the use of the brethren for a long time." And so it happened.

10

MANY from the surrounding regions began to come to the feet of the holy man, and under his rule to take the agreeable road of obedience, by which they afterwards merited to attain heavenly thrones. So much was the fame of his sanctity spread abroad, that not only laymen and canons flocked to him, but also some bishops left their sees and joined themselves to his community. So you might see the place as land cleared of thorns producing new growth and new fruits, and sending the corn, as it were separated from the straw of vices by the frequent blows of words, from the threshing-floor to the granary of the Lord.

11

ON another occasion the feast of St. Benedict was approaching, and our father wanted to go from the monastery where he then was to the aforesaid monastery [of Fleury], so that he might celebrate the night vigils devoutly before the body of the saint[1]—and this he did. In the night before the feast it happened that the morning office was being celebrated before dawn, and when one of the brethren, tired by the night vigil, had at length given himself to sleep, St. Benedict deigned to appear to him. When he had

---

[1] The body of St. Benedict was traditionally said to be at Fleury. See p. 42, *n.* I.

made himself known, he said, "Tell the brethren that because I was not able to be with them last night, I shall certainly be so to-day." "And where were you, Father?" the brother asked. St. Benedict replied: "In the island of Britain." "What were you doing there?" he said. St. Benedict answered: "Brother Leutfred, who through pride left this place and crossed the sea, died this night and was taken by the demons. I have struggled with them and freed him from their power." When he heard this the brother was amazed, and the holy father said to him, "If you are amazed at this, listen further. You may know for certain that from the time this monastery was founded all the brothers who died here have been received into eternal rest."[1] Then the brother said, "As you promised, father, that you would be with us today, who will make known the hour of your coming that we may go to meet you?" "No one," he replied, "but I will show such a sign to all that they will not doubt of my presence." The brother went on, "With what ceremony shall we be able to receive so great a father, or what honour shall we show to him?" To which St. Benedict replied: "If you are anxious for more delicate food, you have abundant fish." "By no means, father," he said. The saint replied, "Let the fishermen be told that they must not go to the river Loire to fish, but to the pool which lies close to the monastery." After hearing this the brother awoke from his sleep, and when the time of silence was ended he was careful to make known to the brethren all that he had been told. Assured, therefore, of the coming of the father, and instructed by the admonition of our father Odo, they each strove to offer from their hearts spiritual gifts to their spiritual father. So they spent the day in hymns and prayers. Meanwhile the servants of the monastery who had been given the task of fishing did not go to the pool as they had been ordered, but to the river Loire, which fact they kept secret. So it came about that they returned about the third hour tired out, but without any catch. When questioned as to why they had come back empty-handed, in their confusion at their presumptuous disobedience they were

---

[1] Mabillon has a deprecating note at this point—and very rightly. Odo, in his own sermon on St. Benedict (*PL*, cxxxiii, col. 721 ff.) makes no mention of this tradition—if it was one—although he has much to say of St. Benedict's body's being amongst them at Fleury.

ashamed to confess what they had done. But the silence which
their shame imposed was broken by their blushes, and the cellarer
said to them, "I know your presumption. But since at first you
refused what was commanded, go now again a second time to
fish—and go to the pool." Which they did, and soon caught so
many fish that no one could doubt that He who had given quails
to the people in the desert [Exod. xvi] was even then providing
this same pool with fish. To this day they abound there, so that
there is never any lack of them; and thus it came about that the
pool, which was previously full of frogs, henceforth abounded with
fish. Our father, in the book which he wrote about the arrival of
the body of St. Benedict in Orleans,[1] described this miracle most
clearly, to the same effect, but not in the same words, as others.
Great crowds from the surrounding districts came to the solemnity.
Many were blind or lame or paralysed or suffering from some
disease, and they came expecting relief. Odo ordered that no food
should be given to these people before the Mass. When it was
time they all went in to the Mass, and such is the size of the
church, that nobody was compelled to stand outside. As they were
beginning to sing the hymn of the angels, Glory be to God on high,
the doors of the church were suddenly broken open with a great
noise, so that all looked round horror-struck. But at this noise all
the sick who were present were restored to their former health, the
blind received sight, the deaf hearing, the lame the power of walking. The lamps of the church, too, were all illuminated. Then
everyone understood that St. Benedict had come according to his
promise. Such spiritual fervour filled the hearts of all that they
could not refrain from tears because of the great joy they felt.

[1] This book of Odo's has been lost. The mention of it leads John into a
characteristic digression for the rest of the chapter in which he describes the
translation of St. Benedict's body, but, be it noted, to Orleans apparently, and
not to Fleury. Since Odo was himself present at the ceremony he describes (see
below in the text) it obviously cannot have been the original translation of
St. Benedict from Italy to Fleury, which occurred in the seventh century. We
must suppose that St. Benedict's body had been temporarily moved from Fleury
owing to the Norse invasions, and that it was being brought back in stages. So
far as I know there is no other reference to the temporary removal of St. Benedict
from Fleury, but it had been found necessary to remove St. Martin from Tours
(see p. 13, n. 2) and St. Maurus from Glanfeuil during the ninth century (see
McCann, St. Benedict, London, 1938, p. 275), and it is very likely that the same
expedient would be adopted in St. Benedict's case, as the Norsemen seem to
have come up the Loire in force.

Father Odo refused to make known to me the names of the brethren who saw this, so there is doubt whether it was he or another who saw it.

12

THE time of his death was at hand, when a blessed reward from Christ should crown the holy actions which I have described. While staying at Rome he was attacked by a sharp and continuous fever, his limbs were racked by pain, a cold fire consumed his vitals and his flesh; so many and such diverse kinds of suffering appeared in the one person that he might well have been called by the Lord and stripped of the earthly form of a man at that very hour. What did the holy man do? A faithful imitator and vicar of the Apostle, he desired with all his heart to be dissolved and to live with Christ [Phil. i. 23]. He had fought the fight of holy labours and had finished the excellent course of all virtue, so that he might deservedly trust with certain hope that the crown of justice was laid up for him in heaven through the gift of divine love [2 Tim. iv. 7, 8]. While he was held awaiting the divine call, his first desire was to make a pilgrimage again to his Martin, for whom he had, so to speak, imbibed a warm and lasting love with his mother's milk, and to consign to him his last breath together with the ashes of his body. And because the clemency of Almighty God always deigns to answer holy desires, it was so with Odo, who had been set aside as another vessel of election from his mother's womb. For the beloved of God saw in the following night a man remarkable in appearance and in grace saying to him in a vision: "O holy soul, beloved of God, your calling and the final dissolution of your body is indeed at hand. But Martin delays you by his prayers, and affords strength to return to your fatherland. But when you shall have come there, life will soon be given you for death, and the blessed society of the elect will be given you in recompense for your loving labour for Christ." The vision was soon verified by signs. His bodily sickness disappeared for a time, health came back more quickly, he undertook the trial of a long journey, caring nothing for his aged and half-dead limbs. He overcame the hard labour out of his great love for Martin; all the more devout in his spiritual service, as he was sure of his reward. Having made the laborious journey he reached Tours at the time when the departure of the victorious spirit from the body of the holy bishop was about to be celebrated.[1] Then there was twofold rejoicing in the city, while all united in renewing the annual feast of Martin and in reverently welcoming the long desired presence of his fellow-citizen, Odo. How devoutly the holy man assisted at this festivity, what prayers mingled with tears he poured out to Martin, what sacrifices of a humble heart he offered as a living victim at the altar of salvation, it is beyond my powers, weighed down as I am by dullness of mind and uncouth speech, to describe. Anxious for death, his spirit was fixed in God and forgetful of earthly things; as the true servant of Martin, with unclouded gaze he attentively contemplated only heavenly things. So he waited during the whole of the holy bishop's feast: but he lamented anxiously because, contrary to his hope, the promised reward was deferred for three days. But on the fourth day of the festival he was struck by renewed fever, a chill crept into his heart's blood and consumed his strength with a sharp pang. Master, then, of his desire, and assured of the divine mercy, the tired spirit languished indeed in the sick body, but "the joyous mind sees God, aspires to Him, pants after Him. His last words ring out. Do Thou, O Christ, spare those whom Thou hast redeemed. He calls on Martin, looks up to him, prays to him."[2] By word he instructed monks coming to him from all sides and inconsolably lamenting his departure; he consigned them to God with fatherly prayers, protected them with blessings, and bade farewell with loving sighs. When the fourteenth day before December arrived, which is also the octave day of the feast of St. Martin, that blessed spirit, refreshed by the divine and saving food and invigorated by the cup of life, freed from the corruptible flesh, departed freely to the skies, and, led by Martin, faithfully presented the manifold fruit of the talent entrusted to it.

[1] The feast of St. Martin, 11th November.
[2] The passage put in quotation marks appears in the text as three lines of hexameters. It is presumably just a spontaneous outburst on John's part.

There receiving the due reward of loving labour, joined to the ranks of the saints, he shines with the glory of a blessed immortality through Christ our Lord, who lives and reigns for ever and ever. Amen.

THE LIFE OF ST. GERALD OF AURILLAC

by

ST. ODO OF CLUNY

THE LIFE OF ST. GERALD OF AURILLAC
BY ST. ODO OF CLUNY

DEDICATORY EPISTLE OF THE AUTHOR

To the Father Abbot Aymo[1] in affectionate remembrance of his merits, Odo the servant of the brethren, everlasting salvation in Christ. I am undertaking, venerable Father, as best I can and with much trepidation, the little book which you recently urged me so strongly to write concerning the life and miracles of the holy man Gerald. On the one hand I fear to be presumptuous in undertaking something beyond my capacity; on the other hand, in not doing it I fear greatly to be contumacious by being disobedient. I undertake the task, however, relying on the obedience and the goodness of Christ, and I beseech you to implore His mercy, that for the love of His servant Gerald He would deign so to guide what I say, that it may not be entirely unworthy of the man He has seen fit to glorify, and that to me it may not be a cause of transgression. To avoid such transgression I pass over some things for which perhaps you will blame me, and set down those things only which were made known to me by sure authorities and when you also were present. Farewell.

[1] He was the abbot of the monastery of St. Martial at Limoges from 936 to his death in 942 (Sackur, vol. i, p. 81). The "canons" of St. Martial at Limoges became monks in the middle of the ninth century. The monastery evidently suffered in the invasions of the Norsemen, for we learn later (ch. 39) that the treasury of the abbey was removed to Turenne. Odo was instrumental in the restoration of monastic life there (Sackur, vol. i, p. 81).

MANY doubt whether the things that are said about the blessed
Gerald are true, and some think that they are certainly not true
but fantastic. Others, as though seeking excuses for their sins,
extol him indiscreetly, saying that Gerald was powerful and rich,
and lived well, and is certainly a saint. They strive indeed to excuse
their luxurious lives by his example. It seemed to me therefore
that I ought to reply a little to these according to my ability. For
I too, formerly, hearing the fame of his miracles, was nevertheless
in doubt, and for this reason chiefly, that stories get about here and
there, through I know not what channels, and are then gradually
discredited as empty. But when cause arose that I should visit the
community of the monastery at Tulle,[1] I was glad to go to his
tomb, and then having summoned four of those whom he had
brought up, namely the monk Hugh, the priest Hildebert, and
two well-born laymen, Witard and another Hildebert, along with
many others, I investigated his behaviour and the quality of his
life in detail. Now with the others, now alone, I carefully investigated what each one said and whether they agreed, silently
pondering if his life was one in which miracles were fitting. Having
learnt how religiously he lived and that God had shown this man
to be in His grace by many signs, I could no longer doubt of his
sanctity. I marvel rather, that in this age of ours, when charity has
almost entirely grown cold, and the time of anti-Christ is at hand,
the miracles of the saints should not cease, but He is mindful of the
promise, that He makes by Jeremias: *I will not cease to do good to
my people.* [Jer. xxxii. 40.] And of this good that He has done the
Apostle bears witness, when he says that God, not leaving Himself
in any age without a witness [Acts xiv. 16], in His kindness fills
the hearts of men with joy. If, therefore, it pleases the divine
goodness, that He who did wonderful things for our fathers,

---

[1] This was another of the monasteries which Odo restored (Sackur, vol. i,
p. 78), and it was no doubt in connexion with this that he was visiting it when
he became interested in the history of St. Gerald. Tulle lies about fifty miles
north-west of Aurillac, and half-way between that town and Limoges.

should be glorified also in our times, we ought by no means to be incredulous. For it seems that the divine dispensation performs these things in our age and through a man of our time, because everything which the saints did or said in the past has been forgotten. And since, as in the days of Noe, a man of God was found, who lived according to the law, God set him up as an example to those who saw him, that their hearts should be inspired to imitate one who was their neighbour, and whom they saw to live a just and pious life. And let not the observance of the commandments of God seem hard or impossible, since it is seen to have been achieved by a layman of great position. For nothing more encourages mental cowardice than that the retribution of good or evil works, which is to follow in the next life, should not be meditated upon in the present. And against this Scripture warns us that in all our actions we should remember our last end [Ecclus. vii. 40]. God, therefore, exalts on earth in the sight of his contemporaries the servant whom He rewards in heaven, so that by that which is done outwardly the contemners of God may see inwardly that God is not served in vain, but that as He Himself testifies, He will glorify those who glorify Him, and bring down in shame those who despise Him. [1 Kings ii. 30.] Since, therefore, I believe this man of God to have been given as an example to the mighty, let them see how they may imitate him as one of themselves held up for their example, lest perchance, as the Queen of the South the Jews, he shall condemn them in the day of judgement [Luke xi, 31]. Taking occasion from his actions, I have added something by way of admonition to those same mighty ones, where opportunity has arisen, as you asked me. And indeed Bishop Turpio[1] and the venerable Abbot Aymo, who is most dear to me, with many others, have driven me with urgent prayers to undertake this. When I would have put forward the true excuse of lack of skill, they said that they preferred matter such as this to be put forth in an unpolished style, and I considering that a grandiose style little

---

[1] He was Bishop of Limoges. We learn from the dedicatory epistle to Odo's *Collations* that he was the bishop at whose instigation Odo wrote, and as the *Collations* is evidently the work referred to in John's *Life*, bk. i, ch. 37, he was the bishop who ordained Odo priest. He was the brother of Abbot Aymo (Duchesne, annotations to *Bibliotheca Cluniacensis* (Marrier) *ad. loc.*; PL cxxxiii, 639).

fitted a humble man, have put my faith in the words of witnesses, who have recorded not many of the miracles, which ordinary men think of great moment, but rather a disciplined way of life, and not a few works of mercy pleasing to God. For in the judgement the king will say to many who prophesied and who did great things: *I know you not*. [Matt. xxv. 12.] But those who execute justice, in which Gerald excelled, are to hear *Come ye, blessed of my father* [Matt. xxv. 34]. And in truth the things which were done by Job, David, and Tobias, and many others, and through which they are blessed, are not those which Gerald is shown to have done. Having considered all this I was persuaded to believe that Gerald (through whom the heavenly Giver of gifts deigns to work miracles) is worthy of the company of the saints. But in making this apology in the preface I have spoken too long; now in the name of Christ let us come to the beginning of our tale.

BOOK I

I

THE man of God, Gerald, took his origin from that part of Gaul which was called by the ancients *Celtica*,[1] in the territory which marches with that of Auvergne and Cahors and Albi, in the town or village of Aurillac. His father was Gerald, his mother Adaltruda.[2] He was so illustrious by the nobility of his birth, that among the families of Gaul his lineage is outstanding both for its possessions and the excellence of its life. For it is said that his parents held modesty and religion as a sort of hereditary dowry. Two witnesses among his ancestors are themselves sufficient to prove the point: namely St. Caesarius, the Bishop of Arles, and the holy Abbot Aredius.[3] And because the Lord is in the generation of the just [Ps. xiii. 6], the generation of Gerald is of those who seek the Lord; and so the righteous generation is blessed. And indeed the great quantity of estates endowed with serfs, lying in various places, which came to Gerald by right of succession,[4] testifies to

[1] Caesar divided the Gauls into the Aquitani, the Belgae, and the Celticae. The latter occupied the country from the lowlands of Switzerland through the uplands of central France to the Atlantic seaboard north of the Garonne. Aurillac lies in the midst of this country towards the south-west of the *Massif Central*, where the rivers begin to flow away to the West to join the Dordogne and the Atlantic at Bordeaux. One does not know exactly what Odo understood by the territories in question, and Albi particularly would seem rather far to the south, but the position of Aurillac roughly corresponds with his description. It belonged essentially to the Aquitaine of the tenth century. (See p. 6, *n*. 1).

[2] Very little is really known about Gerald's parentage. Odo puts the saints mentioned below among the families of his ancestors, but there is no other authority for this. Mabillon (*Acta*, vol. vii, p. 6, *PL*, cxxxiii, 703) says that others, whom he does not name, state that his grandmother was Mathilda, the daughter of Peppin. However this may be, as he says, it is evident that Gerald's father was a well-to-do landowner, though it appears that he did not have the title of count. (See p. 122, *n*. 1). The date of Gerald's birth appears to be established as 855 (Mabillon, *loc. cit.*).

[3] St. Caesarius (470-543) was the foremost bishop of his day in Gaul, and ruled the Church of Arles for forty years. St. Aredius was Abbot of St. Yrier near Limoges at the end of the sixth century. (Mabillon, *Acta*, vol. i, p. 349.)

[4] The feudal system of land tenure, if followed into all its details, was exceedingly complex, and varied much between different places and times, but the main principles remained unchanged throughout. There were two types of holding. One was completely free and entailed no obligation of any kind to another man. Property held in such a way was said to be allod (*alodus*) and it was, of course, hereditary. Some of Gerald's property was of this nature. (See bk. i, ch. 41). The other type of holding was that which in general entailed a

the extent of their riches. But in him the beauty of mind which he inherited from his parents shone forth much augmented. With what grace were his parents endowed, who merited to beget so excellent an offspring!

2

HIS father was so careful to conduct himself chastely in his marriage, that he frequently slept alone far from the marriage bed, as though for a time giving himself to prayer according to the word of the Apostle [I Cor. vii. 5]. He is said to have been warned in sleep on a certain night that he should know his wife, because he was to beget a son, and they say that it was announced to him that he should call his name Gerald, and that he would be a man of great virtue. When he awoke he was full of joy at the vision. Having fallen asleep again it seemed to him that a rod grew up from the big toe of his right foot, which gradually grew into a great tree, which burst into leaf and spread itself on all sides. Then seeming to call workmen he ordered props in the form of forks or poles to be put underneath it. And even when it grew very great, he felt no weight on his toe. In truth visions of dreams are not always vain. And if faith is to be put in sleep, it seems that this vision agrees in its result with future events. He knew his wife, who conceived a son as the vision foretold. The dream may perhaps be doubted, but the mark of virtue evidently followed.

3

WHEN his mother was near to giving birth, on the ninth day before he was born, it happened that she and her husband were lying

---

certain obligation to another man. This was the characteristic feudal holding, in which property was held as what was known at this time as a benefice, and later became known as a fief. The holder of a benefice did homage for it and was the vassal of the man who was the real owner. Originally it was given to him to provide for his maintenance in return for the military service which he gave the lord, and it was not hereditary, though by this time (end of ninth century) it had probably become so in most cases. Gerald, we know, was a royal vassal (bk. i, ch. 32), which meant that he held some of his estates as a benefice from the king and it is probable that already at this time he would succeed his father in these. When a man became a vassal he was said to *commend* himself to his lord. The vassal was essentially a free man who entered into a free contract carrying mutual obligations, and his service was military.

awake. And while they were talking about I know not what, the child cried out so that both heard it. Lost in astonishment, they were dumbfounded as to what it might be—yet they could not but know that the voice sounded in the womb of the mother. The father called the waiting-woman and ordered her to search with a light for the place where the crying came from. When, equally astonished, she protested that there was no child present to have uttered the cry, the child cried a second time. And after a short interval it cried a third time, as a child recently born is accustomed to cry. Three times, therefore, he was heard in the womb of his mother, and assuredly this is a strange thing which certainly happened against the course of nature. And because it happened not by chance but by the dispensation of God, the Ruler of nature, perhaps that voice presaged that his actions in the prison of his mortality were to be of great moment. For as the child in the womb of his mother lives indeed, but is not conscious, so after the guilt of the first man the whole human race on earth is confined as in the narrowness of the womb, and although by faith it lives in the hope of the glory of the sons of God, nevertheless it scarcely performs, except in a languid manner, any act of the senses like seeing, nor can it make use of the senses in the way that the first man did before sin, or the saints do after this life.[1] Gerald therefore did well to cry in the womb of his mother, because acting in the faith of the Holy Trinity beyond the common vigour of men, he signified by that small voice the happy fame with which he was to fill the world.

4

WHEN he had been born, then, and weaned, and had come to that age in which the character of children may usually be discerned, a certain pleasing quality began to show itself in him, by which those who looked closely conjectured of what virtue the future man should be. For at an early age, as we often see, children through the incitements of their corrupt nature are accustomed to be angry

---

[1] This theologically inexact statement about the saints may be compared with what John of Salerno says of St. Martin and St. Benedict. See introduction, p. xix.

and envious, and to wish to be revenged, or to attempt other things of this sort. But in the child Gerald a certain sweetness and modesty of mind, which especially graces youth, adorned his childish acts. By the grace of divine providence he applied himself to the study of letters, but by the will of his parents only to the extent of going through his psalter; after that he was instructed in the worldly exercises customary for the sons of the nobility; to ride to hounds, become an archer, learn to fly falcons and hawks in the proper manner. But lest given to useless pursuits the time suitable for learning letters should pass without profit the divine will ordained that he should be a long time sick, though with such a sickness that he should be withdrawn from worldly pursuits but not hindered in his application to learning. And for a long time he was so covered with small pimples that it was not thought that he could be cured. For this reason his father and mother decided that he should be put more closely to the study of letters, so that if he should prove unsuited for worldly pursuits, he might be fitted for the ecclesiastical state.[1] So it came about that he not only learnt the chant, but also learnt something of grammar. And this was afterwards of much use to him, since, perfected by that exercise, his wits were sharpened for whatever he might wish to apply them to. He had a lively and discerning mind, and was not slow to learn anything to which he set himself.

5

WHILE he was growing up his bodily strength consumed the harmful humours of his body. So agile was he that he could vault over the backs of horses with ease. And because, endowed with bodily strength as he was, he became very active, it was demanded of him that he accustom himself to military service. But the sweet-

[1] The information about Gerald's education is of interest. It may be noted that his parents did not envisage his being able to read anything beyond the psalter, until it became doubtful whether he would be able to take his place as an upper-class layman—for which physical fitness was essential. The only alternative was the ecclesiastical state, and any further education was necessarily identified with this. The learned layman was apparently not contemplated. Nothing is said about Gerald's learning to write, and it is probable that he never did.

ness of the Scriptures, to the study of which he was greatly attracted, held his mind in pledge, so that, although he excelled in military exercises, nevertheless it was the charm of letters which attracted him. In the former by a voluntary sloth he was a little slow, in the latter he was assiduous.[1] I believe now he began to perceive that according to the testimony of Scripture, wisdom is better than strength [Wisd. vi. 1], and that nothing is more precious. And because it is easily perceived by those that love it, wisdom took possession of his mind to reveal itself to him and to be the sweet expression of his thought. Nothing was able to hinder Gerald from hastening to the love of learning. So it came about that he learnt almost the whole series of the Scriptures and surpassed many clerical smatterers in his knowledge of it.

6

AFTER the death of his parents, when he attained full power over his property, Gerald was not puffed up, as youths often are who boast of their grown-up mastery, nor did he change the modesty which was springing up in his heart. His power of ruling increased, but the humble mind did not grow haughty. He was compelled to be occupied in administering and watching over things[2] which, as I have said, came to him by hereditary right, and to leave that peace of heart, which he had to some extent tasted, to take up the weariness of earthly business. He could scarcely bear to leave the inner solitude of his heart, and he returned to it as soon as he could. But while he seemed to fall headlong from the heights of contemplation to the occupations of earth, as the chamois in its

---

[1] He had evidently recovered from his affliction, but in the meantime had developed a taste for reading the Scriptures. The theological learning of the time was, of course, practically confined to the Scriptures and commentaries on them, mostly taken from the Fathers. See Smalley, ch. 2.

[2] In Merovingian times and under Charles the Great the country was divided into districts in each of which a royal official, called the count, was responsible for judicial, military, and financial matters. By Gerald's time the counts were no longer royal officials, but the large local landowners performed their functions and assumed their titles. Gerald is frequently shown performing the judicial office of a count and it is interesting to see a reference to his actually assuming the title (i, 32, p. 122). In many cases, no doubt, the counts were the descendants of men originally appointed by royal authority. The performance of the functions had become hereditary, but they now did it in their own interests and not those of the king.

fall saves itself from death by its horns, so, turning to the divine love and the meditation of Holy Scripture he escaped the ruin of spiritual death. Inspired, as I think, by the very spirit of David, in his fervour he gave no sleep to his eyes, until freed from daily activities he might find within himself a place for the Lord, and exulting in it secretly he tasted how sweet the Lord is [Ps. xxxiii. 9]. Perchance according to that saying of Job, Christ, the Rock, poured forth rivers of oil for him [Job xxix. 6], lest many waters should be able to extinguish in him the light of charity [Cant. viii. 7]. Dragged down to earth, he yearned for this spiritual refreshment, but his household and dependants demanded that he should break into his repose and give himself to the service of others.

7

HE admitted these gnawing cares unwillingly for the sake of the complaints of those who had recourse to him. For his dependants pleaded querulously saying: "Why should a great man suffer violence from persons of low degree who lay waste his property?", adding that, when these discovered that he did not wish to take vengeance they devoured the more greedily that which was rightfully his. It would be more holy and honest that he should recognize the right of armed force, that he should unsheathe the sword against his enemies, that he should restrain the boldness of the violent; it would be better that the bold should be suppressed by force of arms than that the undefended districts should be unjustly oppressed by them. When Gerald heard this he was moved, not by the attack made on him but by reason, to have mercy and to give help. Committing himself entirely to the will of God and the divine mercy, he sought only how he might visit the fatherless and widows and hold himself unspotted from this world, according to the precept of the Apostle. [James i. 27.]

8

HE therefore exerted himself to repress the insolence of the violent, taking care in the first place to promise peace and most easy reconciliation to his enemies. And he did this by taking care, that either he should overcome evil by good, or if his enemies would not come to terms, he should have in God's eyes the greater right on his side. And sometimes indeed he soothed them and reduced them to peace. When insatiable malice poured scorn on peaceful men, showing severity of heart, he broke the teeth of the wicked [Ps. lvii, 7], that, according to the saying of Job, he might snatch the prey from their jaws. [Job xxix 17.] He was not incited by the desire for revenge, as is the case with many, or led on by love of praise from the multitude, but by love of the poor, who were not able to protect themselves. He acted in this way lest, if he became sluggish through an indolent patience, he should seem to have neglected the precept to care for the poor. He ordered the poor man to be saved and the needy to be freed from the hand of the sinner. Rightly, therefore, he did not allow the sinner to prevail. But sometimes when the unavoidable necessity of fighting lay on him, he commanded his men in imperious tones, to fight with the backs of their swords and with their spears reversed. This would have been ridiculous to the enemy if Gerald, strengthened by divine power, had not been invincible to them. And it would have seemed useless to his own men, if they had not learnt by experience that Gerald, who was carried away by his piety in the very moment of battle, had not always been invincible. When therefore they saw that he triumphed by a new kind of fighting which was mingled with piety, they changed their scorn to admiration, and sure of victory they readily fulfilled his commands. For it was a thing unheard of that he or the soldiers who fought under him were not victorious. But this also is certain, that he himself never wounded anybody, nor was wounded by anyone. For Christ, as it is written, was at his side [Ps. cxvii. 6], who seeing the desire of his heart, saw that for love of Him he was so well-disposed that he had no wish to assail the persons of the enemy, but only to check their audacity. Let no one be worried because a just man sometimes made use of fighting, which seems incompatible with religion. No one who has judged his cause impartially will be able to show that the glory of Gerald is clouded by this. For some of the Fathers, and of these the most holy and most patient, when the cause of justice demanded, valiantly took up arms against their adversaries, as Abraham, who

destroyed a great multitude of the enemy to rescue his nephew
[Gen. xiv], and King David who sent his forces even against his
own son. [2 Kings xviii.] Gerald did not fight invading the
property of others, but defending his own, or rather his people's
rights, knowing that the rhinoceros, that is, any powerful man, is
to be bound with a thong that he may break the clods of the valley,
that is, the oppressors of the lowly. [Job xxxix. 10.]¹ For, as the
Apostle says, *the judge beareth not the sword in vain; for he is God's
avenger* [Rom. xiii. 4]. It was lawful, therefore, for a layman to
carry the sword in battle that he might protect defenceless people,
as the harmless flock from evening wolves according to the saying
of Scripture [Acts xx. 29], and that he might restrain by arms or by
the law those whom ecclesiastical censure was not able to subdue.
It does not darken his glory, then, that he fought for the cause of
God, for whom the whole world fights against the unwise. [Wisd.
v. 21.] Rather is it to his praise that he always won openly without
the help of deceit or ambushes, and nevertheless was so protected
by God, that, as I said before, he never stained his sword with
human blood. Hereafter, let him who by his example shall take up
arms against his enemies, seek also by his example not his own but
the common good. For you may see some who for love of praise
or gain boldly put themselves in danger, gladly sustain the evils of
the world for the sake of the world, and while they encounter its
bitterness lose the joys, so to speak, which they were seeking. But
of these it is another story. The work of Gerald shines forth, because it sprang from simplicity of heart.

9

THE old deceiver had made trial of the virtue of the youth, and
having found I know not what of the divine in him, burst out in
envy, and for this reason strove to overthrow him by all the tricks
of temptation that were in his power. But Gerald had learnt to
flee in prayer to the bosom of the divine love, and relying on the
grace of Christ to refute the fabrications of the evil one. But

---

¹ The application of this curious text is obscure. Surprisingly, Gerald is the
rhinoceros, apparently, who breaks the oppressors of the lowly.

insatiably envious, the enemy, when he had found by experience
that he could exercise no power over him through the delectation
of the flesh, raised up the tempest of war against him by means of
wicked men, as I have described above,[1] so that by this means he
might capture the citadel of his heart, into which by himself he
was in no way able to enter. To return to his youth—the cunning
foe was most actively inflamed against that chastity which Gerald
earnestly loved. For it was something new and unaccustomed to
him that a youth should have avoided completely the shipwreck of
his purity. He constantly suggested lustful thoughts to him therefore, for that is his first and greatest means of leading mankind
astray. When Gerald completely repelled them, the enemy suffered
tortures, because he could not introduce them even to the portals
of his heart. And so he repeated the old fraud and had recourse to
the instrument of deception by which Adam and his posterity are
most often led astray—I mean woman. He brought, it is said, a
certain girl before his eyes and while Gerald incautiously took
notice of the colour of her clear skin, he was softened to take delight in it. O, if he had at once understood what lay hidden beneath the skin! For the beauty of the flesh is nothing but the thin
disguise of the skin. He averted his eyes but the image impressed
on the heart through them remained. He was tortured therefore,
allured, and consumed by a blind fire. Overcome at length, he
sent word to the mother of the girl that he would come by night.
He followed the messenger, violently hastened to the death of his
soul. Meanwhile, as captives in chains remember with groans their
former liberty, with sighs Gerald remembered the familiar sweetness of the divine love. And though but weakly, he asked God that
he should not be entirely swallowed up by this temptation. Gerald
came to the agreed place, and the girl entered the room; because
he was cold he stood at the hearth facing her; divine grace looked
on him, and this same girl appeared to him so deformed that he did
not believe it was she whom he saw, until her father asserted that
it was so. Understanding that this did not happen without the
divine assent, that the same girl should no longer have the same

---

[1] The reference seems to be rather to the anecdotes given in the later chapters
of this book, 35-40.

beauty in his eyes, he soon betook himself once more to the mercy of Christ, and sighing deeply he got on to his horse, and giving thanks to God rode away musing. Perhaps he who had allowed himself to be on fire for a whole night, was now assailed by too great coldness, that a harsh frigidity might punish the warmth of a slight delectation. He ordered the father forthwith to give the girl in marriage, presented her with her liberty, and granted her a small holding.[1] Perhaps suspecting his weakness, he had her marriage hurried on, and this was the reason that, as an alms, he gave her the dowry of her liberty, lest her marriage should be delayed. You who were to grow into a cedar of paradise, how could you be so agitated? Surely that you might learn what you might be, left to yourself. For your patron, the Prince of the Apostles, to whom afterwards you committed yourself and all you possessed, would not have had sufficient knowledge of himself, if the critical moment of temptation had not come upon him. But now that you know by experience what a man may be by himself and what by the grace of God, do not scorn to have compassion on the weakness of your supplicants. We know that it is not unusual for the saints to be tempted, for the vices inherent in their corrupt nature come to life, that wherever they strive they may conquer, and conquering be crowned. For there is a difference between one who feels the delight of vice and gives way, and one who fighting against it conquers, and occupying his mind rather with the pleasure of virtue drives out the poison of an evil delight, which perhaps he has for a time imbibed, with the antidote of pious supplication. And the youth, more discreet for the experience of this danger, like a man who has knocked his foot in a slippery place, walked more cautiously, being careful that the eyes should announce nothing to the heart, by means of which death might find entrance through the windows of the soul. [Jer. ix. 21.]

[1] The parents of the girl were evidently serfs, and it would be normal that she should not be able to marry without the lord's consent.

10

FOR the rest, the kind and just Lord, who by the attractiveness of holiness, kept his servant Gerald from defilement, did not omit to punish his concupiscence by a just punishment. A few days after He struck the offender for a year and more with blindness from cataract, so that the eyes which had looked on unlawful things should not for a time be able to see even that which was lawful. And indeed not the slightest evil could penetrate his eyelids. Those about him knew of the blindness and they concealed it from the peering eyes of strangers with the greatest care. But he, humiliating himself under the chastising hand of the Lord, as though prepared for His scourges, was silent. He neither refused bodily medicines, nor eagerly sought them, but waited patiently for the time and the manner in which his Lord might see fit to remove the scourge, and no longer desire to strike him. For he knew that every son is chastised. [Heb. xii, 6.] The judger of hearts indeed purges even the smallest stains in His elect in this life, lest afterwards there should remain in them anything which might offend His eyes. And for this reason God brought on this affliction, that the youth's mind might be cleansed from that which was past, and be kept more pure in the future. When, therefore, God had fulfilled His will in him, He removed the affliction and restored the sight to his eyes.

11

WITH his senses as it were dried up by suffering, Gerald led an upright life, and departed neither to one side nor the other from the middle path of discretion, so that he neither failed in the duties of his worldly affairs, nor diverted himself from the practice of religion by earthly occupations. He surrounded himself with the better type of men and with clerics of good name, with whom whether at home or abroad he performed the divine Office either in common or privately.[1] On a certain Sunday he had to attend a

---

[1] What we are told about Gerald's devotions in this chapter is of great interest. It is valuable testimony to the practices of the pious layman of the time,

meeting of the law-court which had been arranged and to which certain nobles were going to come. Lest he should keep them waiting by coming late, he took care to go on horseback and set out before dawn. For he was on his guard on this grand court-day not to show himself slow or difficult to anybody, as is now the custom with some, who as though coming from a wedding give themselves to drunkenness before they show themselves to their friends—contrary to that saying of Scripture: *Woe to the land whose princes feast early in the morning* [Isa. v. 11]. But with Gerald it was not so. Very unworthy he thought it, that he who was the lord of many people should become a slave to the domination of vices. He went fasting to the law-court, lest failing in temperance he should be unable to give a reasonable judgement. For he sought what was of Christ, what was of peace, what might further the common good. After the night Office, if he was to go anywhere, the solemnity of Mass followed, and so, committing himself and his followers to the divine mercy he set out. On the above-mentioned Sunday, since it was necessary to start before dawn, he omitted the Mass, hoping to hear one after the court, but it was nowhere possible. He went away therefore very sad looking for a place where there might be some hope of finding a Mass, but when he could not find one, he called the clerics who happened to be present and with them all the soldiers who would sing psalms,[1] saying, "It is my fault that this holy day passes uselessly for us. But there is something which we may do for the praise of God, lest we should seem to have spent the holy day quite in vain." After saying this he went through the psalter from the beginning with them, singing no mortal song. And he made it now his custom to recite the psalter almost daily. And when he had finished it, he was seen to rejoice as though spiritually refreshed, as a man is accustomed to rejoice when he has fulfilled his ambition.

---

about which we know very little, and it illustrates perfectly Mr. Southern's remark that "what is quite clear is that those who set themselves a higher standard than the ordinary looked to the monasteries for their examples." (*The Making of the Middle Ages*, p. 158.) As he goes on to point out, when a layman's prayer-book appeared in the form of the Book of Hours in the fourteenth century, it contained simply the additions to the monastic office which had been introduced between the ninth and thirteenth centuries.

[1] *Psalmistanos milites.*

12

IT seems to be useful to say something of his bodily appearance. For although the flesh "profiteth nothing" [John vi. 64], although beauty is a deceiving grace, because it is often the cause of lust and pride, nevertheless in this man it is to be praised, because it was both attractive and free from the foulness of lust. Gerald, therefore, was of medium height and well-proportioned. And while beauty encompassed all his members, his neck was of such shining white and so adorned to suit the eye, that you would think you had hardly seen another so beautiful. His beauty of mind further adorned the beauty of his body, so that the nature of his disposition shone forth in his appearance. And Scripture gives testimony of this, saying that the laughter of the teeth and the movement of the face show the inner nature of the man. [Ecclus. xix. 27.] For he had tasted that the Lord is sweet [Ps. xxxiii. 9] and how delightful is the embrace of the heavenly Spouse; and for that reason he did not suffer the beautiful image of his soul to be allured by the delectation of the flesh before the eyes of this same Spouse. His vassals delighted to kiss his neck, nor did he object, because pride, which is always intractable, found no place in him. His bodily agility made him very quick in his movements, and he was very strong. What is especially noteworthy, because it shows how admirable he was, is that, having matter for pride, he kept himself humble. How blameworthy are those on the other hand, who, possessing little or nothing, are yet puffed up with pride. After he applied himself more closely to intellectual studies his bodily activity began to fail. It was then that he began to take especial pleasure in conversation, and to give profound advice for the handling and arranging of affairs, and although he avoided words of buffoonery his serious talk was of such a nature that even in that he was pleasing to his hearers. He was neither unduly menacing in his threats, nor tenacious in nursing injuries. But neither was he too easy in conferring benefits, nor changeable in taking away those that he had given. Whatever he said he would do he carried out unhesitatingly, unless by chance he learnt that there was sin in it.

13

HE attached such importance to sobriety, that he preserved not only himself but also his household from drunkenness.[1] For those of his household were neither great eaters nor great drinkers. He never compelled his guests to drink, nor was drink brought to him more frequently than to his household. He so ordered his meals that the company rose from them without having drunk too much but at the same time suitably refreshed. And when sometimes he had made his guests, to whose welfare he gave himself entirely, dine early, he himself did not take anything before the third hour, and on fast days not before the ninth. This happy prince observed the precept of Scripture by eating in due time for his refreshment and not for pleasure. [Prov. xiii. 25.] For what might he guard against more fittingly than drunkenness, which apart from the fact that it is the death of the soul and, by the testimony of the Apostle, excludes, like homicide, from the kingdom of God [1 Cor. vi. 10], also does much harm to the body. For from this come lack of strength, shaking of the limbs, lack of perception in the senses, premature old age. Sight, speech, appearance are all debauched, and the beauty of religion quite disfigured. No one can be filled at once with wine and the Holy Spirit, and by no treaty can Jerusalem be saved from the fire of fornication, if she is not willing to keep Nabuzardan, the prince of cooks, from besieging her.[2]

14

CHAIRS for the poor were always placed in his presence and at intervals meals were put in front of them, that he might see for himself what and how much food was given to them.[3] Nor was he

[1] What we are told about Gerald in this chapter needs to be seen against the social background of the times. The feudal lords of this period seem to have been almost without exception utterly lacking in any sort of refinement. Gerald introduced some, and from religious motives.

[2] This is the same text (from 4 Kings xxv) which John quotes Odo as using in his preaching. See p. 20, n. 1.

[3] Much of Gerald's behaviour as related in this *Life* must to a contemporary reader have appeared most unusual and impressive, while to us, who are the heirs of the civilization he helped to form, it seems only what we should expect. On the other hand his free distribution of alms, as described in this chapter,

limited to receiving a certain number, but when more happened to be present, at least of those who seemed deserving, more were brought in to him. No one was ever turned away from his door without alms being given. His servants so arranged that he always had dishes at hand which he might give. Drink also was brought, which he distributed after inspecting and tasting it, so that those might first drink to whom he gave a portion of his bread. Believing that he received Christ in the poor, and reverencing Him in them, he brought to himself in their persons Him whose delight it is, according to the word of the prophet, to bring refreshment to the weary. [Isa. xxviii. 12.] How much those who send out their alms but do not bring the poor in to themselves diminish the merit they receive! For in this way they seem to exclude from their houses Christ, who says: *I was a stranger and you took me in.* [Matt. xxv. 35.] That he might surpass the justice of the Pharisees as the Lord commanded [Matt. v. 20], he had a ninth part of the produce of his fields set apart, and from this the poor were fed in certain of his houses, and clothes and shoes were provided for them in these places. To those who met him he gave coins which he carried for this purpose, and which he gave secretly either himself or through a reliable servant; sometimes when money was bequeathed for some man, he received it along with the needy, rejoicing and choosing to be joined to the poor; he distributed it at once and compensated those who had given by a generous performance of the divine Office in return for the small gift.

---

would have appeared much less surprising to a contemporary than it does to us. What we should call poor relief was given in no other way, and though no doubt it was the Church, through bishops, priests, and monasteries, which did most in this direction, the lay lords were accustomed to distribute alms freely, though it may have been as much from ostentation and at the same time a desire to acquire a sort of spiritual insurance, as from humanity. Where Gerald must have been exceptional was, as Odo points out, in the personal interest he took in the distribution of his alms. Class distinctions—comparable to the caste system as it existed in India—were immensely strong, and the typical feudal count would have felt the most profound contempt for the poor men he helped. (See Lavisse, *Histoire de France*, vol. ii, 2, p. 18.).

15

AT meal times great respect was paid to him. Chattering or buffoonery had no place at his table but the talk was of necessary or virtuous subjects, or indeed of religious ones. At all times of the year he dined once in the day, unless perhaps in the summer when he supped off something simple and uncooked. At his table there was always reading for some time to begin with; but for the sake of the seculars present he used to suspend the reading at intervals, and ask the clerics what had been said in it—those whom he knew to be able to reply. He had noble clerics at his board to whom he eagerly imparted both good behaviour and learning. To the adolescent he showed himself more austere, saying that that age was very dangerous, when a youth put off the voice and appearance of his mother and began to assume the voice and appearance of his father; and one who took care to guard himself at that time, he said, might easily overcome thenceforth the movements of the flesh. When those whom he asked about the reading requested that he should rather speak himself, he used to offer them not a pompous dissertation, but a speech of learning and simplicity. When those were present who would bring forward something facetious or jocular, as used to happen, he restrained them not with biting indignation, but as though by joking also. But he never allowed idle talk to be protracted in his presence. For he knew that it is commanded to all Christians in general that each should eat his bread in silence. [2 Thess. iii. 12.] At the end of the meal the reader always repeated what had been read. So Gerald spent the greater part of meal times speaking with God, or with God speaking to him through the reading. Let them look to this example of his who, against the reproof of the Prophet, have the harp and the lyre to play at their banquets [Isa. v. 12]. They rejoice in the playing and exult at the voice of the organ. They look not at the work of the Lord, because among the voices of those who make a great noise they do not hear the cry of the poor. What then? That is true which Christ, who is the truth, said, that *out of the abundance of the heart the mouth speaketh.* [Matt. xii. 34.] It is clear what those who are always speaking of worldly things, and little or rarely of God, love most, and what abounds in their hearts. Would that, like Gerald, they might look to the last things, and whether they ate or drank they might do all things to the praise of God according to the precept of the Apostle. [1 Cor. x. 31.] On three days in the week and during the whole time when abstinence is ordered, he abstained from meat. But if one of the annual feasts occurred in these days he so broke the abstinence that he abstained on some free ferial day in place of that which he had broken. And he used then to give a meal to one poor man over and above the usual number in view of the feast. But if a fast occurred on a Sunday, he by no means broke or neglected it on this account, but he kept the fast on the Saturday preceding. And if this should seem incongruous in the holy man, let him who may think so know that to the clean all things are clean [Tit. i. 15], that is, to those who eat without the vice of greed. The Judger of Hearts does not look to the quality of the food, but to the necessity or the appetite with which it is taken. The prophet Elias, and Esau,[1] show this by their example. It was lawful, therefore, for a layman, and especially one so just, to make use of things, which are not lawful to those whose profession forbids them. For the Tree of Paradise did not bring death because it was evil, but because it was presumptuously eaten against God's command.

16

HE always wore woollen or linen clothes of the old fashion, and not in that which the sons of Belial, who are without restraint, have devised and follow in our day.[2] His were so made that they neither suggested pompous affectation, nor drew attention by plebeian rusticity. He took care not to adorn himself more than usual with silken or precious garments either because of the occurrence of any

---

[1] Presumably the idea is that Elias was justified in eating the bread and flesh brought to him by the ravens (3 Kings xvii. 6) both because of its provenance and his dispositions, while Esau is condemned for eating the pottage (good in itself) for which he sold his birthright (Gen. xxv. 30-34).

[2] Odo felt strongly about the fashions of dress in his day, but particularly, and not surprisingly, at their adoption by monks. Cf. John of Salerno's *Life*, bk. iii, 1, and *Collations*, bk. ii, 7.

feast or the presence of any dignitary, and he would not change or renew his sword-belt for twenty years if it would last so long. What shall I say of the belts, the twisted cinctures, the buckles, the decorated medallions for horses, when he not only forbade himself to wear gold, but even to possess it? For it was not in gold nor in the multitude of riches that he believed his strength to lie, but in God. Even those who profess religion, harassed by an unashamed and untiring care for the body after which they strive with every effort, scheme to obtain from those who see them the respect which they have lost by their morals through the display at least of a fine coat. It would be more use to these people to spend their time in the cultivation of the soul, which can equally grow more beautiful.

17

THE poor and the wronged always had free access to him, nor did they need to bring the slightest gift to recommend their cause. For the more fully anyone brought his necessity to his notice, the more closely did he attend to his need. And now his goodness was heard of not only in neighbouring, but also in distant regions. And because everyone knew his kindness to all, many found the solution of their difficulties in him. Nor did he disdain either personally or through his officials to interest himself in the affairs of the poor, and, as occasion offered, to give help. For often when he knew that there was fierce strife between litigants, on the day on which the cause was to be heard he had Mass said for them, and implored the divine assistance for those whom, humanly speaking, he could not help. Nor did he allow any lord to take benefices from a vassal because he was angry with him.[1] But when the case was brought forward, partly by entreaty, partly by command, he allayed the exasperation. You might think the vigour of his justice severe in this one thing alone, that whenever a poor man was brought before a more powerful man, he was at hand to uphold the weaker, in

---

[1] The origin of the feudal benefice was that a man made over his freehold property to a lord in return for his protection. He then held the property as a benefice and became the vassal of the lord. There were strict obligations on both sides, but a domineering overlord might of course repudiate his obligations or even withdraw the benefice altogether. He had no right to do this if the vassal fulfilled his obligations.

such a way that the stronger was overcome without being hurt.[1] For the rest, truly hungering after justice, he insisted on its being carried out not only among his own people but even among strangers.

18

THE thirst for justice burned in him, and hunger too. Neither simplicity nor kindness was lacking to the asperity of his zeal, but neither was the asperity of zeal lacking to the kindness of his simplicity. For as it is said of Job that he was a man simple and upright [Job i. 1], so Gerald, although he had much care for the poor, was never slow in punishing the guil·y. He was aware that it was divinely granted to some that they should wash away crime, which cannot remain unpunished, by temporal suffering. So King David, when he was dying, ordered Joab and Semei to be punished [3 Kings ii. 5 and 8].

Robbers had taken possession of a certain wood, and plundered and murdered both passers-by and those who lived in the vicinity. Gerald, hearing of this, immediately gave orders for them to be captured. It happened, however, that a certain countryman was driven by fear to join them. But the soldiers who captured them, fearing that Gerald would either release them, or blame them for showing him the prisoners unpunished, forthwith put out the eyes of all of them. And so it came about that this countryman was blinded. Later he went into the district of Toulouse, and a long time afterwards, when Gerald heard that he had not been a companion of the robbers, he was very grieved, and asked if he was still alive, and where he had gone. Having learnt that he had gone to the province of Toulouse, he sent him, so they say, a hundred shillings, ordering the messenger to ask pardon for him from the man.

19

How he mercifully consoled the afflicted, and often spared the guilty, may be seen from an example. His neighbours had afflicted

---

[1] We may very easily underrate the significance of Gerald's consideration for the poor. All the history of the times goes to show that it was very exceptional.

a certain priest with increasing quarrels, to the point that they put
out his eyes. The count consoled the man greatly by his words,
urging him to be patient. But lest the consolation of words should
seem meagre, he handed over to him a certain church in his juris-
diction by formal deed.[1] After a little time one of those who had
done violence to the priest was taken by the officers[2] and shut up
in prison, and this was forthwith announced to the count as something over which he would rejoice. And he in haste, as though with
the desire of punishing the man, went to the prison. But other
cases arose which it was necessary to deal with on the next day, and
so he ordered the accused to be kept till then. In the evening when
the officers had gone home, he secretly ordered the jailer to refresh
the man with food and drink. And because he had no shoes he
allowed shoes to be given to him and permitted him to escape.[3] On
the next day when those who were attending the court came to
the count, he ordered the accused to be brought forth, and some
men whom the jailer had prepared to act on his behalf announced
trembling that the accused had escaped. Gerald, wishing to conceal
the truth, made as though to threaten the jailer, but soon he said,
"It is well, for the priest has now forgiven the injury done
to him."

20

So, two men in chains were presented to him accused of a great
crime. The accusers insisted that he should order them forthwith
to be hanged. He dissembled, because he did not wish to free them

---

[1] Small churches, like monasteries, were of course the property of those who
built them or on whose land they stood.
[2] These were presumably the officials of the count referred to in ch. 17.
[3] This apparently very arbitrary behaviour of Gerald's can be better understood, if it is remembered that the population of the whole country must have
been very small by modern standards, and a local count would be likely to have
knowledge of the people with whom he was dealing. Gerald must have known
both the man and his accusers, and have had no doubts about the merits of the
case. Such examples make it clear that the justice administered by the counts
was of a patriarchal character little trammelled by legal forms. No doubt it was
mainly in the interests of the count to see that some sort of justice was done, but
he could as easily act in an arbitrary way, with cruelty and violence, as Gerald
did with clemency. Theoretically the free man had a right of appeal to the king's
court, but it is doubtful if this meant much around the year 900 in Aquitaine.
Another example of the same sort of procedure occurs in the next chapter.

openly. For he so conducted himself in any good work, that the goodness did not appear too much. Looking therefore at the accusers, "If", he said, "they ought to die, as you say, let us first give them a meal in the customary manner." Then he ordered food and drink to be brought to them, and ordered them to be unbound so that they might eat. When they had eaten he gave them his knife saying, "Go yourselves and bring the osier with which you must be hanged." Not far away was a wood which grew up thickly with saplings. Going into this as though looking for osiers and gradually penetrating further they suddenly disappeared, and so escaped the moment of death. Those who were present, understanding that it was with his consent, did not dare to search for them among the bushes. He punished either with fines or branding the accused who were, as far as could be judged from their appearance, confirmed in evil. But those who had done wrong not through seasoned malice but inadvertently, he set free uncondemned. It was unheard of, nevertheless, that anyone was punished by death or maiming in his presence.

21

OF the many things he did let me recall a few particular examples which will suffice to show certain acts of goodness which are known to me. For this reason, too, I insert certain small facts through which his great zeal may be illustrated, as for example the following. Once while he was going along by the road,[1] a country-woman was guiding the plough in an adjoining field. He asked her why she was doing a man's work. She replied that her husband had been long ill, that the time of sowing was passing, she was alone and had no one to help her. Having pity on her calamities, he ordered as many coins to be given her as there were days of sowing left over, so that on each day she might hire a labourer and she herself cease from doing the work of a man. Nature flees from

---

[1] *Agger publicus*. It was the Roman term for a built-up road. Dalton notes its use still in the sixth century (*The History of the Franks*, (trans.), Oxford, 1926, vol. i, p. 151)—less surprising than in the tenth. It very likely refers here to a Roman road.

everything artificial, as Ambrose says,[1] and its author, God, abhors what is unnatural. This is a small thing in itself, but the attitude of a just man in agreement with the laws of nature makes it become great.

22

ON another occasion as he was going along the road a peasant was reaping chick-peas[2] nearby. Some of his retinue, who were in front, took some of it and began to eat it. When he saw this, spurring his horse, he came at full speed to the man, asking if his followers had taken the chick-pea. "I gave it to them freely," he said. "May God reward you!" Gerald replied.

23

AN incident of the same kind is that which occurred when his servants were preparing a meal under the shade of some cherry trees. He bought for silver from a peasant who was claiming them some branches which were hanging down loaded with ripe fruit, which the servants had broken off before he came. Perhaps someone will say that these things are not worth relating: but I am showing the mind of this God-fearing man in small things, that indirectly it may be understood that he who did not despise little things, was not able to be brought low by great ones. Was not the goodwill of the widow with two small coins approved by the Lord? [Mark xii. 43.]

24

To his vassals he was so kind and peaceable that it was a matter of wonder to those who saw it. And they frequently complained that he was soft and timid, because he permitted himself to be injured by persons of low degree as though he had no authority. Nor was

---

[1] This may have been suggested by a rather vague recollection of *De Officiis Ministrorum*, lib. i, cap. xviii, 75: *Nihil enim fucatum placet. Motum natura informet. Fucatum* is the word Odo uses.

[2] The Latin is *cicer*, still the botanical name for a leguminous plant from which the poor made a kind of pulse or porridge.

he easily or lightly annoyed, as lords generally are, by his critics. On one occasion he met a number of countrymen who had left their holdings,[1] and were moving into another province. When he had recognized them and inquired where they were going with their household goods, they replied that they had been wronged by him when he had given them their holdings. The soldiers who were accompanying him urged that he should order them to be beaten and made to go back to the holdings from which they had come. But he was unwilling, for he knew that both he and they had one Lord in heaven, who was accustomed rather, in the words of the Apostle, to forbear threats [Eph. vi. 9], and who was not used to raise the hand of His might against the fatherless [Job xxxi. 21]. He therefore permitted them to go where they thought they would be better off, and gave them permission to live there. Not without shame I recently heard some idle tattle that he used not to remit the debts of a man who was in pledge to him, but that is quite false, as those bear witness who often saw him remit not only the interest but also the capital.[2]

25

HIS tenants and clerics, who loved him dearly as a father, often brought him bundles of wax, which he with many thanks accepted as great gifts. And he did not allow any of this wax to be burnt for his own use, but he ordered it all to be burnt in lights before the altar or the relics of the saints, which he had carried about with him. The servants of his bedchamber, when it happened that there was no wax ready for his service, prepared birch bark or pinewood torches. But how could one who was so careful that private people should not use the gifts which had been freely given him, exact strict payment from those who had pledged themselves? Rather,

---

[1] *Colonia* is the word used. The *coloni* were theoretically free and were *ingenui*, persons before the law, but they were in effect only the highest grade of serfs, for they were bound to their holdings, as we see here. These, presumably, were men whom Gerald had recently settled for some reason on part of his estates. See *Cambridge Medieval History*, vol. ii, p. 150, and Dalton, vol. i, p. 391.

[2] A man who owed Gerald money gave him some piece of property as a pledge of surety, and this was regarded as cancelling the debt. Gerald is accused of accepting the pledge and also demanding payment of the debt.

he often remitted to the debtors more than they owed to him by right. In the same way he forbore to threaten his servants, according to the precept of the Apostle [Eph. vi. 9]. Sometimes he was defrauded, and according to the saying of the same Apostle [I Cor. vi. 7], he suffered his goods to be seized.

26

To prove this by an example: a thief once entered his tent at night; a candle was burning before his bed as was usual and Gerald happened to be awake, for it was his custom in bed to be nourished with the love and the sweetness of Christ through the practice of prayer. Curiously peering about, the thief was looking to see if there was anything that he could carry away. He saw a little cushion with a silk cover and stretching out his hand drew it to him. "Who are you?", said Gerald. The thief was terrified and hesitated in a dazed way. Then Gerald said, "Go on with what you are doing, and depart carefully lest anyone hear." So he persuaded him that he might lawfully depart with what he had stolen. Who except Gerald would have done this? Certainly it seems to me that this is much more worthy of admiration than if he had caused the man to grow stiff in a stone prison.

27

How careful he was to fulfil that command of the Apostle: *You shall not circumvent your brother in business* [I Thess. iv. 6] will be clear from this example. Once on his way back from Rome as he was going past Pavia he made his camp not far from the city. The Venetians[1] and many others hearing of this immediately went out to him, for he was quite the most celebrated traveller on that road, and was known to all as a religious and generous man. When therefore the traders, as their manner is, were going about among the tents and enquiring if anybody wanted to buy anything, some of

---

[1] Venice was already the clearing-house for trade with Byzantium and the East. Charles the Great conceded this trade in north Italy to the Venetians in 812, and Otto I renewed the concession in 967. This chapter, with its direct reference to Constantinople, provides evidence for its operation between these two dates. See Ganshof, *Mélanges offerts à N. Iorga*, Paris, 1933, pp. 295-307.

the more considerable among them came to Gerald's tent and asked the retainers whether the lord count (for so they all called him) would order some cloaks or spices. He himself called them and said, "I bought what I wanted in Rome; but I should like you to tell me whether I bought wisely." Then he ordered the cloaks that he had got to be brought out. Now, one of them was very valuable, and a Venetian looking at it, asked what he had given for it. When he had learnt the price, "Indeed," he said, "if it was at Constantinople it would be worth even more." When the count heard this he was horrified, as though in dread of a great crime. Afterwards, therefore, when he met some Roman pilgrims whom he knew, he gave them as many shillings as the Venetian had said the cloak was worth more than the price he had given for it, telling them where they could find the seller of the cloak. Truly, while men are accustomed to have compunction for other kinds of sin, and to consider amendment, rarely or never will you see anyone except Gerald who regrets having transgressed in a sin of this kind. But indeed he knew that God is offended by all sin, and he did not wish to offend even in the smallest things Him whom he loved with his whole heart.

28

NOT unmindful that the justice of Christians ought to surpass the justice of the Pharisees [Matt. v. 20], when all his produce had been rightly tithed, he ordered a ninth part to be set aside so that it might be used to buy various necessaries for the poor, and from this, as occasion demanded, clothes also were bought for the needy who presented themselves from time to time. In addition he always carried money with him, of which he secretly gave as much as he could to poor people whom he met, either himself or through somebody who knew of the case. And though the returns from his fields and vineyards were large, it was never heard that his stewards lent anything.[1] He himself never bought land, except one small field which happened to be surrounded by one of his properties. Some rich men become very ardent over this, forgetting the

---

[1] This is presumably regarded as proof of Gerald's control.

terrible threat of the prophet: *Woe to you that join house to house and lay field to field* [Isa. v. 8]. For Gerald, according to the precept of the Gospel, was contented with his wages. [Luke iii. 14.] And as he never injured or calumniated anyone, so, like the Lord, the Disposer of all things, he kept those things which were his by right safe from the wicked and perverse. For he was lord of so many estates in different provinces, that in those places in which he had full authority he might truly be said to be rich. Nor did the number of his properties make him proud, for as the psalmist says, there was nothing on the earth that he wished from the Lord. [Ps. lxxii. 25.] And the Lord indeed added all these things to him, because he sought first the kingdom of God [Matt. vi. 33]. By the grace of God he so prospered, and went on his way so safely and unharmed, that the saying of Job would seem to apply to him: *Thou hast made a fence for him, and his possession has increased on the earth.* [Job i. 10.]

29

LET me relate this fact as an example of how he used to overcome evil by good, according to the precept of the Apostle. [Rom. xii. 21.] When he came on one occasion to Piacenza, a certain cleric arrived who was in charge of the port.[1] As is usual there, this man was expecting very lucrative passage-money from the Roman pilgrims. For some reason he was in a very bad temper, and was flinging angry words about, attacking the Bishop of Rodez[2] and other distinguished men in opprobrious terms. The man of God happened to be standing opposite him, and, fearing a quarrel would start, restrained his fellow-travellers from using hard words in reply. But the cleric he subdued by gentle words, and gave him

---

[1] The word is *portus*, which was used for the regular stopping-places for traffic on the rivers (Boissonade, *Life and Work in Medieval Europe*, trans. Power, London, 1927, p. 110). Piacenza is close to the river Po. The official in charge of such a stopping-place might well be a cleric in minor orders. Odo calls him simply *clericus*.

[2] Rodez is about fifty miles south of Aurillac, which lay just outside the diocese. The first bishop, St. Amantius, is said to have been a disciple of St. Martial. The thirteenth bishop of the see (c. 900-9) was called Gausbert and is evidently the man referred to by that name as a close friend of Gerald's in ii, 2. It was no doubt Gausbert who was with him on this occasion. See *Gallia Christiana*, ed. Sainte-Marthe, Paris, 1720, vol. i, pp. 195 ff.

some small gifts. Noticing the graceful words with which Gerald restrained the bishop and the others from replying to his insults, the cleric returned to a more gentle frame of mind, and asked who he was. When Gerald replied that he was from Aquitaine and a person of moderate position, the cleric noting his appearance and his speech, gave way entirely to his graciousness. He remitted whatever was owed of passage-money for all his company, and filled his flasks and bottles and those of all his party with wine. For the count had this gift from God, that both he and what he said were most pleasing, and not only to chance persons, but to great men. Even by kings he was always liked and respected.

30

AND rightly indeed was he loved by all, for he himself loved everybody. Let me relate what he did for a certain fugitive as for a friend. On this same journey he found a man who had left his protection some years before.[1] This man was considered to be rich and of some standing by the people among whom he dwelt. Gerald's retainers finding the man brought him trembling and in great fear into his presence. But Gerald privately inquired of him how things were going with him, and when he had learnt that he was held in no small esteem in that place, he replied, "And neither will I bring you into discredit." He ordered his men not to betray what the man had been in his own country, and then in the presence of his neighbours he gave him some little gifts and paid him considerable respect in talking to him and at table, and sent him away in peace. Who but Gerald would have done this? Yet this is what he did who was no servant of avarice, but had dedicated himself entirely to mercy.

31

AGAIN on this same journey, a certain man from the neighbourhood of Bourges[2] had broken his hip not far from Rome. Abandoned by his companions, he remained alone with his wife. One of Gerald's soldiers, a certain Boniface, found him by chance, and

---

[1] The man was evidently a serf.
[2] The town lies some 160 miles due north of Aurillac.

hearing of his necessity brought him to Gerald saying: "Look, my lord, I have found something after your heart's desire which I present for your pleasure: here is a man needing help." The man of God joyfully took him into his protection and supplying all his wants conducted him to Brioude.[1] Then he gave him ten shillings more with which he might get back to his own people. This and similar facts witness to the desire of showing mercy with which he was generously filled by divine inspiration.

32

WE know indeed that the corn for the harvest must grow along with the cockle [Matt. xiii. 30] and the grain of wheat be kept down by the straw above it for a time; so it was necessary that the malicious Cain should exercise the just Abel in patience. Gerald also, who like Job may be said to have been the brother of dragons and the companion of ostriches [Job xxx. 29], was often attacked by certain men of his provinces. For, the state being in a most disturbed condition,[2] the marquises in their insolence had subjected the royal vassals to themselves.[3] But it had been proved by

[1] In the Auvergne uplands some forty miles south of Clermont-Ferrand. It was more or less on Gerald's way home, though north of the direct route, but it was still some 130 miles from Bourges. I make no attempt to assess the value of the *solidus*, which I have translated "shilling".

[2] Odo gives us no indication of date, but it is almost certain that the period to which he is referring was the reign of King Odo of France. The Emperor Charles the Fat, who was the last of his line to rule over the whole of the Empire of Charles the Great, died in 887. For three years before he died the Vikings had been making particularly heavy raids into France and had almost succeeded in capturing Paris. The only Carolingian of the direct line, the future Charles the Simple, was a boy of eight, but it was out of the question for a child to rule at that time, and Odo, the Count of Paris, who had saved his city, though abandoned by the Emperor, was elected king. Many of the great lords, who regarded him as one of themselves, were never really loyal to him, and in 893 some of them sent for the boy Charles from England. There followed six years of civil war (893-9) before Odo died. We have no indication of the part played by Gerald in this, and we do not even know to which king, Odo or Charles the Simple, he gave his allegiance, but it seems most likely to have been Charles, for his friend William of Aquitaine was certainly hostile to Odo. William's support of Charles would not necessarily have prevented him from trying to withdraw Gerald's immediate allegiance from that king. (See next note).

[3] This is the process known as mediatizing. There were a number of men who held estates in various parts of the kingdom as benefices direct from the king himself. The local magnates, given the circumstances of the time, naturally preferred these men to be directly subject to themselves, and in the end they did in fact succeed in mediatizing nearly all the royal vassals.

We have an interesting example of the thing actually happening a little lower

experience in many cases that, as has been said, the Almighty opposed the enemies of Gerald. He appeared so invincible to them that the trouble which they strove to make for him came back rather on their own heads, as it is written: *He that diggeth a pit for his neighbour shall fall into it* [Prov. xxvi. 27]. Duke William of Aquitaine indeed, a good man and praiseworthy for many things, when he had already become very powerful, urged Gerald not by threats but by entreaties to leave the king's service and *commend* himself to him. But Gerald would not agree since he had only recently assumed the title of Count.[1] He commended his nephew, Rainald, to him, however, with a great number of his men. But the same William was not at all annoyed with him, remembering that his father Bernard had recommended[2] him as a youth to this same Lord Gerald for the love he bore him. And therefore he always held him in great veneration and as a dear companion. When the matter came up William went to talk with him, and, always delighted by the gentleness of this gracious man, by force of entreaties exacted that he should remain with him for some time. And in discussing what was to be done he often made him walk for a long time with him.

33

It happened once, since the occasion demanded it, that he spent a long time with William in a district to which he had gone to wage

down in the text. Gerald was evidently a royal vassal, and we are told explicitly that William of Aquitaine tried hard to make him leave the king's service and become his own vassal. Gerald refused, but the course he followed was really a compromise. He commended his nephew, who was also his heir, to William, and in this way, although he maintained his personal allegiance to the king, the eventual mediatization of his estates would be brought about. Thus Ganshof (*Feudalism*, trans. P. Grierson, London, 1952, p. 55) where this passage is referred to and parts of the text quoted, but it is not clear how far Gerald did make Rainald his heir. See p. 136, *n.* 2.

[1] It is difficult to know just what this means and what Gerald's title to be called Count really was, for it appears that there was no Count of Aurillac before or after him. The phrase used in the text is *favore comitis nuper usurpato*. Odo seems to imply (i, 6) that Gerald exercised the functions of a count from when he succeeded to his estates, and it would seem that he did simply adopt the title.

[2] The Latin is *commendavit*, but I have translated it "recommended", in the general sense that we use the word today, for it is evidently not used in its technical feudal sense. William of Aquitaine could never have been a vassal of Gerald's.

war. During this time the pay, which was carried on Gerald's pack-horses, gradually gave out, and the army turned to looting. Under the pretext of pursuing William's enemies it laid waste the whole region, with the result that the inhabitants, fearing for their safety, left their property and fled, and no one could be found to pay Gerald's retainers. As they found nothing to buy, and they were not allowed to touch any of the booty, they suffered great want in that expedition. For he would not allow anything to be received from those who were plundering, lest by participating with them he should be party to sin. He stayed, however, in the company of his friend, and in spite of his troubles did not desert him. Some mocked, because he and his men were in want while others enjoyed the booty, but many, who were sensible, blessed him lamenting greatly that they were not fit to imitate such an example. From this he earned the name of Gerald the Good, by which he was afterwards always known.

34

WILLIAM thought so well of him that he wished to give him his sister in marriage, and their mother, Ermengard, desired it also without delay, for she loved this man with great affection. But Christ, the Son of the Virgin, had ever imbued him with the love of chastity, which he so embraced from his earliest years that he would not allow himself to be diverted from it even by the prospect of so excellent a marriage. The horror he felt for carnal obscenity may be judged from the fact that he never incurred a nocturnal illusion without grief. Whenever this human misfortune happened to him in sleep, a confidential servant brought him privately a change of clothes, kept ready for this emergency, and cloths and a vessel of water. When the servant had brought these, he immediately retired and shut the door, for Gerald would not allow him to see him naked. This follower of interior purity so fled from the staining of the body that he washed away what happened to him in sleep not only with water but with tears. This may seem foolish, but only to those whose unclean minds reek with the foulness of vice, and who, when they soil themselves naturally or voluntarily, disdain to wash away their uncleanness. But Gerald knew the Scripture, *With all watchfulness keep thy heart* [Prov. iv. 23], and again, *He that condemneth small things shall fall by little and little.* [Ecclus. xix. 1.] Only consider how great this man is to be held who, placed amidst wordly riches and at the height of earthly position, preserved chastity. What could he have done more splendid? One could demand nothing more, or more excellent, for as St. Martin asserts, nothing is to be compared with virginity.

35

COUNT Ademarus[1] was very insistent that Gerald should give him his allegiance, but he was not able to extract any agreement from him. Gerald refused to commend himself not only to Ademarus but even to Duke William, who had greater possessions, and I believe he had in mind Mardochai who scorned to submit himself to the proud Aman and to show to princes an honour due to God (Esther iii. 2]. Indeed, when he was enjoying the friendship of William and apparently in peace, that persecution might not be lacking to one living in Christ, Satan stirred up the above-mentioned Count Ademarus against him whom he had tried to reach by many and various temptations, but whom he had never been able to subject to himself. On one occasion it happened that Gerald camped at night in a meadow with a few soldiers, and Ademarus, having sent a spy, ascertained where he was and how many he had with him. Delighted at having found an opportunity of capturing him, he collected a force of armed men, and directed it to the place. Gerald, it is said, was asleep with all his men in a part of the meadow. But He who guards Israel did not sleep in guarding an innocent man. As it is written of the prophet Jeremias that the Lord hid him on the way [Jer. xxxvi. 26], so God concealed Gerald, and the men, having made a circle round the whole

---

[1] According to Duchesne this was the Count of Poitiers of that name, while Bouange (i, pp. 457-63) thinks that it was one Ademarus de Scalis, so called from a castle of the same name which he possessed in the city of Tulle. The relations of these feudal lords with each other and with the kings, Odo and Charles the Simple, were so complicated at this time (888-98), and the evidence that we have concerning them is so fragmentary, that it is impossible to be sure who this man was, or of the reason for his hostility to Gerald.

meadow, and then a smaller one in the centre, were not able to find him. Ademarus, his effort having been foiled, and with regret that his wickedness was brought to nothing, departed. The just man, as it is written, with clean hands has become stronger to praise the Lord [Job xvii. 9].

36

In the same way the followers of Count Ademarus occupied his castle.[1] When Gerald heard this he took a few soldiers who happened to be with him at the time, and hastened to the place. Ademarus, with a strong body of troops, prepared to follow the attackers. But when the troops which Gerald was leading were not far from the castle, Ademarus held back his hastening army, saying, "We must find out by how many fighting men this Gerald is defended, who has dared to come before us and lay siege to the castle, for he would not have put himself into this danger unless he had been guarded by forces from the countryside." He then sent some evil vassals to investigate. Night came on, and the spies hastened without delay and carefully sought out the nature of Gerald's encampment. But as happens at night, they mistook some white stones seen at a distance in the uncertain light for the tents of the besiegers. They forthwith returned, pale and trembling, to Ademarus and told him that they had seen an enormous encampment. On their way back they passed a certain married woman to whom they told the same thing, and it was through her that what had appeared to the spies was afterwards made known to the man of God. Ademarus, therefore, his army having been overthrown by the divine will, returned to his own part of the country, and when the invaders of the castle learnt next day that he was no longer present, they sought peace from Gerald, begging that he would permit them to retire without disgrace. And that the man of God, Gerald, immediately did. But his soldiers, who were greatly

---

[1] In this and the following chapters Odo uses *castellum*, *castrum*, and *oppidum* to describe what is evidently Gerald's castle at Aurillac. The castle at this time would be a primitive affair, probably of timber, standing on a mound surrounded by a palisade and moat. (See Lavisse, vol. ii, (2), p. 15.) In general all these stories give a good picture—and it is a contemporary one—of the lawlessness of the nobility of the time.

roused, would hardly suffer them to go unless they were despoiled of their arms. The goodness of Gerald, however, prevailed, and he compelled his men to stand aside while the fleeing enemy came out through a postern. Nevertheless he ordered two of his men to stand there armed, and see that no one dared to take any of their belongings as they went out. In this way Gerald triumphed without bloodshed over his discomfited enemy, and Christ, as His manner is, brought greater honour to His soldier through this adversity.

37

GODFRED, the Count of Turenne,[1] on one occasion collected a force of troops and hastened to provoke the man of God to war, and to lay waste the districts under him. But it happened that he was so wounded by the very sword with which he had armed himself, that he was not able to carry out the expedition he had undertaken. Understanding at length that he had been wounded on account of the wrong to the man of God, he gave up his malice, rightly seeing that the saying of Moses held good: *Let us flee from Israel: for the Lord fighteth for them against us.* [Exod. xiv. 25.]

38

NEVERTHELESS, the brother of the aforesaid Ademarus secretly broke into the castle which overlooks the monastery.[2] But because he had learnt from the experience of others that, with God on his side, Gerald always prevailed over his enemies, he did not dare to remain there. Nevertheless, he took everything that could be carried away, before fleeing as fast as he could. Not long afterwards he gave back everything to some honest men who were reproaching him for his crime, and coming to the man of God he asked pardon

[1] Nothing certain seems to be known about this man. Duchesne doubtfully identifies him with a Count of Turenne who was active some fifteen years before. He was a comparatively near neighbour of Gerald's, Turenne being some forty-five miles west of Aurillac. (Cf. p. 124, n. 1).

[2] The castle of Aurillac still stands on an eminence overlooking the town with the church of St. Gerald at its centre. This church is on the site of the one he put up himself (cf. p. 137, n. 1) and the monastery was beside it. Unsightly modern buildings have been added to the castle, and the whole is now used as a school.

for his boldness. For Gerald was held in such reverence by all who knew him that anyone who injured him, as though he had committed a sacrilege, might be assured that he would not prosper. Although the sons of darkness molested the son of light in the ways which I have related and in many others, he did not fail to protect the poor wherever he was able. He pardoned those who injured him so easily that you would think that he was more willing to pardon than they were to be reconciled. The harder case for him was always one involving the poor, since he had much sympathy for them, and he could more easily neglect his own interest than theirs. Like a skilful doctor who chances to be wounded himself but is careful to heal the wounds of others, he did not fail to protect the weak even when he was suffering injury himself.

39

HE was so invincible to his enemies that the harm which they tried to inflict on him came back rather on their own heads, as may be seen from what has been said above and from the following example. Count Adalelmus, the brother of Ademarus, apart from the injury which he did to Gerald when he attacked the castle of Aurillac (which injury Gerald gladly forgave him), was still inflamed with malice and was persistently driven to harm the holy man.[1] Having collected, therefore, a force of his followers he tried to break into the castle at a time when Gerald happened to be hearing Mass. When he was still some distance off, those inside saw him coming and quickly shut the gate. A great noise of people shouting arose in the castle and the soldiers who were at Mass with the count wanted to go out, but he stopped them with a word and would not allow them to go until Mass was finished. Meanwhile the followers of Adalelmus, going round the castle walls, found nothing except seven horses, which they drove off, and seeing they

---

[1] This sentence presumably refers to the attack on Aurillac described in the last chapter. We are told there that Adalelmus—presuming that there is only one brother of Ademarus in question—repented of his hostility to Gerald, so we must suppose the repentance was of short duration. These chapters illustrate Odo's insufficiency as an historian. He is only concerned with the incidents as examples of Gerald's edifying behaviour and not at all with relating them to the story of his life.

had made their attack to no purpose they began shamefacedly to retire. It is said that the man of God, after he had restrained his soldiers, took his psalter and straightway went up above the gate and recited I know not which of the psalms to the Lord. The tyrant who had made the heart of the just man to mourn [Ezech. xiii. 22] was nevertheless permitted to retire rejoicing. I am about to relate marvellous things and almost unbelievable, unless they had been asserted on such good testimony. Nearly sixty of their horses died in a short time, and Adalelmus after fourteen days died so terrible a death, that in whatever place he was buried a violent whirlwind uncovered his body. Adalbert bears witness to this, that same monk who preaches the word of God to the people at Limoges. He used to look after the treasury of St. Martial at Turenne,[1] when it had been moved there for fear of the pagan peoples. Seeing what had happened, the robbers sent back to the man of God the horses which they had taken.

40

SOMETIMES he was compelled unwillingly to show his strength and to bow the neck of the wicked by force of arms, as happened in the case of a most evil man called Arlaldus. This man held a certain small castle which is called St. Céré,[2] and coming out from this like a wolf in the evening he made attacks on the retainers of Gerald, who as a peaceable man talked to him who hated peace, and also gave him some little gifts, and arms for his soldiers, as though to soften his fierce manners by kindness. But the foolish and brutal man, attributing this not to goodness but to cowardice, acted still more audaciously against his retainers. At length Gerald, considering that he could not restrain the madness of the foolish man without punishing him, collected a force of soldiers and went

---

[1] This was no doubt the treasury of the church of St. Martial at Limoges, which had been moved to Turenne (some sixty miles south) to escape the invasions of the Norsemen. The relics of St. Martin, and doubtless other treasures along with them, had been removed in a similar way from Tours (cf. p. 84, n. 1). In the tenth century, with the settling of the Norsemen in Normandy, conditions improved and treasuries were able to be restored.

[2] A small town in the Department of Lot lying about twenty-seven miles west and a little south of Aurillac. The ruins of a castle stand on a hill above the town to this day.

to his castle. And by a remarkable stroke of victory, he drew the beast from his lair without killing any of his men. When Arlaldus stood before him full of confusion, Gerald, as befitted him, spoke not abusively but reasonably. Trembling he replied with humble and appealing words, and the man of God said to him: "Now you have learnt that you and your forces cannot resist me: be careful therefore how you rage, be careful how you continue to act with malice, lest something worse comes on your head. I will let you go without troubling to take a hostage or an oath from you. Nor will I permit any of your goods to be taken in compensation for the booty which you habitually take." So he sent the man away with a rebuke, and he henceforth was careful not to presume to injure Gerald's people.

41

Now, as I said above, his adversaries, dismayed by the fear of God, gave in, for although after the example of Job he was the brother of dragons and the companion of ostriches [Job xxx. 29], the beasts of the field were peaceable to him. He had a freehold property at Pousthomy,[1] and from there his estates so lay that in going and returning from the Puy de Griou[2] he was always able to stay at his own chapels.[3] Moreover he did not need to commend any village to another lord for its safety, except one small place called Talizat,[4] which was situated far from the rest of his property among bad neighbours. The officers permitted him,[5] though he was

[1] A township which lies about seventy-five miles south of Aurillac in the Department of L'Aveyron. It is about twenty-five miles east of Albi.

[2] *Ad montem magnum Greon.* This seems to be the Puy de Griou, one of the heights in the Monts du Cantal lying about sixteen miles north east of Aurillac The distance in a direct line from there to Pousthomy would be about ninety-five miles, which gives a good idea of the extent of Gerald's estates.

[3] The word *capella* used here presumably means some small oratory or country church on his estates.

[4] *Taladiciacus.* The little hamlet of Talizat lying some thirty-seven miles north-east of Aurillac. Odo's statement that it was isolated from Gerald's other property is borne out by the fact that all the other places named except the Puy de Griou lie south or west of Aurillac.

[5] It is difficult to know what this passage means. Odo says that the officials permitted him *invito et nolenti* to commend the property (that is, he held in future as a vassal of Bernard's). It is hard to see how they could have permitted him, or the transaction could have been made at all, if he did not know of it, and I have omitted the word *nolenti* in the translation. As he was a royal vassal, it is

unwilling, to commend this to a certain Bernard for safety. He bore this patiently with a certain amusement, saying: "It is well that I should learn that it is better to trust in the Lord than in man." [Ps. cxvii. 8.] It is good to relate this, so that it may be seen that whenever God permitted something to happen for his trial, he did not let it lead to sadness but to humility. This demonstrates that he lived by faith [Rom. i. 17], and knowing how to subject everything to the divine dispensation, was aware that nothing is done without reason, as it is written. [Job v. 6.]

42

I HAVE now treated of his external actions and his ordinary way of life, from which it may easily be seen, that he was a man who cultivated justice, and, according to the apostolic precept, lived soberly and piously and justly [Tit. ii. 12]. Since therefore he fulfilled uncomplainingly all that justified him in the eyes of the Lord it ought not to seem incredible that the Lord multiplied His mercies on him. For this reason I exhort those to whom all that report says of this holy man seems unworthy of credence to reconsider his case more cautiously and more diligently. For if it seems to be a difficulty, that he was a man of great position in the world, it is to be considered that that man is especially worthy of praise who has matter for pride and attains the height of power but is nevertheless humble. For power is only from God, who, according to the Scripture, does not cast away the mighty, whereas He himself also is mighty. [Job xxxvi. 5.] Although Gerald was raised on high by the glory of the world, it ought not to seem incredible that God should glorify the man who glorified Him in the observance of His commandments [1 Kings ii. 30]. Were not king David, Ezechias, and Josias mighty and warlike? The same things have been heard in this age of those who took care to glorify Him by keeping His commandments, and whom God honours

---

possible that the officials were those of the king, but the whole passage is obscure in detail. Bouange (p. i, 42) supposes that the officials were his own, and that they suggested the arrangement, to which he reluctantly agreed. The difficulty in the text as it stands is the word *permiserunt*, which is hardly compatible with Bouange's interpretation. It was evidently regarded as a humiliation for him that he should have to commend any property at all.

with miracles, as King Oswald of the English.[1] For in every age the divine mercy does many things to foster religion, which has been despised and forgotten. Whence the Apostle says that God leaves no age without a witness of Him [Acts xiv. 16], and this is some-times given by the wicked, as under Moses they performed many signs, of whom it is written, that with most of them God was not well pleased [1 Cor. x. 5]. Faithful witnesses assert things which are hardly to be believed, as St. Jerome of a man who was formerly violent and a robber, that after he had been converted to Christ he made the sun to stand still so that he might complete his journey, and then entered in to his disciples in bodily form through a closed door. If therefore God, who did wonderful things for the Fathers, even in our time deigns to work miracles in order to revive enthusiasm for downtrodden religion through a man who, as in the days of Noe, was found just, it ought not to seem in-credible. But He rather is to be glorified who, leaving no time without a witness of His goodness, and mindful of His promise, does not cease to do good to His people. Keeping for the next book what has to be said about the actions of this man after he had given himself entirely to the cult of the divine service, let me bring this one to an end in the name of the Lord.

[1] The story of St. Oswald, the King of Northumbria, who was slain fighting against the pagan Penda, is told by Bede (*Hist. Eccl.*, iii 1-3, 9-13).

BOOK II

Preface

THOSE who rashly dispute about Gerald's merits may satisfy themselves if they will consider the nature of his life. As if seated on a judgement-seat they may determine whether he ought to be a saint or not; for this depends upon the will of God, which brings it about that even by the reprobate marvels are often performed for the benefit of the good. Let them therefore be satisfied by the testimony of the miracles[1] which Christ deigned to work through him both in his lifetime and after his death. To those who find satisfaction in remarking that Gerald was both a man of great position and holy, I would point out (lest they congratulate themselves on this) that unless they become poor in spirit and, as he did, season their power with religion, their little house will not be able to stand. They will be condemned by a comparison with him, for they could have lived righteously as he did, but they would not. There are some professed religious, great eaters and drinkers, who making excuses for their own sins assert in their cups that Gerald used to eat meat and yet was holy, but their profession clearly condemns them. For many things are lawful to a layman which are not lawful to a monk. Adam was condemned, not because the tree in Paradise was evil in itself, but because he did that which had been forbidden. Gerald was quite justified in using those things which are allowed to his state in life, for he both abstained from what is not allowed and took his food with the poor. He knew that wine was made to be drunk soberly. Elias too ate meat and was worthy of being carried up into heaven. But through the greed which drives some men Esau lost his first birthright for a pottage of lentils. [Gen. xxv. 31-4.] Gerald's case therefore is different from these. But let

---

[1] In one sentence Odo seems to repudiate miracles as a witness to sanctity and in the next to appeal to them. In the first sentence he uses the word *signa*, in the second *miracula*, but the distinction could only be made presumably in the light of the character of the man who performed them, *signa* being performed by the reprobate and *miracula* by the holy.

those who say foolishly that he can neither be called a martyr nor a confessor know that he can be called both, and not only he but all those who carry the Cross by resisting vice, or who glorify God by doing good. God indeed is confessed by deeds, as John bears witness: *By this we know that we have known him, if we keep his commandments.* [1 John ii. 3.] By deeds also He is denied, as the Apostle says of some: *They profess that they know God, but in their works they deny him* [Tit. i. 16]. Since therefore a confessor is so called because he confesses, and God is either denied or confessed by deeds, Gerald can all the more truly be called a confessor as he confessed God by more righteous deeds. What do those who, like the Jews, seek signs, do about John the Baptist, who is not reported to have worked any miracle after his nativity? With regard to this man, although miracles are by no means absent, I say one thing, that as he did not put his hope in money or riches, he performed, as it is written, wonderful things in his life. [Ecclus. xxxi. 9.]

I

THE athlete of the heavenly hosts long struggling in the arena of this earthly life fought manfully against the forces of evil. And indeed keeping the word of life in the midst of a wicked nation [Phil. ii. 15], he shone out as a lamp. And since it was necessary that he should be tested in the darkness of the storm, the malignant enemy tried by all the tricks in his power to put out this light both directly and through his ministers. But as a flame fanned by the wind burns more fiercely, so the fire of divine love, which glowed in the heart of Gerald from his youth, could not be extinguished by the rain of temptation. On the contrary, as he grew more mature, and any vices which he had were gradually suppressed, he daily grew stronger in virtues. Now he set his heart on rising upwards [Ps. lxxxiii. 6], now according to the saying of the Prophet he towered above the high places of the earth [Isa. lviii. 14]. You may see the dawn of his sanctity break on the festival day, you may see the lily spring up among the thorns [Cant. ii. 2], and that the nearer he came to maturity the more did the flowers of his virtue unfold. And therefore as though resting on the highest point, he had fixed the desire of his mind on the happiness of heaven. And since through this desire of heaven an inward light illumined him, he was able to distinguish the darkness of earthly desire. Should I not have called earthly desire a darkness which blinds the lovers of the world, so that they love vanity? But Gerald had learnt to distinguish the precious from the valueless, and thought it very unworthy that he should lick the dust who knew himself to be called to the banquet of the heavenly Lamb. He grieved much over those whose love of the world makes them enemies of God. And after he had tasted how sweet the Lord is [Ps. xxxiii. 9], he disdained to drink of the stolen waters which are sweeter [Prov. ix. 17]. He lamented rather those who, according to the saying of Job, run eagerly to gnaw the roots of juniper [Job xxx. 4], that is, a cupidity full of thorns. He scorned worldly power, which was abundantly offered to him. But nevertheless, as it is the part of the wise to turn all things to their use, he took thought how he might so dispose of his temporal possessions that they might profit him in eternity.

2

He called, therefore, the venerable and most praiseworthy Bishop Gausbert,[1] with some other honest men, and told them privately what was in his mind. For this Gausbert was very dear to the man of God, and he and Gerald were intimate friends, united as they were by the common bonds of holiness. Gerald, therefore, stated that he was weary of the life he was leading, that he desired to enter religion, to go to Rome, and to make over his property by will to the blessed Peter, Prince of the Apostles. When the matter had been discussed for a long time, the holy man Gausbert, considering the case more deeply, finally recommended that for the sake of the general welfare he should continue to wear secular dress, but that he should dedicate the property to the blessed Peter as he wished. And so as not to appear disobedient by adhering obstinately to his plan Gerald agreed. Mindful of that saying of

---

1 He was the Bishop of Rodez. See p. 119, n. 2.

the Apostle that the Jew (which is interpreted *one who confesses*)[1] becomes greater and better in secret than in public,[2] he was tonsured in such a way that it remained hidden from men, though known to God. For he shaved off part of his beard, and continuing round his head shaved off part of his hair in the form of a tonsure. But in order that this should be quite unknown, he bound some of his chamberlains, who were aware of it, by an oath, that as long as he lived they should never betray the fact. He seems in the end to have won a double reward by this action of his, for on the one hand, glowing with the love of the Lord, he showed to God the sign of his conversion, on the other, filled with the love of his neighbour, he compelled himself against his inclination to remain for his sake in a dress which he did not desire. For what way of life could he show more pleasing to God than that in which he neither neglected the help of his fellow-men nor diminished the perfection of his own life? And what way of life could be more valuable? For it was useful to many, and known only to God, who, according to the Scripture, so directed his purpose that, although He made him enter into marriage with Lia, He did not deprive him of the desired embraces of Rachel. [Gen. xxix and xxx.]

3

HE easily found a means of hiding his tonsure. He shaved off his beard as though it were troublesome to him, since the hair from the back of his head hung down, and he concealed the tonsure on the top of his head by wearing a cap.[3] He wore clothes of skin above his linen ones, because both clerics and laymen are accustomed to use clothes of this sort.[4] But he never had two skin

[1] The interpretation was standard. See Jerome's *De Nominibus Hebraicis*, *PL*, xxiii, 781.

[2] I think Odo must have had the text in Rom. ii. 28-9, in mind, which says, "It is not he is a Jew who is so outwardly ... but he is a Jew that is one inwardly".

[3] The word used is *tiara*, which generally meant a mitre, and is now only used of the papal mitre, but it could also mean some sort of clerical cap. See Ducange.

[4] Duchesne (*ad. loc.*) quotes references to the use of skin garments by the Cluny monks in the time of Peter the Venerable (twelfth century). They must have done a good deal to ward off the rigours of cold in the unheated churches and the open cloisters.

garments at once. When a new one had to be got, he ordered the
old one to be given away immediately. When he rode his sword
was carried in front of him, but he himself never laid a hand on
it. From early on he had a golden cross made for his belt, and he
never rode a horse adorned with medallions. In ways like this it
appeared how much he studied moderation and despised the
trappings of his position.

4

AFTER he had freed himself from everything to serve God, he went
to Rome to consecrate his possessions to the Lord, and assigned
the notable property of Aurillac to the blessed Peter,[1] Prince of
the Apostles, by formal will,[2] with as many additional properties as
would suffice the monks he had decided to gather there for their
whole income. For he very much desired to establish a monastic
foundation in that place, where the monks might lead the common
life with an abbot of their order. He assigned also dues to be paid
each year at the tomb of St. Peter. And what he had conceived in

[1] In spite of the rather depressing account which Odo goes on to give of
Gerald's efforts to found a monastery at Aurillac, he did in fact found one which
lasted until the second half of the sixteenth century, when discipline grew relaxed and it was taken over by the bishop and turned into a house of canons.
Towards the end of the tenth century it had a very eminent member in the
person of Gerbert, perhaps the foremost scholar of his day, who eventually became an outstanding Pope as Sylvester II (999-1003). Gerbert, it is true, does
not seem to have stayed long at Aurillac, but he certainly began his monastic life
there, before going on to become, on the way to the papacy, Abbot of Bobbio
and Archbishop of Rheims.
    Mabillon printed a tenth-century chronicle of Aurillac which states that
Gerald obtained from Charles the Simple the privilege that the monastery
should be directly under the see of Rome (*Vetera Analecta*, Paris, 1675-   , vol.
ii, 237). According to the same authority (*Annales*, iii, 332) the second Abbot of
Aurillac, John, obtained confirmation of this privilege of exemption from
Pope John X (914-28). This must have been, therefore, after Gerald's death,
which occurred in 909.
[2] A will of Gerald's is quoted in full by Duchesne (*ad. loc.*). This deals with
the foundation of the Abbey of Aurillac, and the lands given to it, and is dated
September of the seventeenth year of Charles (the Simple), that is 909, shortly
before the death of Gerald therefore (see p. 165, *n.* 2). No mention is made in
this will of the dues to be paid to Rome (see below in text), and Mabillon
thought that the will referred to here by Odo was made earlier, at the time of
the foundation, which he puts about 894 (see *PL*, cxxxiii, col. 705).
    It may be noted that the extant will leaves a good deal of property to Gerald's
nephew, Rainald, for his lifetime, but with reversion to the abbey after his death.
It does not appear from this source that he left any property to Rainald absolutely
as Ganshof supposes (see p. 121, *n.* 3).

the fervour of his heart he carried out according to plan, and by the favour of God he performed what he had decreed. When he got back he ordered quarrymen and masons to be collected from all round, and commanded the foundation to be laid for a church in honour of St. Peter. But Satan, envious of all good, by what device I know not, made the judgement of the masters to err. For they laid the foundation unsoundly and, when a great sum of money had been spent and the walls raised to a considerable height, the joining of the dressed stones suddenly came apart, and they fell to the ground. But Gerald was not unduly saddened by this. As it is written, *Whatsoever shall befall the just man, it shall not make him sad* [Prov. xii. 21]. For he had complete trust that, although the work would be retarded by this happening, the reward of the wasted effort would by no means be lost. He saw that this collapse came about with the permission of God, for it almost always happens that when anything pleasing is offered to God, it is carried through with difficulty. And certainly in natural things that which grows most quickly withers most quickly; that which grows with difficulty lasts longer.

5

THE season of Lent had arrived and the milder weather favoured the building operations. One morning after he had finished his accustomed prayers Gerald went out from the castle which overlooks the site, and when he had gone a little way, looking about here and there, he began to consider where he could best lay the foundations of a church. Eventually by the will of God he chose the destined place. So he ordered workmen to come once more and to set about making plans to start the interrupted work again. When they had begun, they were to carry on wisely and to build a church of suitable size and in rounded form,[1] such as his father had

---

[1] *Arcuato schemate.* This is evidently meant to refer to the rounded (bow-like) apse and arches of a Romanesque church. Excavations carried out in 1944 in the church of St. Gerald at Aurillac revealed part of what is certainly the church built by the saint himself. Sufficient was discovered to give the approximate plan and size of the church, which was built on the model of the ancient basilicas with a semi-circular apse. (Beaufrère, *L'Église carolingienne du bon comte Géraud*, Aurillac, 1945.)

formerly built in honour of St. Clement. For, as I have said, his father was a religious man, as befitted one descended from a religious stock.

6

WHILE he went on with building the monastery he was always turning over in his mind where to find monks of good character who would live in the place according to their rule. But when the rareness[1] with which they were to be found brought home the difficulty of his task, he became anxious and did not know what to do. Then he sent some noble youths to the monastery at Vabres,[2] where a fervent regular observance was growing up, that they might be trained in the rule with the community there. One of them still survives and he states, and also in writing, that he has himself witnessed those actions which I have ascribed to blessed Gerald. When these same youths were ordered to return, they became relaxed with a feminine softness through lack of masters, and neglected the rigour of their rule, and so the plan came to nothing. Compelled, however, by necessity he put one of them in charge of the rest. But when this man led a dissolute life, the man of God was much troubled, because he was not able to correct him, and he did not have another whom he could put in his place. When he saw him and his associates entering on the path of a corrupt life, sighing profoundly, he repeated that saying of David, *O Lord, defeat the counsel of Achitophel.* [2 Kings xv. 34.]

7

SOMETIMES he broke out in lamentation at the sight of men giving themselves to evil. In his disgust he sighed complainingly that these men were perishing through love of the world, that piety was failing and iniquity abounded, that innocence had almost entirely

---

[1] With this may be compared what John of Salerno has to say about Odo's own difficulty in finding a monastery of good observance (i, 22). That was some ten or more years later, and it would be more rather than less difficult when Gerald was trying to do it.

[2] The monastery was founded by Raymund, Count of Toulouse, in the twenty-third year of Charles the Bald, 866. It lay about twenty miles west-north-west of Toulouse.

departed from the hearts of men, and truth from their lips. He did not wish to be involved in their quarrels, but prayed that almighty God would bring peace to all, ordering Masses to be said, frequently repeating that saying of Ezechias: *O Lord, only let peace and truth be in my days* [Isa. xxxix. 8], and *There is now no saint; truths are decayed from among the children of men.* [Ps. xi. 2.]

8

He hoped that the desire by which he aspired after heavenly things and despised those of earth might be a consolation to him, if he found some to share in it. Consequently his mind was in a turmoil day and night, and he could not forget his wish to gather a community of monks. He often spoke of it with his household and friends. He was so moved by his desire for this that sometimes he exclaimed, "O, if it might be granted me by some means to obtain religious monks. How I would give them all I possess, and then go through life begging. I would make no delay in taking the necessary steps." Sometimes his friends would say, "Are there not many monks to be found in these regions from whom you can choose a community at will?" But speaking with great vehemence he would reply, "If monks are perfect, they are like the blessed angels, but if they return to the desire of the world they are rightly compared to the apostate angels, who by their apostasy did not keep to their home. I tell you that a good layman is far better than a monk who does not keep his vows." When they rejoined, "Why then have you been accustomed to show such favours not only to neighbouring monks, but to those from a distance?", making little of his deeds, with his usual humility he would reply, "What I do is nothing; but if, as you say, I do anything, I am certain that He is true who promised to reward a cup of cold water given in His name [Matt. x. 42]. Let them understand what they are in the eyes of God. Certainly it is true that he who receives a just man in the name of a just man shall receive the reward of a just man [Matt. x. 41]." These and similar words of his make it clear that he despised the pleasures of this present life, that he burned with the desire of heaven, that he wished to leave all his possessions, if there had been anyone to whom he could reasonably hand them over. The common saying that the will is taken for the deed is true. Whence it comes also that he who hates his brother is considered a murderer, and John the Evangelist drank the chalice of the passion [Matt. xx, 22] though he died in peace. If therefore the will is taken for the deed, Gerald is certainly not to be deprived of the reward promised to those who give up all things. [Matt. xix. 29.]

9

IT was against his will, therefore, that he was kept in the world. And although companions were lacking with whom he might renounce the world, he occupied himself entirely in a wonderful way with the work of God. To such an extent was he occupied alternately listening to reading and saying prayers, now with others now alone, that the marvel was how he could devote so much effort to this, and that he always wanted to say such a large number of psalms, especially as he got through much other business in between whiles. He was not obstinate in absenting himself unduly from necessary cases, but giving himself to these for a little as occasion demanded he soon hurried back to the sweetness of the psalmody. How reverent he was in church cannot be adequately expressed, for he appeared to be contemplating divine things and with rapt expression imitating that saying of the prophet *As the Lord liveth in whose sight I stand* [3 Kings xvii. 1]. To make this clear from an example: the festival day of our Lord's ascension had come round and he went to celebrate it, as it is a great feast, at the monastery of Solignac.[1] He would not suffer the Office of so great a festival to be recited other than solemnly, nor did he allow, as many do, the service to be shortened in celebration. The monks, therefore, came and prepared a throne and *prie-dieu* arrayed as was fitting for so great a person, and when he had come to this after visiting the altars, the brethren began to say the Office in a protracted manner, as the custom is. The count stood so lost in con-

---

[1] Not far from Limoges. The monastery is said to have been founded by St. Eligius at the time of King Dagobert (630-8). It was laid waste in the troubled times which followed, but was refounded by Louis the Pious, the son of Charles the Great. (Duchesne, *ad. loc.*).

templation that he neither sat nor reclined,[1] or only very slightly, until it was finished, showing by the immobility of his body the devotion and constancy of his mind. With us it is not so, for we sing the divine praises before the face of God as though concealing the fact that we are praying, with a pompous voice rather than with simplicity of heart. And when the understanding of the mind ought to be in harmony with the voice, we make the voice keep pace with the quickness of the mind. But Gerald, recalling the saying of the Apostle, *to God we are manifest* [2 Cor. v. 11], so comported himself as in the sight of the Judge who sees all things.

10

THAT it might honour him in the sight of men, who honoured God before the wicked by carrying out His commandments—although the time of Anti-Christ is now at hand and the miracles of the saints ought to cease—the divine mercy, mindful of the promise which says *Whoever shall glorify me, him will I glorify* [1 Kings ii. 30], deigned to honour this His servant with the gift of healing. And the manner of healing was such, that although he refused through humility to lay hands on the sick, he nevertheless frequently helped them, although he was absent and was not desiring to do so. The sick used to steal the water with which he had washed his hands; and many were cured. That this may seem more credible it is right that certain persons should be called to mind. For a certain countryman near the monastery of Solignac had a son who was blind, and lamenting for a long time that he was oppressed by both blindness and poverty, he was warned in a vision that he should go to the count Gerald and bathe the eyes of his son with the water in which he had washed his hands. The man believed the vision, and coming made known the content of his dream. When the count heard this he was much afraid and troubled in his mind, and refusing to be so presumptuous said it

---

[1] This is the technical term for leaning back on the *misericord* of a choir stall. It might appear that Gerald had some sort of throne or faldstool on which it would be impossible to recline, but this position is contrasted with that of sitting. *In antipodium recubaret* is Odo's phrase. Ducange explains *antipodium* as the back part of monastic stalls *quae anteriori seu podio opponitur*, and Odo's phrase suggests our use of reclining.

was an illusion which had deceived the man and would deceive him, that he might attempt things which had not been granted. The man was in error in asking such things with a vain hope. The father, made anxious by the blindness of his son, burst forth in lamentations, and understanding that the holy man would not agree out of humility, pretending to go away he obtained the water from one of the servants. Returning home and invoking the name of Christ he bathed the blind eyes of his son, who received his sight. And another deed followed this one.

II

A CERTAIN boy in Aurillac was lame, and he was handed over to a smith to learn a trade by which he might live. Warned in sleep that he should beg the water in the same way, the smith, who had to obtain it, knowing that the man of God was very strict in this matter, did not dare to ask for the water openly, but got it secretly from the servants. He sprinkled the useless member with the water, and the divine power immediately restored it to its proper use. When the report of this fact became gradually spread abroad, it eventually reached the ears of the count. Struck by the strangeness of the event, he said it had not come about by his merits, but by the faith of those who had given the water to the smith. This had been kept secret from him, and unable to discover who had given it, he was moved to violent threats that no one should presume to do such a thing again, saying that if a serf did it he should be maimed, if a free man he should be reduced to servitude. For he feared nothing more than praise. And while he was kind to his enemies, he was severe to those who praised him.

12

AT Pousthomy,[1] a considerable freehold property of his, a blind woman received her sight from the water in which he had washed his hands. This became known to all, but was most carefully concealed from him for the sake of one of the servants who had given

---

[1] See p. 129, n. 1.

the water to the woman. For his people could not make light of the mutilation which he had threatened, knowing that he would not yield in the matter of punishment, if he caught the man who had given it.

13

AGAIN, he was staying at a chapel near the village called Crucicula,[1] when another woman, who was one of his servants, was given her sight by the water from his hands. When he learnt this he urgently interrogated the man, Rabboldus, who had given the water, found out that he had done it, and immediately dismissed him from his service. After a little time, however, a certain nobleman called Ebbo came to reason with the count, saying that perhaps he was acting against the will of God, when he neglected a grace given from heaven under the pretext of indiscreet humility, and sent away in sadness those whom he might have helped. It was better to give those who asked what they needed, since perhaps this grace was given to him for their sakes. There was no fear of pride, since he was not covetous of praise; nor of presumption, because those who asked for help had stated that they were divinely urged; and a special reason for granting it was that it had been proved by experiment that the gift of health asked from him had often been granted, though without his knowledge. He set all this out in a very reasonable way. But with sighs and tears Gerald replied that he feared it might rather be a deceit of the devil wishing to make use of the occasion to deceive him, and plotting to deprive him of the reward of any good he had done. At length, convinced by reason and by entreaty, he took back the man he had dismissed, and ordered the woman to be given twelve coins.

14

KNOWING that the condition of the mind is best preserved by alternate reading and prayer, he had the Scriptures read to him, as

[1] "Little Cross", *Croizette*. The place cannot be identified with certainty, but there is today a Croizette not far from Argentat in the Department of Corrèze, thirty miles west of Aurillac, which may well have been the place as Gerald's estates lay in that direction.

I have said. And so it was that he adopted the practice of having reading at his dinner, and this was not omitted even if guests were present. At intervals he graciously ordered the reader to stop, and to ask the meaning of the reading[1] from those who might know. When those whom he asked used to beg him rather to speak himself, he would reply clearly and knowledgeably, as one well versed in the subject, but in such a way as not to put his clerics to shame. When the meal was finished and the others had departed, he generally had those passages which were left over from the lessons recited in church read to him. While he was listening to reading no one easily presumed to break in on him for any reason, for according to the saying of Job he was terrible to those beneath him, and the light of his countenance fell not on the earth. [Job xxix. 24.] It is wonderful to recall his words and talk. When he spoke from a joyous mind his words were most pleasing, but when he spoke rebukingly, they seemed like goads and were feared almost more than mere words. He was slow to give anything, but when he had once given it, he did not take it back. If he heard a priest was of evil repute, he did not disdain his Mass, because he knew that the sacred mystery cannot be invalidated by a man who is a sinner. And whereas he judged the deeds of others severely or mildly as the case deserved, he held his own deeds to be of little value, and the less value he attached to them the more he commended them to the divine regard.

15

BECAUSE he gave himself wholeheartedly to the desire of heaven, his mouth was so filled from the abundance of his heart [Matt. xii. 34], that the law of God sounded almost continuously on his lips. For he had marked certain holy words which seemed to fit bodily duties. Thus, before he spoke in the morning he said: *Set a watch, O Lord, before my mouth, and a door round about my lips* [Ps. cxl. 3], and there were other sayings of this sort which he

---

[1] According to the Latin here it is the reader who is to ask the meaning of what has been read, but where the reading at meals is described in bk. i (ch. 15), it is Gerald who asks, and this seems to be implied here lower down. It seems more likely.

adapted to particular actions, for example when he awoke, when he got out of bed, when he put on his shoes, his clothes, or his belt, or certainly when he went on a journey or began any other action, so that in the words of the Apostle he seemed to do all in the name of the Lord [Col. iii. 17]. Sometimes when he happened to be sitting with few companions or alone, he meditated on I know not what for long in silence, and, bathed in tears, he sighed from the depths of his heart so as to shake his whole body; it was easy to see that his mind dwelt on other things and he found no consolation in the present time. His speech and his silence were such that his mouth declared the praise of the Lord [Ps. l. 17] and the meditation of his heart was always in His sight [Ps. xviii. 15].

16

HIS followers knew that he greatly desired to be a religious, but being a prudent man and realizing that those who set a high ideal before themselves only fall the more grievously when the love of the world corrupts them, he judged it better to remain as he was than to attempt so difficult an undertaking without tried assistants. If therefore one considers his desire, he was true to the monastic profession through his devotion to Christ. And it is indeed high praise for a man in secular dress to keep the rule of religious, as on the other hand it is a very shameful thing to follow the world in the habit of a monk. Since, therefore, as I said above, he had no brethren with whom it was good to live together in unity [Ps. cxxxii. 1], life on earth was irksome to him. But as, long ago, Noe's dove, not finding where she might rest, returned to Noe in the ark [Gen. viii. 9], so this man, amidst the waves of the world, retiring into his inmost heart, took his rest in the joy of Christ. He did not, like the crow, settle on the carrion of bodily pleasure, for his soul refused to be consoled with this life's glory, but took its delight in the memory of its God, and coming back to the sanctuary of the heart as though to the ark, gave voice to its joy. For he did not allow iniquity to dwell in his heart, fearing lest the Lord should be unwilling to hear him. Rather, the sins which human nature cannot escape and which, though slight to us, seemed great

to him, he was always careful to keep before his eyes, so that he
might with confidence look to receive from the mercy of God forgiveness for the evil dispositions of his heart. And so his King and
Lord mercifully directed his ways in His sight [Ps. v, 9], and kindly
hearkened to the voice of his prayer [Ps. v. 3]. He took so much
trouble always to have his lodging next the church that for many
years he went to the oratory every night, except once on the feast
of the Innocents on account of a journey. A number of clerics
always accompanied him and with these he laboured at the work
of God. All the ecclesiastical equipment necessary for the service
was carried with him, and with this he performed the divine
service with great care and reverence, especially on the festivals.
For the night Office he used to come to the oratory a long time
before the others, and when it was finished he remained alone. And
then all the more sweetly as it was more in private he tasted the
savour of internal sweetness. After a time he came out joyous and
brisk, and either went to his bed or joined his household. He had
established such a way of life that any wise man must have
marvelled at the great grace which had come to him. He so clung
to this manner of life in externals, that his servants knew how he
would conduct himself at every season of the year.

17

HE established a custom of going frequently to Rome.[1] It is said
that he went there again and again; my informants are certain of
seven times. For it is a quality of human nature always to wish to
see the light, and being a spiritual man, he went to gaze spiritually
on those two lights of the world, Peter and Paul. And since he was
not yet able[2] to contemplate them directly, he often visited their
tombs and shrines, and he made over his possessions to St. Peter.
He made it a rule to go every second year to their tombs as a serf

---

[1] The close relationship which the Franks maintained with Rome dates from
the reform of the Frankish Church by St. Boniface. It was no doubt strengthened
after Charles the Great's coronation there, and seems to have been maintained
throughout Carolingian times. (See Duchesne, note *ad loc.*).

[2] The text reads *quoniam ipsos necdum volebat intueri*, which does not make
very good sense. The change to *valebat* is made without comment by M. Abel
Beaufrère, *Enigmes d'Aurillac* (p. 26), and I have adopted it here.

with ten shillings hung round his neck that he might pay them as a due to his lord.[1] Who can describe the devotion with which he performed this ? He was so good to those in want, that his bounty hardly passed a poor man by, and they abounded in that place, for he was confident that he himself would be heard, if he heard the cry of the poor. He gave generously also to the monasteries that lay on the road, and the fame of his great generosity sounded far and wide, so that monks, as well as pilgrims and the needy who were his guests, used to inquire anxiously, at the time when the pilgrims to Rome are accustomed to pass by, if and when Count Gerald was coming. Even the Marruci,[2] the fierce inhabitants of the Alps, thought nothing more profitable than to carry Gerald's baggage through the pass of Mont Joux.[3]

18

ONCE when he was making this journey and came to the city of Asti[4] a thief made off with two of his pack-horses, but coming to a river he was not able to get them across before he was taken by Count Gerald's men. Having got back the pack-horses he took no action against the thief.

19

ANOTHER time when he was going that way he had a certain monk called Aribert with him, a man of great abstemiousness. For it was always a sweet companionship for him, when he found men of religious life, and he used to take great delight in their company. Now it happened on one occasion that there was none of the food[5]

---

[1] Mr. R. W. Southern points out that "the ceremonies of initiation into serfdom were often used to symbolize initiation into the liberty of religion" (*The Making of the Middle Ages*, p. 105), and he quotes this passage in illustration, though wrongly attributing the action to St. Gerard of Brogne.

[2] These were the Saracens based on Fraxinetum (St. Tropez) on the south coast of France, whence they had spread into the Southern Alps. (See p. 61, *n.* 3.)

[3] *Juga montis Jovina*. Duchesne in a note calls this Mont Joux, which I have put in the text, but the only place of the name I can find is in the Jura, and would hardly have been on Gerald's way to Rome. The Jou-sous-Monjou in the Department of Cantal, near Aurillac, can hardly be the place, as the Marucci would not have been found so far to the west, I think.

[4] About thirty-five miles east and a little south of Turin.

[5] *Pulmentarium* is the word used. According to Ducange this is anything that may be added to bread. He quotes the passage and connects the word with

which this abstemious man ate with his bread. The count asked
carefully whether the servants had prepared the usual food for
him, and when they replied that they had nothing except bread,
he became most anxious, saying: "What has happened to us today?
We have all we want to eat, and this servant of God will go short."
It was an abstinence day; the time to wash hands had arrived, and
Samuel, who tells the story, running to fetch the water, found a
small fish lying gasping on the bank, which had jumped out of the
water when it saw him. He caught it and returned joyfully to the
count. "Look," he said, "God sends you this fish; for I found it
lying near the water." "Thanks be to God", he replied. And while
it was being cooked he went into his tent and kneeling down
prayed for a while in tears. His character was such that he preferred nothing to Christ,[1] but rather devoutly returned thanks to
Him for everything that happened. When he arose from prayer he
cheerfully joined himself to the company. The abstemious man,
however, sitting down at table with the rest, ate till he was satisfied,
and since there was still a part of the fish left over, the count urged
him, saying, "Why do you hold back, brother, from eating the little
fish, you will have nothing else?" When he replied that he had
already had enough, the count took some to try its quality. Finding
it to be of excellent flavour he ate as much as he wanted, and to all
those present he gave a morsel as a token of devotion.[2] All gave
thanks to God, recognizing the divine gift both in the finding of
the fish and in the amount which was left over. For it had been
six inches long.

20

IN the same way, when he was going to Rome and arrived at the
city of Tuscany called Lucca, a certain woman came up to him

---

the fish described lower in the text as jumping on to the bank. The fish does
indeed seem to have provided the *pulmentarium*, but Odo's story would have
had more point, if he had made this clear from the start.

[1] Cf. the *Rule* of St. Benedict, ch. 4, "To prefer nothing to the love of
Christ".

[2] *Pro benedictione.* This was evidently what was more usually called a *eulo-
gium*. It generally took the form of blessed bread given as a sign of union and
charity. Cf. the *Rule* of St. Benedict, ch. 54, and the note in Abbot Justin
McCann's edition (Orchard Series, 1952).

saying that she had been warned in a vision that he would give back his sight to her son. When he heard this he rebuked the woman, and setting the mule he was riding in motion, he fled, much disturbed. The woman asked everyone she could find how she might obtain the hoped-for benefit from the man of God. Perhaps it was one of the servants who told her that miracles had been worked by the water from his hands. But the count had been put on his guard by the woman, and whenever he washed his hands had the water poured out on the ground in front of him. Still she kept on following him, until he became less careful about the water being poured away. At length she obtained some without his knowledge and bathed the eyes of her blind son, who immediately received his sight. When, therefore, the holy man came back from the city, the woman presented him with her son, now able to see. And when all were praising this deed, Gerald went away silent and in tears, nor did anyone dare to refer to this or anything of the kind in his hearing.

21

WHAT I am going to relate is remarkable, and it may seem incredible, but I believe the two witnesses who assert it. They say that this same holy man was returning from Italy by the road which goes to Lyons from Turin. He had crossed the Alps, and the way led through some country which, they state, is without water. It happened too that the supply of wine ran out. There was no water, and, since the district had long been laid waste by the Saracens, wine could not be found there either, so the party began to suffer greatly from thirst. They tried as best they might to get over this part of the journey quickly, but they were short of servants and pack-horses, so the count had to order a short halt. The dispirited men threw themselves on the turf, while the pack-horses, driven by thirst, wandered in all directions over the grazing-ground. When one of the clerics, not wishing to continue the halt, went to collect and saddle them again, he found a little hole full of some liquid. He was very surprised, and wishing to find out what it was, stooped down. The liquid smelt to him like wine. Greatly rejoicing, he ran back to the count and told him that he had discovered something like wine. "What, are you mad?" said the count: "I wish you might have found water. Where could wine come from here?" The cleric, however, taking a vessel, drew some of this liquid and brought it to him. That which was brought certainly had the colour and smell of wine. Then the count ordered his chaplains to take the cross and the reliquaries and to say the exorcism for the blessing of water over the hole with the liquid. Then he ordered that in the name of Christ they should find out what it was by tasting it. When they found it was wine the holy man joined them all in giving thanks to God with great admiration and joy, and before he drank himself, he ordered it to be given to all the others, but he did not allow any of it to be put into flagons. I have related this on the word of those who say they saw it. Nevertheless, those things which now happen at his tomb persuade one to believe everything that one hears of him.

22

THE holy man often took this road [to Rome]. It was not that he wished to approach the palaces of kings, or the halls of marquises, and certainly not the assemblies of princes, but it was the heavenly rulers Peter and Paul, as I said before, that he was on fire to see more frequently. But he sought out too with keen devotion other holy places, namely the tomb of the most holy Saint Martin, and of St. Martial.[1] I believe he saw in contemplation how the ranks of the blessed rejoice in the court of heaven. With those to whom he was soon to be joined he had to some extent a foretaste of the joy of his Lord.

23

ON the other side of Sutri, next to the town, there is a rushy field called Saint Martin's, where the Roman pilgrims are accustomed

---

[1] We have seen much about the tomb of St. Martin at Tours as a place of pilgrimage in John's *Life* of Odo. St. Martial was a Bishop of Limoges in the third century, though an early legend enshrined in an eleventh-century *Life* makes him out to have been a disciple of our Lord. Great devotion was paid to him at Limoges.

to camp.[1] The servants had put up the tents there, and the count happened to be standing alone, when a blind man had himself led up to him. Begging suppliantly he asked if he would deign to give him some water which had touched his hands. The count ordered him to remain where he was and be silent. Then he went into his tent and prayed for a little time before the relics of the saints. The servants were going about their work, and while they were occupied, seeing that he could be unobserved, he called up somebody to lead the man in unnoticed. Then he carefully washed his hands, and soaked his fingers in the water, and made the sign of the cross over it with the holy relics. When the blind man poured it on his sightless eyes, he was immediately able to see. The man of God stopped him from crying out, and joined him in giving thanks to the divine majesty. He then clothed him with one of his garments, a tunic, and had him conducted in secret from the tents.

24

IT was the same when he came back from the city. He arrived one Saturday at a certain church, at the place where heaps of sulphur are to be seen.[2] When his people wished to go on the next day, he kept them back, saying that out of reverence for the Lord's day they should stay at least till None. And this delay was not without even a temporal advantage, for when the High Mass was over and they were setting out on their journey after having something to eat, a man came in mounted on a broken-down horse, who had got lost on his journey, and the Count Gerald ordered him to be received without charge to the resident priest. Before they had reached Abricola,[3] a blind man sitting by the roadside asked them as they passed, if there was anybody in the company called Gerald. One of our brethren, who at that time was still a canon, happened

---

[1] I think this must be the meaning in spite of the Latin—*scirposus ager habetur ultra Sutriam, juxta burgum videlicet, qui vocantur* [sic] *sancti Martini, quo Romei castrametari solent.* Sutri is the ancient Etruscan city between Rome and Viterbo, about twenty miles from Viterbo.

[2] There are sulphurous springs at Bagni di Stigliano near Manziana on this same road from Viterbo to Rome.

[3] Unidentified. There is a place called Abriola about five miles east of Salerno, but this incident is expressly said to have occurred on Gerald's way back from Rome. There is no evidence that he ever went south of the city.

to be travelling in Count Gerald's party, and out of devotion he
was travelling on foot. Being weary he came up to the blind man,
and to his enquiry about Count Gerald answered that he was
following behind. "But why are you seeking him so earnestly?"
he said. "I have been afflicted with blindness for nine years, and
last night I was warned in sleep to come here and seek Gerald, the
pilgrim of St. Peter, that I might ask him to wash his hands, and
then pour the water on my blind eyes." When the cleric heard this,
he stood still till Count Gerald came up. Now it was Gerald's
custom to ride alone with his head covered that he might be more
free to say his psalms. When he came up, therefore the cleric
whispered to the blind man, "Here he is", and the latter asked him
if he would mind stopping for a short time, and he added what he
had been told in sleep. The count blushed, and with a changed
countenance rejecting what he heard, started to go on. But the
blind man, adjuring him strongly, begged him to stop and help a
man in misfortune, and not to refuse the hoped-for benefit. Those
who were present implored the same thing. But he deliberating a
little, and remembering, as I think, that, according to the saying of
the Apostle, he ought not to neglect the grace that was given to
him [1 Tim. iv. 14], replied with his usual words, saying, "Help
me, ye saints of God", and stopped. And since, as is usual among
those small hills, a stream flowed by, water was forthwith brought.
He dismounted and washed his hands saying, "The will of God
be done." Then, much moved, he started to go on. The blind man
did not delay in taking the water, nor did the outcome of the
miracle fail him. He received his sight so promptly that he immediately ran after Gerald crying, "O holy Gerald, O holy Gerald,
thanks be to God I see." But Gerald put spurs to his mule so as
not to hear the cries of those who were praising him, and passed
through Abricola, nor could his fellow-travellers catch up with him
for two days! Indeed, it is not hard to believe that those hands
through which this power of healing was conferred shone with
purity and were without stain, and that every gift was shaken from
them [Isa. xxxiii. 15]. On the other hand how unhappy are they
whose right hand is filled with gifts [Ps. xxv. 10], for it is written
that fire devours those who love to take bribes. [Job xv. 34.]

25

OTHER things are related of his journeying which I pass over for fear of being too lengthy, but let me add one, because it shows a miracle of another sort. On one of his journeys to Rome, when he was already in Italy, he heard the voice of a man crying out and announcing his death. It seemed to him that it was the voice of a certain Girbald whom he had left at home. So he called some of his followers and asked them if they knew anything of Girbald. They replied that he was sick when they left him. He ordered the time to be noted, and the psalms for the dead to be recited for him. When he came home and inquired about this man, he found that he had died on the very day that the voice had been heard.

26

AFTER his journey of devotion he liked to go to some quiet place, as though to fulfil that word of the psalmist which says: *I have gone far off, flying away; and I abode in the wilderness.* [Ps. liv. 8.] He wished to rest from the comings and goings of the world and the noise of the law-courts, that he might give himself more freely to the service of God. Now when he was staying for this reason at the chapel called Catuserias,[1] on the feast of Saints John and Paul[2] a certain countrywoman came into the garden to do some work or other, when suddenly a great drop of blood appeared on her hand, which immediately began to swell. The terrified woman ran lamenting to the man of God, and showing him her hand begged him to have mercy on her. He immediately ordered clerics to come and say Mass for her, and then to bless water and to wash away the drop of blood with it. He himself stood aside out of humility, lest the miracle should be attributed to his virtue. When the woman's hand was washed, the blood and the swelling disappeared, and she went away healed.

[1] Catus, about ten miles north-west of Cahors in the Department of Lot and some sixty-five miles south-west of Aurillac.
[2] These saints were martyred under Julian the Apostate about the year 362, and their feast is kept on June 26th.

27

BECAUSE that place, which I have said was dear to him, was remote and little-known, he often stayed there. On one occasion he had been celebrating the Assumption of the holy Mother of God, Mary, in this church, and after Mass he went out to his followers, for it was his custom after long-continued prayers to give himself to general conversation, so that anyone who had cause to speak with him might have the opportunity of doing so. When he had gone out among his people, therefore, the man who was in charge of the preparation of the food said to him: "We are very sorry, my lord, that we cannot find anything for your meal on this feast except salted meat." "Do not let that worry you," he said, "for if it pleases the Mother of God we shall not lack on her feast." He spoke, and from a rock which overhung the place a stag threw itself down. Rejoicing and lost in admiration the servants seized it, and from it, as the flesh of stags is tender at that season, they prepared a delicate meal for the count. And it should not seem incredible that the divine bounty provided him with food in this unexpected manner, because, acting according to the saying of the Apostle, he ate his morsel with the poor to the glory of God. [1 Cor. x. 31.] As those of his followers who are still here attest, he never turned his ear from the cry of the poor. The holy man, according to the saying of the psalmist: *Blessed is he that understandeth concerning the needy and the poor* [Ps. xl. 2], when he heard the voices of those who cried out, used to sigh deeply and reply with words of compassion.

28

YOU knew Count Raymund, the son of Odo.[1] This man treacherously held captive Count Gerald's nephew, Benedict, who was

---

[1] This may have been the Count of Toulouse contemporary with William the Pious of Aquitaine. It was only a little more than a hundred years after this that the County of Toulouse was to become the centre of that fierce yet highly civilized society of which the lasting monument is the poetry of the troubadours, but its counts were already powerful men, and they were hereditary enemies of the dukes of Aquitaine. We know nothing of how Benedict came to be Viscount of Toulouse, nor of the cause of Raymund's hostility.

Viscount of Toulouse. But his brother, Rainald, gave himself up as a hostage and won him back his freedom. When Count Gerald heard that Rainald had given himself up in his brother's place, he did all he could to help his nephew. But Raymund delayed making restitution, secretly plotting to capture Benedict again and hold them both. Seven months had passed without the holy man Gerald's being able to make any progress in the rescue of his nephew, and one day he complained to his sister, Avigerna, about this: "Why do you cease to implore Christ for your son? Certainly, either we are lacking in faith, or what is more true, we do not deserve to be heard"—and he wept as he said the words. From that time on Gerald gave himself wholeheartedly to the Lord in prayer. And he also sent Abbot Rudolf to Raymund at once, but he was not able to make any headway and soon returned. But on the following night it seemed to Raymund that the holy man Gerald stood beside his bed and struck him with his hand, saying, "Why do you not listen when I ask so often? Know for sure that if you hold the hostage any longer, misfortune will come upon you." At these words Raymund woke up and was greatly terrified by the memory of the vision. He called his household and told them what he had dreamt. One of them, from whom up till then most opposition had come, was for some reason equally afraid, and urged him to grant Count Gerald's petition at once, saying that otherwise they would certainly die. Raymund immediately sent to the lodging of Abbot Rudolf and ordered him to come back. When he did so, he told him plainly how the man of God had terrified him in a vision, forthwith gave back the hostage, and humbly asked Rudolf to bring him back into the good graces of Count Gerald. So by the help of God Gerald prevailed, and according to the word of Scripture humbled the great ones of the earth. [Isa. xlv. 2.]

29

ONCE when he was going to meet this same Count Raymund and was approaching the river Aveyron,[1] someone happened to mention

---

[1] This river flows into the Tarn and thence into the Garonne not far from Moissac, in the country south of Aurillac.

that he had no fish to eat that day. While they were speaking of this those who were walking with the count saw a fish called a mullet[1] swimming towards them. One of them, who tells the story, threw out a cast-net and wounded it. When it was wounded it withdrew a little and then came again to the bank towards which it had been swimming, and there it remained till one of them put out his hand and caught it. It was of no small size. The holy man giving thanks to God tried to make the others, who were extolling the fact as a miracle, keep quiet; as though it had happened by accident. And perhaps someone may say that this could have happened by accident, but I think he will not remember having seen a fish in a broad river like the Aveyron rushing in to men on the bank.

30

IF it is rightly considered a miracle, either that a fish should have jumped out of the water, or a stag fallen unexpectedly from a rock, so should it that a fish in a river offered itself to be caught. But much more wonderful is something which the divine agency brought on another occasion to bring food to the man of God. Not far from the monastery of Figeac[2] there is a hamlet dedicated to St. Gregory, in charge of which was a certain priest called Gerald, who on account of his sanctity was a very dear friend to the man of God, and who before the end of his life went to live as a recluse. Gerald, therefore, on one occasion turned aside to visit this man, and after they had prayed together and kissed each other, he said, "What are you going to give us to eat, Brother Gerald? For we have come to have dinner with you." He spoke like this on account of the easy relations that this priest had with him. But with pleasure the priest replied, "If it pleases your piety, my lord, you shall not go away fasting. Nevertheless I have only bread and wine

---

[1] The Latin is *capito*. According to Ducange this seems to mean what we call a bull-head or miller's thumb, a small fish which is common in the rivers of France, but too small to be appropriate to the story. The grey mullet, *mugilida capito*, would seem a more likely species to play the part.

[2] In the Department of Lot, about thirty miles south-west of Aurillac. The text reads *Friacus*, but according to Bouange (i, 28) this is an error for *Fiaco*, which is the reading in a manuscript formerly preserved at Aurillac.

to put before you, but I will see if by chance I can find some cheese or eggs." "Do not trouble yourself," the count said, "because it is an abstinence day and it will be good for us to eat more sparingly on this occasion, since there is nothing to provide a banquet." The priest hurried away to prepare, and going into his inner room he saw a fish lying on a plate. Astounded, he asked his servant privately who had brought it. The servant replied that he did not know, and said that nobody had been there who could have done so. The priest, therefore, going out to the count asked him if he would mind coming in to his inner room, and when he followed him in showed him the fish. Astonished and full of admiration, Gerald joined the priest in giving thanks to God. But he bound him and his servant, nevertheless, under oath not to betray this fact to anyone during his lifetime. But gradually the fact did become known to many, for the divine dispensation, which glorifies holy men, sometimes makes them known against their will. Truly the Lord is still mindful of His promise and does not deprive of all good those who seek Him [Ps. xxxiii. 11]. For the rest, this should not seem incredible, since we often read that God has deigned to supplement the food or the drink of his servants miraculously.

31

Not far from Aurillac in a district called Marcolez,[1] there is to be found a naturally round stone. On one occasion when Count Gerald was passing through the district, one of his followers called Adraldus told his companions that he could jump on to the top of the stone, and he forthwith did so to the amazement of all. But it was said that this Adraldus had a knowledge of incantations and magic. When the count came up, those in front stopped and pointed the jump out to him. He thought that it could not possibly have been made by any natural agility, and raising his hand he made the sign of the cross. After that the man, though he tried many times, was quite unable to jump on to the stone. And so it was manifest that this activity of his was the result of an incantation, which

[1] *Marculiscus*, clearly, I think, to be identified with Marcolez, which is about ten miles south of Aurillac.

could no longer aid him after the sign of the cross, and that the power of Count Gerald was great, since the power of the enemy had no force against his sign.

32

SINCE I have related this about his making the sign of the cross, let me add something else that he did in this way. It was the feast of St. Laurence and he was keeping it in a certain chapel not far from Argentat.[1] Now one of his serving-women there was grievously afflicted. Since he had already prayed for her, and in the midst of the people, as she was, she was still mouthing and raving, they asked if the man of God would deign to make the sign of the cross over her. Out of his usual humility he was unwilling to do this for a long time, but as she never stopped raving, and those who were present asked more insistently, he at length raised his hand and made the sign of the cross over her, and she, vomiting forth blood and matter, was straightway healed. When all were sounding the praises of God and glorifying His servant, Gerald ordered them with many reproaches to be quiet, saying that they should glorify God alone, and St. Peter whose church it was. For it is that same church at which he was stopping when the blind woman mentioned above[2] received her sight from the water in which he had washed his hands.

33

A MAN called Herloard fell from his horse and badly damaged one of his knees. The pain was such that for six days he went without eating. Not being able to find a remedy he sent to Capdenac[3] and had some of the water from Count Gerald's hands secretly brought to him. Wonderful to relate, as soon as he had sprinkled this water on his knee, he got up cured and free from all pain. Other things are told of him which deserve both to be related and admired, but

[1] About thirty miles west of Aurillac. The chapel may possibly have been that of Crucicula, cf. p. 143, n. 1.
[2] Ch. 13 above.
[3] Some thirty miles south-west of Aurillac.

because they rest on common report and not on the four witnesses I mentioned, I prefer to keep silent about them, for I am not ignorant that he did many things which none, or few, know about. Like all pious and good men he was careful always to guard humility as the apple of his eye, and for that reason, as far as he could, he concealed his good works. But of those which became known against his will he would hear no praise.

34

LET this suffice for his miracles, and it may satisfy those who assess the glory of a saint not from the amount of his good works, but from the number of the signs which he performed. To such as these perhaps his sanctity would have seemed less, if they had heard nothing about the miracles which he did in his lifetime. But the righteous works which he performed will be more pleasing to those who are held by his holy love, and who revere him with a discerning admiration. But since both are to be found in him, namely a holy justice and the glorification of miracles, they honour him with a more secure and lively devotion. If he had happened to have the spirit of prophecy, no one, I think, would have denied that he was a saint. But he accomplished more than this, because he conquered avarice. For what profit was it to Balaam that he prophesied so profound a mystery, when he was rejected on account of avarice? [Num. xxii-xxiv.] Do not look for any great miracle in Gerald, therefore, because this is he who did not put his hope in money or in treasures. [Ecclus. xxxi. 8.] This is he, who, as I have said, did wonderful things. So rarely will you find one who does not put his hope of happiness in riches, that on account of that very rarity the divine word must have interposed. Who is such a one? When he is found he is worthy of praise, and as the text goes on, we will praise him for he has done wonderful things in his life. [Ecclus. xxxi. 9.] There is much evidence for the wonderful things which Gerald did. For it is well known that he preserved those things which were given him by his parents and by kings, so that he might dispense them not as to servants but as to masters, that he increased his property without injuring anyone,

that he laid up treasure for himself in heaven, that he was exalted
in power but nevertheless remained poor in spirit. For this reason
it should seem neither wonderful nor unbelievable, if, as the text
goes on, his goods were established in the Lord [Ecclus. xxxi. 11].
Although by far the most outstanding of his deeds is that he preserved his chastity to old age. For it is chastity alone which imitates
the purity of the angels. Since, therefore, he overcame lust, which
is Satan's chief weapon, it is not remarkable that he had power
over Satan, whom he conquered in preserving chastity. It is not
incredible that he who cast the Prince of Mammon out of his heart
by overcoming avarice now frees those who are possessed by
devils. Rightly is the spirit of pride now subject to him, who at
the very summit of earthly power showed himself humble.

BOOK III

Preface

SINCE what I have already said has shown clearly that the venerable man, Gerald, was outstanding for the power of working miracles, it remains now for me to describe by way of conclusion how he gave up his spirit from its bodily habitation. It is beyond doubt that, although he had brought his bodily appetites into subjection through spare living, he had great vigour. Nor, when his strength failed, did he lack fortitude. But when, in view of his age, the time approached for him to be freed from the service he had faithfully performed, he began gradually to lose his accustomed vigour. The fact was not hidden from him, and indeed the loss of his strength made it clear that he was failing. When he looked around at the many who were habitually in close attendance on him, he began to speak with deep sighs and failing breath: "Alas, my poor followers and most dear friends, do you not see that I am without my former strength? Know that the time of my death is approaching, when my spirit at the will of its Creator will be transferred to its destined habitation, and weak nature will return to dust." Suffering and weakness did not keep him from his usual abstinence. It is a remarkable thing, but the feebleness which normally takes possession of old people was not able to move his indomitable spirit out of its usual course. The weakness of the flesh was by no means able to relax the strictness of his mind. While, therefore, the soul was increasing in virtues, his bodily strength was ebbing away. But since, thinking meanly of himself, he did not recognize his own virtues, he did not rightly understand whence his bodily weakness sprang. For the power of the spirit, which was always growing in him, had almost cut off his bodily strength. And indeed this is the way with the saints, for the divine power would have been less strong in them, if the bodily power had not grown weaker. So Daniel, seeing the vision of angels, was sick for many days [Daniel x. 8], and Jacob became lame when he wrestled with an angel [Gen. xxxii. 25]. For he who is filled with spiritual grace is deprived of bodily strength. So the exterior man failed, while the interior was renewed from day to day.

I

ONE day he was in the castle which overlooks Aurillac, and looking at the monastery he wept copiously. When one of his followers asked why he wept, he replied, "Because I can by no means bring into effect the desire which I have long had for this place. For here is my resting place, here will I dwell [Ps. cxxxi. 14]. By the help of God I have easily provided all those things suitable for the use of monks; only the monks are missing; they alone could not be found, and so alone and bereaved I am worn out with sorrow. Nevertheless I hope that Almighty God in His own good time will deign to fulfil my desire. Nor is it strange if I, a sinner, am left with my desire unfulfilled, since King David was forbidden to build the temple of the Lord, while God provided the one who was to carry out the work after him [3 Kings v. 3]. And though I may not see it in my lifetime, the mercy of Christ will grant what I long for when it pleases Him, for you know my desire that the walls of this house may be too narrow for all those who will come to it." How he came to this knowledge he did not say. But seeing the place full of people as he foretold, those who know him to have made the remark have formed the opinion that he was inspired to say what he did by the power of God. For truly his mouth was filled from the abundance of his heart [Matt. xii. 34], that the law of God might ever resound in it. For the rest, according to the example of David aforesaid, he foresaw all that would be necessary for the future inhabitants, and took care to provide for them in relics of the saints, ornaments and vestments for the church, and in the produce of the fields.

2

AND truly, as the Scripture says that he who is holy shall be sanctified still [Apoc. xxii. 11], it was fitting that this man of God should be brought to naught through suffering before his death.

To him it happened as to blessed Job and Tobias that he was chosen to be proved by trial. And so for seven years and more he lost the sight of his eyes. But so sharp-witted was he that it was unbelievable that he suffered from blindness. He not only did not grieve over this affliction, but even rejoiced in the Lord that He had deigned to scourge him. For he knew, indeed, that not every one who is chastised is a son, but nevertheless there is no son who does not suffer the rod. And this was a consolation to him, that the Judge on high should raise His hand to strike him, and that his sins, without which no man may live, should be punished in this life. For assured of the mercy of the Lord, he trusted that He would deign to free him whom He had deigned to afflict in this life from everlasting chastisement. If it had been possible to add to his previous practices, the more he retired from exterior activity by reason of his blindness the more attentively he gave himself to prayer. In proportion as he was not able to gaze on the face of the world, by so much he contemplated more clearly the true light of the heart. Outside business ceased, and he applied himself entirely to the practice of prayer and reading.

3

TWO years before he died he had the church solemnly consecrated. So many relics of saints[1] were enclosed within the altars that those who knew the number were amazed. To those who only know by hearsay it may seem incredible. For this holy father set himself to collect them from all sides, whenever opportunity offered, during his whole life. He obtained them at Rome and everywhere, for he was pleasing in speech and manner, generous in the price he paid and, what is more, supported by divine grace in whatever he undertook. It is known that in obtaining relics he often gave precious tents and well-conditioned horses, as well as great sums of money. He placed the tooth of St. Martial at the

[1] Something has already been said in the introduction (p. xxii) about the attitude to relics at this time. It is interesting to note that Gerald had no inhibitions about paying for them, a characteristic which he shared with his contemporary, St. Gerard of Brogne and all the men of his time. (See Sackur, vol. i, p. 123).

right-hand side of the altar with the relics of St. Martin and St. Hilary. None of the benefactors had been able to loosen this tooth from the holy man's jaw, though they had long tried, but after praying he withdrew it at once. In connexion with this same altar a marvellous thing happened on the day of the consecration. Crowds of people were pressing around and a boy took the covering from it to give to one of the ministers. Those who were standing near told him not to do so, but he did not let go of it, and was forthwith seized by violent pains. First the skin came off his hands, then gradually off his whole body, so that he had scarcely recovered in six weeks. Gerald, as he had formerly decided, handed the church over to the control of monks, of whom up till then few were living there.[1]

4

WHILE he still lived he took the greatest care to ensure that he should leave all those dependent on him in peace, lest any occasion of strife should arise among them. The farms and estates which he had not handed over to St. Peter[2] he left to relations and soldiers, and even serfs; to some of them in such a manner that after their death they should return to Aurillac. At this time he only gave their liberty to a hundred serfs, but they are innumerable whom he emancipated at different times and places. Many through their love of him refused their liberty and preferred rather to remain as his serfs. It shows how mild a dominion he exercised over them that they sometimes preferred being his serfs to being free. He was warned by some of his followers that as far as concerned his household, and it was very large, he should not free a greater number from the yoke of servitude. "It is right", he said to these, "that the civil law should be observed in this, and therefore the number appointed in that law should not be passed." Let this be told that hence it may be clear how closely he adhered to the divine precepts, when he submitted in this way to legal and human ones.

[1] See page 136, n. 1.　　　　　[2] See p. 136, n. 2.

5

WHEN the time of his departure drew near he was staying at Cezerviacum,[1] a certain church which belonged to him, dedicated to St. Siricius. More than usually full of compunction he sighed profoundly, so that it was evident that his heart's desire was elsewhere and that he would never have consolation in the present life. Tears were mingled with the sighs, and with eyes raised to heaven he prayed that he might be freed from this world, repeating often the invocation *Help, ye saints of God*. This expression had always been familiar in his mouth, and it was what he was accustomed to exclaim at any unexpected event. Not long after this he lost much strength by a convulsion, and the strength of his limbs and the harmony of the whole body gradually disappeared. Knowing that the time of his dissolution was at hand he ordered Bishop Amblardus[2] to be called that he might fortify him in death by his prayers, and that the pastor might hand over the sheep seeking the pastures of paradise to Christ the Pastor of all. Meanwhile, with his faculties clear and no lack of memory, he arranged everything necessary for his funeral and the needs of those he was leaving. When swift fame suddenly spread all around the rumour that the man of God, Gerald, was near his end, men came together as though lamenting a common loss, crowds of clerics and monks with nobles mingling among them, groups of the poor, and people from the countryside; all these by their lamentations incited the grief of others. They broke out into sighs and tears as though they had a grievance. They raised their voices in lamentation over his piety, his charity, his care for the poor, his protection of the weak.

[1] According to Bouange (*Histoire de l'Abbaye d'Aurillac, précédée de la vie de Saint Géraud*, Paris, 1899, vol. i, p. 163, *n.* 3) this is Saint-Cirgues in the *arrondissement* of Figeac (Lot), about twenty-five miles south-west of Aurillac. The church mentioned below as already dedicated to St. Siricius in St. Gerald's time has given its name to the place.

[2] Bishop of Clermont (Mabillon, *Acta O.S.B.*, vol. vii, p. 9, *PL*, cxxxiii, col. 708). He died in 912, and the fact enables us to place Gerald's death between that year and September 909 when he made his will (see p. 136, *n.* 2). Mabillon points out that according to Odo Gerald died on a Friday, and the 13th October (the date on which his feast was kept at Aurillac and throughout Aquitaine) fell on a Friday in the year 909, which seems satisfactorily to place Gerald's death in that year.

In tears some declared, "How great a comfort is the world losing", others, "O Gerald, rightly called good, who will help the needy as you have done? Who will be a father to orphans or the defender of widows? Who will give such comfort to the sorrowful? Who will use your great authority on behalf of the poor? Who will consider the necessities of individuals and help them as you did? Most indulgent father, how kind, how gentle you always were! You won the thanks of all; the fame of so great goodness drew to you the affections even of those who were unknown to you." Expressions of this sort, which a great sorrow usually elicits among the sighs, poured in with such deep lamentation that you would think these tears could never cease. So it went on each day until the end of his time on earth arrived. To the last he could not give up his custom of ordering alms to be given to all wishing to receive them.

6

TRULY I may call that man blessed and happy whose character was such that even on earth he did not lose the love due to his good works, and in heaven is received in the love of the saints. Truly he is happy who, although at the height of worldly power, nevertheless injured none, oppressed none, and against whom none brought the smallest complaint. For if Nathanael is called a true Israelite because guile was not found in him [John i. 47], rightly may I call this man an Israelite whom, in the words of blessed Job [xxix. 11], the ear that heard blesses, to whom the eye that saw gives testimony. When, therefore, all were mourning, he alone continued joyous, as one indeed who knew that the splendour of the noon-day shall arise in the evening for those who hope in the Lord [Job xi. 17], and when He has given them sleep, this is their inheritance. Therefore, although the flesh might fear on account of its mortal state, the spirit, confirmed in the sight of glory, exulted, trusting that it would now receive in fact the hope so long desired. For as it is written that the just man has confidence in his death [Prov. xiv. 32], so you would judge that he was confirmed in hope and had no fear of death. He seemed joyous therefore, since not the slightest word betrayed that he feared. During the whole time of his illness he forced his failing limbs to the divine service, so that he would not allow the night Office to be celebrated once except in church. Placed before the altar he always heard both the Mass of the day and a black Mass. And indeed when his limbs became too stiff and he was no longer able to walk by himself, the fervour of his spirit was such that it forced the body to be carried by the hands of bearers to the oratory; moreover, as if extending the tunic of good works to the heels, he sang the praise of God's might to the end.

7

AT dawn on a Friday, feeling himself grow worse he ordered his chaplains to recite the night Office in his presence, while the bishop was reciting it in church with his. He himself sang the psalms with the others, and after Lauds he finished the day Hours also. Then as he came to the end of Compline he armed himself with the sign of the cross and adding the expression so long familiar to him— Help, ye saints of God—for the last time, he closed his eyes in silence. Seeing that he had ceased to speak, those who were present called the bishop. They clothed his holy limbs in sackcloth, and while the rest were singing the psalms for the dying, one of the priests celebrated Mass and brought him Holy Viaticum. Some were saying that he was already dead, but he still retained the use of his senses and opening his eyes showed that he was still alive. Then of his own will he received the body of the Lord for which he was waiting, and so that happy soul departed to heaven. It is as though the order of the day in the week symbolized his own situation, for it showed that the good work, which is proper to the number six, had been completed, and that he had passed on to the true Sabbath which signifies rest.[1] And he, as we believe, now sees what he craved for, now possesses what he hoped for. But to many his passing meant no little grief, and although it was relieved by a certain sweetness in as much as they knew that for him rejoicing

---

[1] The meaning is obscure in English, but we were told at the beginning of the chapter that Gerald died on a Friday, and in Church Latin Friday is *Feria Sexta* and Saturday *Sabbatum*; hence the symbolism of the number six and the Sabbath rest.

rather than grief was called for, nevertheless they lamented loudly that they were deprived of his companionship, the like of whom they did not hope to see again. They, because of their human nature, were sad, but the angels, as we believe, rejoiced. For if there shall be joy among the angels on one sinner doing penance [Luke xv. 7], how much more for this just man who grew old in performing works of virtue. Faith sees the joy of the Lord in which he is received by the angels, but this is hidden from the bodily eyes, which have only seen the body paying its debt of death; and it has not yet appeared how greatly the soul is glorified in heaven. Gerald dies therefore, but according to the saying of David by no means as cowards are accustomed to do, for his lot is among the saints. [Wisd. v. 5.] And if he fulfilled that saying of the psalmist, *But you like men shall die* [Ps. lxxxi. 7], nevertheless that applies to him which is said before, *I have said: You are gods and all of you sons of the Most High.* [Ps. lxxxi. 6.] The Evangelist bears witness: *We are sons of God, and it hath not yet appeared what we shall be.* [1 John iii. 2.] Happy, then, Gerald who distinguished the precious from the worthless. After he had tasted how sweet the Lord is, he gave himself not at all to the pleasures of this life to the contempt of the Lord. Life on earth, which is precious to the reprobate, he held to be of little value, and death, which to them is the worst of evils, he found precious. Truly blessed is he whose days passed in sorrow and whose years in lamentation, because he has now experienced how great is the multitude of the sweetness, which the Lord has in store for those who fear Him [Ps. xxx. 20]. And even in the sight of men he demonstrates this to some extent by daily signs. How great is the difference between him and the evil rich! To him tears were as bread, and he took his drink with tears in full measure. [Ps. lxxix. 6]. These live their days in good things and have their consolation, according to the saying of the Gospel, in this life. But he with the voice of exultation has passed over to the tabernacle of God [Ps. xlii. 3]. Of them it is said that in a moment they are brought down to hell. [Ps. xxx. 18.] For the rest, even if anyone should be able to say anything worthy of his external way of life, none of us could, I do not say expound, but even touch, the meaning of the delights which fill him everlastingly in the right hand of the Lord, unless perchance somebody feels in himself what it is to delight in the salvation of God.

8

BUT since God is wonderful in His saints, in whom we are commanded to praise Him, by the saying of Scripture, *Praise the Lord in his saints* [Ps. cl. 1], therefore, O blessed Gerald, as far as we can we will praise God for you. I will praise Him because He chose and justified you, because He made glorious His mercy in you [Rom. viii. 30], and led you by straight paths [Ps. xxii. 3], because He made known the fruit of your labour, and did not desert you even to old age, and what is more, because He counted you among the sons of God, and finally glorifies you in the sight of all. And because praise becomes the saints [Ps. xxxii. 1], to the glory of God I also praise you, because according to the saying of Jeremias you bore the yoke of Christ from your youth [Lam. iii. 27], and did not spurn the grace of His calling; because you did not give anything in exchange for your soul [Mark viii. 37], and did not receive His salvation in vain; because you did not expose the secret thoughts of your heart, which you conceived of the love of Christ, and did not fail in the hour of temptation; because you did not give yourself to the external joys of this life, and did not falter in doing good. But, nevertheless, do Thou, O Lord, pardon my presumption through him. For I fear to exaggerate in what I say, because I have attempted what I was by no means fitted to do. For although he in whom Thou art praised is worthy of praise, I, O Lord, am unworthy to give it, because *praise is not seemly in the mouth of a sinner*. [Ecclus. xv. 9.] Let Thy saints, therefore, bless Thee as it is written [Ps. cxliv. 10], and let Thy works confess Thee. But because Thine eyes see the imperfect being of the Church [Ps. cxxxviii. 16], and its stones shall have pity on the earth [Ps. ci. 15], we beg that those who on account of the solidity of their morals are called stones may deign to help us who, because of our wickedness, are earth; that we who have not the garment of justice may embrace the stones and be able to cover our nakedness with their merits. May this servant of Thine direct to us the loving mercy with which Thy charity endowed him, and may he look lovingly from the eternal court of heaven, in which he resides among the heavenly rulers, into this vale of tears which he has left. May he hear the prayers of each, and with Thee may he meet the necessities of all, our Lord Jesus Christ Thy Son assisting, who with Thee and the Holy Ghost liveth and is glorified, God for ever and ever. Amen.

9

SWIFTLY, as happens in the case of people of great virtue, the news of his death was spread far and wide. A vast multitude of men soon began to come together from all sides, nobles in great numbers, innumerable crowds of country people and the poor, many monks, and bands of priests. All of them mourned him with a brotherly and tender devotion, and wept for him with I know not what divine instinct of compunction and love, because they knew that he was pleasing to God.

10

WHEN his body had been stripped for washing, Ragembertus and other servants who were performing the duty put both his hands on his breast, when suddenly his right arm extended itself, and his hand was applied to his private parts so as to cover them. Thinking this had happened by chance they bent the hand back to the breast. But again it was extended in the same way and covered his private parts. They were amazed, but wishing to understand the matter more carefully they bent the arm back a third time and put the hand back with the other on his breast. Immediately with lightning speed it sought the same parts and covered them. Those who were laying him out, struck at once by admiration and fear, realized then that this was not happening without divine power. Perhaps it was being divinely shown that this flesh when alive was always anxious to preserve the modesty of chastity. They quickly covered the body, and when it had received a covering the hand no more stretched out.

11

WITH great crowds accompanying them his people carried the holy body to Aurillac, as he had ordered, and placed it under a stone monument on the left-hand side of the church—near and to the right of the altar of St. Peter.[1]

But let me bring this little book to an end lest it should displease both by its unpolished style and its length. If anything in it has pleased the reader, let him attribute that to the merits of the Count Gerald. Whatever is displeasing he shall put down to my lack of skill, but let him find in it nevertheless an occasion for forgiveness. And for this reason, and in view of the fact that I only presumed to undertake the work by order, I humbly beg that he may intercede for me with Him who judges the hearts of men.

12

FOR blessed Gerald it is more than enough that the faithful Witness in heaven, whom he always sought to please, recompenses him in paradise, but nevertheless this same Witness, Christ, deigns to manifest outwardly how great is the glory which he possesses within. For it is written that God renews His witnesses against us [Job x. 17], and whoever keeps His commandments is His witness against us, that we too are able to keep those same commandments but are not willing. For to speak of people like myself, we scorn to read all the sayings of holy men and neglect to imitate their example, while nevertheless we are tirelessly occupied with idle and worldly speech. But acting in this way we prove ourselves to be those of whom the Apostle says, *They will turn away their hearing from the truth, but will be turned unto fables.* [2 Tim. iv. 4.] And so

---

[1] This is followed by a phrase—*et ipsum nihilominus in dextrorsum*—which as M. Abel Beaufrère (*Sépultures antiques du monastère bénédictin d'Aurillac*, Aurillac, 1944, p. 8, *n.* 8) says is evidently meant to give greater precision, but which *est si confuse qu'on n'ose pas en proposer la traduction.* The excavations in 1944 in the church of St. Gerald at Aurillac (p. 137, *n.* 1) disclosed what appears to have been a vault under the floor of the Carolingian church, and this may have been the crypt referred to in iv, 4, and the first burial-place of St. Gerald, but the evidence is still too fragmentary to permit of certainty. Beaufrère, *L'Église carolingienne*, pp. 12 and 22.

to reprimand somewhat our laziness and other manifestations of vice Christ, the Ruler of the Ages, raises this witness of His against us, making him glorious in our sight with many miracles, so that, because we close our eyes, as has been said, to the consideration of the example of holy men, we may turn our gaze to the splendour of this man, as to one resplendent with His own merits. In our own day he kept the divine precepts, but because the dead quickly depart from our hearts, we forthwith forget this, and not remembering the reward due to his good works we are sinfully slothful in imitating them. And for this reason He deigns to work miracles, which occur perhaps for a time, that so we may understand the glory which he has within, and may turn our minds to those recently performed works by which he attained that glory, and that we may strive to grow strong to imitate them. But now with the help of God let me say something of these same miracles, as may seem reasonable.

Book IV

1

ON the Sunday after his death he was carried to Aurillac, as I said, with great crowds accompanying him. While the choir was singing the psalms round the bier during the night, a certain noble called Gibbo placed his daughter, who was afflicted with epilepsy, under the bier, and afterwards she suffered no more from her infirmity. She is now the mother of a family and her perfect health bears witness to this miracle.

2

A CERTAIN man living on the estate called Grimaldus saw himself in a dream trying to lift the lid off the coffin. When he woke up he found his hands and arms from the elbow downward withered, so that he could do nothing with them. Remaining stricken like this for nearly a fortnight, he came as a suppliant to the tomb and was immediately healed.

3

THE lunatic maid of a certain man called Lambert was warned in a dream that she should come as a suppliant to his tomb. She told this to her master, but he, fearing that it was an illusion and that he would be ridiculous, if no miraculous result followed the vision, forbade her. But warned a second and a third time in a vision she again asked her master to be allowed to go there, and this he now granted. The woman went, and after praying at the tomb departed completely healed.

4

IN the meantime a little round plot of grass appeared before the crypt. Although the plot was covered with grass, the earth round about was bare and dusty. When those who passed through the cemetery[1] saw the little plot and the dusty path which surrounded it, they were astonished, for they knew that neither man nor beast had trodden out the path. For a time it was there and then it disappeared. Next summer the same thing was seen in the same place, but much larger. There was a dusty path worn round as before. The third summer in the same way a round plot of grass surrounded by a dusty path appeared, but it was larger still. And thenceforth it was seen for many years gradually spreading itself outwards. Those who considered the cause carefully believed it to be some prodigy, and conjectured that the green circle was perhaps a symbol of the fame of the blessed Gerald full of the greenness of virtue. This fame spreads itself around among the people, who are barren of good works and are signified by the dusty circle, and makes them fertile by its good example. When for love of him they gladly undertake the labour of pilgrimages, when they offer gifts, and some of them return new men, they are like the circle extending itself forward and partly replacing the aridity of the circle of dust. Whether it really signified this the Ruler of all things knows, but it is certain that nothing is done on this earth without a cause.

5

THERE was a certain cleric of good name who lived in the city of Rodez. This man, if faith is to be put in dreams, saw the following vision. There was as it were a high place from which a great light shone forth, and four steps led up to this light. Before the first step was a footpace of iron, before the second one of brass. The third had a footpace of silver, the fourth of gold. He saw two men, glorious in appearance and dress, come to the first step, and they were followed by two more who were leading a third between them by the hand. It was revealed to the cleric who saw this that the first two were St. Paul and St. Martial, the two who followed

---

[1] It is of interest that in 1939, when some gardens were being laid out adjoining the church of St. Gerald at Aurillac, a large number of stone sarcophagi were found lying close to the present church, and in 1944 several were found under the floor of the existing building, but outside the walls of the Carolingian church. (Beaufrère, *Sépultures*, and *L'Église carolingienne*, p. 13).

St. Peter and St. Andrew, but the third whom they were leading was St. Gerald, whom the cleric had not known in this life. But when afterwards he described the figure and face he had seen, those who had known Gerald recognized the likeness. When these had come to the first step they appeared to recite a psalm, after which St. Peter said a collect to which the others replied Amen. This was done a second, a third, and a fourth time. With the others still standing St. Peter went towards the bright light mentioned above, and having prostrated himself on the earth lay for a little while in adoration. Then he got up and prostrated three times, and a voice replied from the light asking what he wanted. "Lord," he said, "I beg Thy mercy for Thy servant Gerald." And then one, I know not who, holding a book, seemed to recite his life story. When he had been reading for a little time the cleric was only able to distinguish the words, *He that could have transgressed and hath not transgressed, and could do evil things and hath not done them.* [Ecclus. xxxi. 10.] Then the voice was heard to say, "Do what you will with him", and a sceptre was brought forth and given to St. Peter, and he had the power of raising Gerald with it. The cleric heard the voice of Him who gave, but saw only the sceptre. Then St. Peter returned rejoicing to those who were waiting, and a steep path leading up to heaven appeared at the place where they were standing. St. Peter, taking the beloved of God, Gerald, by the hand and beginning to go up the steps, intoned in a loud voice *Te Deum laudamus*, and so singing they departed into heaven with him.

And another sign from his tomb followed this vision.

6

IN the seventh year after his death the coffin[1] began gradually to rise above the ground, but the earth which surrounded it did not seem to be either raised or depressed. Those who dwelt in the place had not yet noticed this, but a certain cleric coming from the

---

[1] *Sarcophagus, qui usque medium cooperculi terra contusa calcibus fuerat contactus.* It is impossible to get a satisfactory rendering of this passage, and I have omitted it. The general sense does not seem to be affected.

district of Limoges asked the monks whether the coffin of Count Gerald had come out of the ground, and added that he had been warned in a dream to come to his tomb, because his coffin had begun to appear. Then the monks going with him to the tomb and taking away the hanging with which it was covered found all as the cleric had seen in his sleep. At that time it stood out a little, now considerably more. Whoever knows this cannot but be aware of some divine power. After this miracles began to occur frequently.

7

THE feast of the Circumcision had come round, and a certain vassal called Adraldus ordered a witch's fire to be kept all night in his house. But in the dead of the night demons attacked the guardians of the fire and did such harm to them that they killed one and deprived the other of the use of his limbs. Afterwards this man, who eked out his living by begging, was carried to Aurillac. When a few days later some lawless men made an attack upon the place, and the monks began to sound the alarm and to recite litanies, the maimed man begged that those around him should carry him to the tomb of Count Gerald. When they had done this, he prayed that the saint would deign to help him, and in a short time he arose healed, and with all his limbs instantly restored he had his full health. Miracles followed and the fame of Gerald's virtues became more widely and better known. If anyone doubts the facts, for in the sick the same things are often repeated, he can put them to the test with his own eyes and so gain credence of the past. I omit what the divine mercy often deigns to repeat in those who are afflicted by various diseases, for fear of being too long, but I have touched lightly upon some things which redound to the glory of this blessed man, lest I should seem to have passed over them thoughtlessly.

8

IT is known that this same holy man in his lifetime brought many relics of the saints to Aurillac. Indeed, as was said before, he was most assiduous in this cause, and he had no small help from God to obtain what he wished. Among other relics of the saints which were there is a certain relic of the True Cross which was known by frequent trial to have such power that if a man who was carrying it rode on horseback, the horse shortly died, or if he perjured himself he became an epileptic. Not a few became epileptics on account of this sin. The inhabitants of that region had truly ferocious habits,[1] but gradually by his example and the reverence they have for the holy man they seem to be gentler. When they make any agreement or solemn oath in law they have the relic brought by some monk or cleric, who, however, comes on foot.

9

SOME disputing rashly about the glory of St. Gerald assert that this grace of healing was conferred not through his merits, but through the power of these relics. Considering the case carefully, I believe that the benefits of health are conferred through the holy relics in such a way as not to deny the co-operating virtue of St. Gerald. The nature of the things which happen suggests this, for he himself is accustomed to appear in a vision to the sick, and the benefit of health is especially conferred before his tomb, as happened in the case of the son of John, the Viscount of Auvergne. Bringing the boy, who was deaf and dumb and had a withered hand, the father prostrated himself before the tomb and gave himself to prayer. In the middle of the night blood burst forth from the child's ears, and reaching out his hand he put it healed round

---

[1] *Mores valde ferinos habere solebant.* I think this means a good deal more than that they were uncouth; they were dangerous. In a semi-suburbanized England it is difficult to imagine what the inhabitants of the Frankish kingdoms must have been like in Odo's day, but we get some idea perhaps when we read about the people who murdered an English family, the Drummonds, who stopped to camp for the night in a lonely district of Upper Provence in 1952. The French poet and *littérateur*, Jean Giono, has written an illuminating essay (see Bibliography) on these descendants of mixed races (including the Marruci) who inhabit the mountainous March country between France and Italy. Admittedly this is not the district to which Odo is referring in the present passage, but it is one which was well known to him and Gerald on their journeys to Rome. Its inhabitants, who, as M. Giono tells us, in their little walled towns have interbred for a thousand years, untouched by those who hurry through on their way to the Côte d'Azur, would appear to have changed remarkably little from Odo's day, and doubtless at that time their type of behaviour was more widespread.

the neck of his father, and speaking for the first time he asked for bread. The church was filled with the voice of the father giving thanks for his son, and he made over a freehold property of his to the saint. I mention names in this case because the miracle, being performed for a person of standing, came to the notice of many. Different miracles, or those of another kind, were noted by the inhabitants, but since the number grew very great no care was taken to keep count.

10

IN the castle of Aurillac there was a mounting-block before the doors of the church[1] from which he used to mount his horse. The sick who kiss this for love of him recover their health, and for this reason the inhabitants have now moved it into the church and covered it with a hanging like an altar. Not far from the town which the country-people call *Mulsedonum*[2] the man of God had a small country-house. Some citizens of the town agreed together that they would take his table, which was still there, to eat their meals off, and this they did. The bearers chanced to set it down in front of a certain house, and in the middle of the day a man tried to go to sleep on it, but he was immediately struck blind and senseless, and when a dog jumped on the table it immediately became paralyzed. Nobody realized as yet the cause, and someone else threw himself on the table, but he too was immediately struck blind. Understanding at length that these things were happening because the table had been consecrated by the many meals of the holy man, they carried it covered with a linen cloth into the church of St. Martin which is near by, and it is to be seen there to this day suspended from the roof. A certain priest, with some of his neighbours, came to hold a feast on another of his tables which was in the village of *le bex*[3]. When they were chattering and making

---

[1] The church of St. Stephen stood on the north side of the castle with which it communicated by a staircase, traces of which are still to be seen (Bouange, vol. i, p. 90, *n*. 1). The church and doubtless other buildings would be enclosed within the wall or palisade.

[2] According to Bouange (vol. i, p. 32, *n*. 1) this is Monceaux, two miles from Argentat (Corrèze), and about thirty miles west of Aurillac.

[3] A few miles from Aurillac (Bouange, vol. i, p. 33, *n* 1).

jokes among themselves as is customary, suddenly a great fear
struck them all, so that, stopping their jesting, they went to eat in
another place. But the table they carried into an oratory[1] which
had been built in a place where the bearers had put down the bier
[of Gerald] to change the pall. (When some grazing cattle came
on the little space where the bier had been set down they immediately began to be tormented and some of them died. The natives
realized the cause of what had happened to the cattle, and built
this oratory in the place.) It is certain that from that time many sick
people recovered their health there. And moreover a remarkable
and almost unbelievable thing happened, if experience had not
proved it, for a little spring burst forth in that place sufficient for
wayfarers to drink from.

II

WHILE he was still living the man of God bound Rainald,[2] whom
he suspected, by an oath, but Rainald broke his oath and with his
followers greatly troubled the community which Gerald had
assigned to the monastery. In the pillaging which they were suffering some invoked the name of Count Gerald, and one night it
seemed to Rainald that he saw the man of God standing by him
and demanding that he kept his oath, at the same time warning him
to cease from troubling the community any more. Roused by the
vision he told it to his wife, and she persuaded him that having
been warned in this way he should keep the oath. Full of compunction, he related this in due course to his followers, ordering
them, but in a half-hearted way, not to molest the community, but
they in a short time returned to their accustomed rapacity. Nor
did Rainald stop them, for he was prone to evil, and although he
was a blood relation of the holy man, he was very far from having

[1] Bouange (vol. i, p. 33, *n.* 2) perpetuating what I suppose is a local tradition
states that the oratory (or its successor) dedicated to our Lady under the title
Notre-Dame-de-Grâces still exists in the hamlet of Bourgnioux, not more than
ten miles from Aurillac.
[2] This is apparently the nephew (he is called a blood-relation below) whom
Gerald had commended to William of Aquitaine (i, 32) and rescued from
Raymund of Toulouse (ii, 28), but we have had no previous indication that he
was unsatisfactory.

his piety. Then the holy man appeared to him again in a threatening manner, and full of anger reproached him with the good he had done to him, for which he had received only evil, and striking him on the head he threatened him with death to follow.

12

IN the province which is called Alemannia[1] a certain noble was possessed by demons. His parents and retainers took him to many relics of the saints, that at least by their intercession the divine grace might liberate him. But the Giver of all goods, who had decreed to glorify His chosen one, reserved this miracle for him. The name of the blessed man had not yet been heard in that province, and when the parents took their son to the bodies of the saints, the demons often exclaimed that they would never go out of him but through the intercession of St. Gerald. The parents of the demoniac went in all directions to see if they could hear of the province in which St. Gerald was. It may have been one of the Roman pilgrims, or another, who told them the province and the place. They hurried to Aurillac and as soon as they came to the tomb the demons began to cry out through the possessed man, "O Gerald, for what reason do you make game of us? For what reason do we burn in your power?" Forthwith the man fell to the ground and spewed them out together with a quantity of blood. Ever after he remained sound.

[1] St. Gerald seems to have had a considerable local cult from the time of his death, and still has, though he is little known outside Auvergne. It is of interest, however, that churches are found dedicated to him in the French Alps (Bouange, vol. i, pp. 98-9) in the country that he must have gone through on his way to Rome, and in which Odo tells us that he was well-known (ii, 17). Alemannia, lying well to the north in what is now south-west Germany and Switzerland, would not be likely to have heard of him. (See below in text.)

INDEX

INDEX